Conducting Rese
Online and Blen~~ ~~ ~~ ~~
Environments

Conducting Research in Online and Blended Learning Environments-New Pedagogical Frontiers examines various perspectives, issues, and methods for conducting research in online and blended learning environments. The book provides in-depth examinations of the perspectives and issues that anyone considering research in online or blended learning will find insightful as they plan their own inquiries. Grounded in educational research theory, this is invaluable to both the serious researcher and the occasional evaluator.

Conducting Research in Online and Blended Learning Environments provides comprehensive, useful information on research paradigms, methodologies, and methods that should be considered in designing and conducting studies in this area. Examples of the most respected research in the field enhance each chapter's presentation.

Charles D. Dziuban is Director of the Research Initiative for Teaching Effectiveness, Center for Distributed Learning, at the University of Central Florida, USA.

Anthony G. Picciano is Professor and Executive Officer of the Ph.D. Program in Urban Education at the Graduate Center of the City University of New York, USA.

Charles R. Graham is Professor of Instructional Psychology and Technology at Brigham Young University, USA. He currently serves as department chair.

Patsy D. Moskal is the Associate Director for the Research Initiative for Teaching Effectiveness, Center for Distributed Learning, at the University of Central Florida, USA.

"Inquiry into online and blended learning is critical. This book helps us see how to combine old and new research methodologies to ensure our methods are keeping pace with an increasingly complex higher education environment where the future rests on how well students engage and learn. The authors provide us tools to ensure we are effective."

Diana Oblinger
President Emeritus, EDUCAUSE

"This new analysis explores how the perennial issues of research in higher education are applied to the emerging and rapidly changing world of online and blended learning. At a time when institutional effectiveness and student success have become paramount, this volume provides critical insights and thoughtful guidance for the higher education research community."

George L. Mehaffy
Vice President for Academic Leadership and Change
American Association of State Colleges and Universities (AASCU)

"'What is working, what is not working, and what will make it better?' These questions vex developers of blended learning courses who want to improve their students' learning outcomes and experiences. As the authors say, 'Good Research is Just Plain Hard,' but this book makes it a little easier to answer these questions. The authors supply tools and techniques that span a range of research disciplines, and they offer guidance on how to apply the techniques thoughtfully and accurately."

Irvin R. Katz
Director, Cognitive Sciences Research Group,
Educational Testing Service

"All animals can be said to learn, but so far as we know, we are the only species that asks the question, 'what do we know about learning?' As the complexities of our civilization's digital age continue to grow, our answers to that big question will determine our future. This book asks that big question, across every educational modality, and it never shrinks from the subtlety, nuance, rigor, and imagination required of all who ask it."

Gardner Campbell, Ph.D.
Vice Provost for Learning Innovation and Student Success
Virginia Commonwealth University

"The authors note that 'online technology has opened up new possibilities for how teachers teach and how students learn' and they couldn't be more on target. They have given us intellectual handholds by which we can take this journey with them and their colleagues. This guide to specific aspects of education research as applied to online and blended learning with examples of the 'best research' conducted in it will give the reader ideas and insights into good practice. The careful choice of topics and the quality of the authors will give this book shelf life. Hop on board for the ride or selected excursions. An informative guide to the future of educational research in online learning awaits you."

Phillip D. Long, Ph.D.
Associate Vice Provost for Learning Sciences
Deputy Director, Center for Teaching and Learning/Continuing and
Innovative Education
The University of Texas at Austin

"I was amazed by the range of research methods covered in this book as well as the breadth of the theoretical underpinnings for blended and fully online learning. The authors offer interesting analyses related to many of the seminal pieces that have been written over the past couple of decades since the emergence of Web-based instruction."

Curtis J. Bonk
Professor, Instructional Systems Technology Department
Indiana University Bloomington

"Research into our practices in teaching and learning is more critical than ever. This book is an indispensable guide for best practices for research in the burgeoning domain of blended and online learning in higher education."

Malcolm Brown
Director, EDUCAUSE Learning Initiative

"The authors are experts in crafting a comprehensive and insightful text on online and blended learning research. Contemporary researchers and practitioners will find in this text extensive and useful research-based and practical guidance for conducting research. Beyond a 'how-to' text, the collective wisdom and perspectives shared by the authors inspires researchers to think about what they should research and why they should do it. Understanding 'what drives the agenda' in online and blended learning research is far more promising than trying to predict its future."

Laurie P. Dringus, Ph.D.
Professor, Graduate School of Computer and Information Sciences
Nova Southeastern University
Past Editor-in-Chief (1998–2015) of *The Internet and Higher Education*

"What is absolutely valuable in this book is the compendium of research methods for online and blended learning. Indeed, this work is about new frontiers in education and research—very few books are. I will do all I can to see that this volume is published in Poland. It should be accessible to all students, researchers, and educational practitioners interested in exploring digital learning spaces."

Stanisław Dylak, Ph.D.
Professor at Adam Mickiewicz University–Poznan, Poland
Head of Department of Research on Teacher and Teacher Education
(Pedeutology)
Faculty of Educational Studies

"This is an immensely useful and important guide. It can serve as an accessible and helpful handbook to introduce online and blended learning practitioners to research or to refresh and extend the expertise of established researchers. But it can also stimulate thinking and understanding about the role of online and blended learning in higher education. The final chapter provides a remarkably thoughtful exploration of considerations for the future that will appeal to theorists and pragmatists alike."

Susan Grajek
Vice President, Data, Research, and Analytics, EDUCAUSE

"In this work, the authors take the reader through a highly thoughtful and practical narrative of how we can conceptualize and apply research to this dynamic field. Simply put, this is one of those rare books that I believe should be part of the curriculum for every graduate student in this field and on the shelf of every serious practitioner."

Phil Ice
Vice President, Research & Development
American Public University System

"A much needed comprehensive and valuable look at research issues in blended and online learning. A definite asset in building coherency in the field. If there is one book to guide future research, make it this one."

Tanya Joosten
Director, eLearning Research and Development, Academic Affairs
Codirector, National Research Center for Distance Education and
Technological Advancements
University of Wisconsin–Milwaukee

"This book is a call for action. It asks researchers to examine the long view as they create contextual research questions, embrace a multiplicity of research methods, conduct research in expected and unexpected places, and above all promote collaborative research amongst a 'coalition of educational professionals.' Keep this book conveniently close. It will inspire, invigorate, and refresh your desire and ability to conduct research while greatly benefiting from the authors' wisdom."

Linda Jorn
University of Wisconsin–Madison
Associate Vice Provost for Learning Technologies
DoIT Director of Academic Technology

"This book is a must read for faculty, instructional designers, and researchers interested in learning about or conducting research in online and blended learning. The authors delve into an emerging and unique research culture that encompasses various perspectives, issues, and methods for both small sample and big data studies. This book is timely, insightful and comprehensive—a one-of-a-kind approach for anyone interested in exploring or advancing pedagogical research processes."

Susan E. Metros
Chief Information Officer, The USC Marshall School of Business
Associate Dean, The USC Jimmy Iovine and Andre Young Academy
Professor of Design Practice, The USC Roski School of Art and Design
The University of Southern California, Los Angeles, California

"Conducting Research in Online and Blended Learning Environments is a tremendous resource for institutions, researchers and faculty looking to do just that. The strength of this book is in its authors—some of the most respected researchers of online and blended learning in higher education today. Kudos and thank you for the comprehensive roadmap you provide for those interested in quality and blended research."

Mary Niemiec
Associate Vice President for Distance Education
Director, University of Nebraska Online Worldwide

"Online and blended learning as a reorientation of teaching and learning practices seems to demand a careful rethinking of research design including choice and combination of research methods. This book will become a most valuable resource for us who want to understand the present and future of teaching and learning."

Anders Norberg, Strategist for the Multi-Institutional Campus
Skellefteå, Sweden

"Co-authored by four of the top people in the field, this book will fill a major gap in the online and blended learning research literature. With an appropriate emphasis on pedagogical design over technology, this volume will provide thought-provoking inspiration as well as invaluable guidance to both experienced and emerging researchers and practitioners."

Thomas C. Reeves, Ph.D.
Professor Emeritus of Learning, Design, and Technology
University of Georgia

"This book is both timely and useful. In an era in which pedagogy needs to proactively respond to complex and rapidly changing social, economic and technological landscapes, here is a contribution which provides contextualised, foundational knowledge and advice on constructing meaningful research frameworks, gathering data and analysing evidence to answer primary and applied educational questions associated with contemporary online and blended teaching and learning."

Gavin Sanderson
Senior Lecturer, Teaching Excellence & Innovation
University of South Australia

"The range of themes addressed in the thirteen chapters presented in this new volume is truly impressive. This book stands as an authoritative and comprehensive resource for doctoral students and new faculty in online learning research and as a welcome tool for more senior scholars. We need more work like this to continue to advance the field, but in this collection the authors have set a high bar for those who would follow."

Peter Shea, Ph.D.
Editor of *Online Learning* (formerly *JALN*)
Associate Provost for Online Education &
Associate Professor, Educational Theory and Practice and CCI
University of Albany, State University of New York

"The authors, who are all top tier researchers in the area themselves, have developed self-contained chapters that provide clear explanations of a variety of research approaches and include examples of best practices of each drawn from the online and blended learning literature. This book is a must read for both researchers working in the field and practitioners wishing to investigate some aspect of their work."

Karen Swan
Stukel Distinguished Professor of Educational Leadership
University of Illinois–Springfield

"This book is a must read for anyone interested in conducting research in the rapidly growing field of online and blended learning in higher education. Not only do these highly accomplished authors provide pedagogically informed frameworks and strategies for conducting such educational research but they also offer ideas, insights, and cautions for future research directions based on their own extensive experiences in this field."

Norm Vaughan
Professor, Mount Royal University
Coauthor of *Teaching in Blended Learning Environments: Creating and Sustaining Communities of Inquiry* and *Blended Learning in Higher Education*

Conducting Research in Online and Blended Learning Environments

New Pedagogical Frontiers

Charles D. Dziuban, Anthony G. Picciano, Charles R. Graham, and Patsy D. Moskal

Routledge
Taylor & Francis Group

NEW YORK AND LONDON

First published 2016
by Routledge
711 Third Avenue, New York, NY 10017

and by Routledge
2 Park Square, Milton Park, Abingdon, Oxon OX14 4RN

Routledge is an imprint of the Taylor & Francis Group, an informa business

Library of Congress Cataloging-in-Publication Data
Dziuban, Charles.
   Conducting research in online and blended learning environments : new pedagogical frontiers / Charles D. Dziuban, Anthony G. Picciano, Charles R. Graham, Patsy D. Moskal.
      pages cm
   Includes bibliographical references and index.
   1. Web-based instruction—Research.   2. Internet in education—Research.   3. Blended learning—Research.   I. Picciano, Anthony G.   II. Graham, Charles R.   III. Moskal, Patsy D.   IV. Title.
   LB1044.87.D98 2016
   371.33′44678—dc23
   2015007621

ISBN: 978-0-415-74246-7 (hbk)
ISBN: 978-0-415-74247-4 (pbk)
ISBN: 978-1-315-81460-5 (ebk)

Typeset in Bembo
by Apex CoVantage, LLC

Printed and bound in the United States of America by Publishers Graphics, LLC on sustainably sourced paper.

To all those faculty, students, and researchers who explore the role of technology in education and invest their intellectual resources in order to improve teaching and learning in our schools, colleges, and universities. Because of your efforts the new frontier is bright indeed.

Contents

List of Illustrations

FIGURES

TABLES

BOXES

.

Preface

The idea for this project originated in 2006 when Tony Picciano and Chuck Dziuban began receiving manuscripts for their book *Blended Learning: Research Perspectives*. Those chapters made it clear that researchers throughout the country were exploring improved research designs that would assess the impact of blended learning on teaching and learning. Authors were incorporating the best of traditional methods while simultaneously developing research techniques and data analysis procedures that pushed the boundaries of impact evaluation. That original project published by the Sloan Consortium (now the Online Learning Consortium) led to extended conversations among researchers in blended learning about new directions for educational inquiry.

Quickly, effective research became a global conversation that convinced Tony and Chuck to pursue a sequel to the original volume with Charles Graham of Brigham Young University. That second book appeared in 2014. *Blended Learning: Research Perspectives, Volume 2* confirmed the original conclusion that rapid adoption of blended learning throughout the world was creating enthusiasm for transforming research methods. However, not only was this reexamination taking place in the blended learning arena, an equally vigorous initiative was developing in fully online learning. Investigators were experimenting with improving study designs, collecting and analyzing information (not just data), and trying to account for the highly interactive nature of blended and online learning. In addition, they were developing models for how research might inform pedagogy by using instructional technologies.

Presentations at scientific meetings, conversations with the authors in those original two volumes, and discussions with the editors at Routledge led Charles, Anthony, and Charles to invite Patsy Moskal from the University of Central Florida to join them in describing the principles, methods, and issues they have encountered while conducting research in online and blended learning over several years. As our readers might suspect, this was a daunting task. Trying to distill pedagogy and research methods into this small volume forced difficult choices, such as what to include, what to omit, and which examples to provide. In addition, after extended discussion, the authors decided to minimize the use of URLs for the resources in the book because of their tendency to go dark and frustrate readers. Our assumption was that virtually everyone who reads this will have little trouble finding the resources we mention. Further, rapidly changing resources for online and blended learning research create challenges for any author to keep up with emerging developments.

Finally, we (Charles, Anthony, Charles, and Patsy) hope that our readers will find this work helpful as they approach the new research frontier. Further, we hope that they understand and forgive that this is not a metaphorical turn-by-turn GPS for conducting research, but rather a general guidepost for heading in the right direction. The four of us have enjoyed working on this project immensely because we have gotten to know and learn from each other more than we could have ever imagined. From this interchange we have a much better picture of what we know, what we don't know, and what we need to know. Anyone who has written a book is abjectly aware that it never quite lives up to the expectations that were held for it. That is certainly the case for the four of us. The only consolation will be that somehow it lives up to your expectations in some small measure. We wish you much success in your research endeavors.

Acknowledgments

The authors owe a debt of gratitude to all those individuals who saw to it that this project came to fruition. Without their encouragement and support this book most certainly would not be in your hands. Marcella Bush, Andrea Hermsdorfer, and Genny DeCantis of the Research Initiative for Teaching Effectiveness at the University of Central Florida spent untold hours editing, formatting, and fixing errors in the manuscript. There is no way that we can thank them properly for the way that they have gone above and beyond anything that could have been expected. Second, our profound gratitude goes to our esteemed colleagues throughout the world who contributed their time and effort reading and critiquing these chapters. Their efforts have humbled us, sharpened our insights, and improved our research skills at so many levels. You are an amazing community of scholars. In addition we so much appreciate the continued support of our colleague and friend Alex Masulis and his staff at Taylor & Francis who had faith in our ability to pull off this little adventure. Alex was the driving force that helped us persevere in those difficult times that every author faces. We would also like to acknowledge and thank our families, who patiently encouraged us to complete this journey! Finally, each of us is so grateful to all of our students and colleagues who twisted our roots and stretched our vectors, forcing us to learn what we don't know and better understand what we do know. You above all have made it clear that learning to conduct research in online and blended learning is a lifelong process. Without you there would be no frontier for us.

Charles, Anthony, Charles, and Patsy

About the Authors

Charles D. Dziuban is director of the Research Initiative for Teaching Effectiveness at the University of Central Florida (UCF), where he has been a faculty member since 1970, teaching research design and statistics, as well as the founding director of the university's Faculty Center for Teaching and Learning. He received his Ph.D. from the University of Wisconsin. Since 1996, he has directed the impact evaluation of UCF's distributed learning initiative, examining student and faculty outcomes as well as gauging the impact of online, blended, and lecture capture courses on the university. Charles has published in numerous journals, including *Multivariate Behavioral Research*, *The Psychological Bulletin*, *Educational and Psychological Measurement*, the *American Education Research Journal*, *Phi Delta Kappa*, *The Internet in Higher Education*, the *Journal of Asynchronous Learning Networks* (now *Online Learning*), and the *Sloan-C View*. He has received funding from several government and industrial agencies, including the Ford Foundation, Centers for Disease Control, National Science Foundation, and the Alfred P. Sloan Foundation. In 2000, Charles was named UCF's first ever Pegasus Professor for extraordinary research, teaching, and service, and in 2005 received the honor of Professor Emeritus. In 2005, he received the Sloan Consortium (now the Online Learning Consortium) award for "Most Outstanding Achievement in Online Learning by an Individual." In 2007 he was appointed to the National Information and Communication Technology (ICT) Literacy Policy Council. Charles has coauthored, coedited, or contributed to numerous books and chapters on blended and online learning and is a regular invited speaker at national and international conferences and universities. In 2011, UCF established the Charles D. Dziuban award for excellence in online teaching in recognition of his impact on the field.

Anthony G. Picciano is a professor and executive officer of the Ph.D. Program in Urban Education at the Graduate Center of the City University of New York. He is also a member of the faculty in the graduate program in education leadership at Hunter College, the doctoral certificate program in interactive pedagogy and technology at the City University of New York Graduate Center, and the CUNY online BA program in communication and culture. In 1998, Dr. Picciano cofounded CUNY Online, a multimillion-dollar initiative funded by the Alfred P. Sloan Foundation that provides support services to faculty using the Internet for course development. He was a founding member and continues to serve on the board of directors of the Online Learning Consortium (formerly the Sloan Consortium). Dr. Picciano's research interests are school leadership, education policy, Internet-based teaching and learning, and multimedia instructional models.

Dr. Picciano has conducted major national studies with Jeff Seaman on the extent and nature of online and blended learning in American K–12 school districts. He has authored numerous articles and books, including *Educational Leadership and Planning for Technology*, 5th edition (2010, Pearson), *Data-Driven Decision Making for Effective School Leadership* (2006, Pearson), *Distance Learning: Making Connections across Virtual Space and Time* (2001, Pearson), *Educational Research Primer* (2004, Continuum), *The Great Education-Industrial Complex: Ideology, Technology, and Profit* (2013, Routledge/Taylor & Francis), and *Blended Learning: Research Perspectives, Volume 2* (2014, Routledge/Taylor & Francis). In 2010, Dr. Picciano received the Sloan Consortium's "National Award for Outstanding Achievement in Online Education by an Individual." Visit Dr. Picciano's website at http://anthonypicciano.com.

Charles R. Graham is a Professor of Instructional Psychology and Technology at Brigham Young University with interest in technology-mediated teaching and learning. Charles studies the design and evaluation of blended learning environments and the use of technology to enhance teaching and learning. Charles has authored 50+ articles in over two dozen journals, many with graduate students whom he loves to work with and mentor. He has also published 20+ chapters related to online and blended learning environments in edited books, including *Online Collaborative Learning: Theory and Practice*, *Blended Learning: Research Perspectives*, *The Encyclopedia of Distance Learning*, and the *AECT Handbook of Research on Educational Communications and Technology*. Charles also coedited the *Handbook of Blended Learning: Global Perspectives, Local Designs*, which contains thirty-nine chapters with examples of blended learning in higher education, corporate, and military contexts from around the world. He coedited a volume titled *Blended Learning: Research Perspectives, Volume 2*, with twenty-one chapters on current research practices in blended learning. He has also coauthored a book for teachers and practitioners interested in designing blended learning environments, titled *Essentials for Blended Learning*. His research publications can be found online at https://sites.google.com/site/charlesrgraham/.

Patsy D. Moskal is the associate director for the Research Initiative for Teaching Effectiveness at the University of Central Florida (UCF). Since 1996, she has served as the liaison for faculty research of distributed learning and teaching effectiveness at UCF. Patsy specializes in statistics, graphics, program evaluation, and applied data analysis. She has extensive experience in research methods including survey development, interviewing, and conducting focus groups, and frequently serves as an evaluation consultant to school districts and industry and government organizations. She has also served as a co-principal investigator on grants from several government and industrial agencies, including the National Science Foundation, the Alfred P. Sloan Foundation, and the Gates Foundation–funded Next Generation Learning Challenges (NGLC). She frequently serves as a proposal reviewer for conferences and journals, and has also been a reviewer for NSF SBIR/STTR and DoE proposals. Patsy has coauthored numerous articles and chapters on blended and online learning and frequently presents on these topics. In 2011 she was named a Sloan-C Fellow "in recognition of her groundbreaking work in the assessment of the impact and efficacy of online and blended learning." Patsy is very active in both EDUCAUSE and Online Learning Consortium, serving as the Online Learning Consortium International Conference Program chair in 2014 and conference chair in 2015.

Chapter 1

Research in Online and Blended Learning

New Challenges, New Opportunities

Anthony G. Picciano

In April 2014, I received an email from a colleague, an assistant professor at the George Washington University who has been instrumental in leading blended learning course development projects in the School of Health Sciences. She was emailing to ask my opinion on research and publication possibilities for her and her colleagues who were in the midst of collecting data on these projects. Specifically, she envisioned at least four studies based on data they were collecting on blended learning and communities of practice, blended learning and reflective practice, and blended learning and increased interaction in relation to higher levels of learning.

In May 2014, I was at North-West University in South Africa to lecture and conduct workshops on online and blended learning in higher education. North-West University was under a federal government mandate to expand higher education opportunities to its citizens and had asked the public universities for strategies for doing so. Among the strategies being considered was to expand the use of online and blended learning technologies. The specific topics of my workshops related to conducting research in instructional technology, design of blended learning environments, massive open online courses (MOOCs), and technology planning. For the workshop on conducting research in instructional technology, the participants represented a group of fifteen (mostly younger) faculty members who were contemplating conducting studies related to work they were doing in their own courses and with their own students. Their topics related to student outcomes, faculty workload, and blended learning in large section classes. They were interested, and had expertise, in qualitative and/or quantitative research methods, but had never published in the area of instructional technology.

On the sixteen-hour flight to South Africa, I started reading a recently published book, entitled *Learning Online: What Research Tells Us Whether, When, and How*, sent to me by the authors, Barbara Means, Marianne Bakia, and Robert Murphy. I was familiar with their earlier work, a meta-analysis on "evidence-based practices" in online learning they conducted for the U.S. Department of Education, and published in 2010. The purpose of their new book was to describe the available research on online learning, and specifically on how best to implement different forms of online learning for different kinds of students, subject areas, and contexts (Means, Bakia, & Murphy, 2014).

As I reflected on the above, all of which occurred within a thirty-day period between April and May 2014, I thought how it would have been unheard of to consider any of these scenarios as little as twenty years ago. The Internet was just beginning, and no one predicted the rapidity with which it would permeate all aspects of society, including education. Since the mid-1990s, a significant change has occurred in the delivery of instruction in schools and colleges throughout the world. Traditional face-to-face courses are being redesigned and augmented by online and blended learning modalities. Teachers and students can meet at any time and in any place to participate in a class. In the United States in 2013, more than seven million students, or approximately one-third of the higher education population, were enrolled in fully online college courses (Allen & Seaman, 2014). Millions of additional college students were enrolled in blended courses. However, accurate data on the extent of blended learning in American higher education is nonexistent, mainly because of problems with a standardized definition and accurate data reporting at the individual college level. Fully online colleges, both for profit and not for profit, have been the fastest growing segment of the higher education market. Since 2008, MOOCs have appeared in higher education programs that enroll as many as 150,000 international students in a single course. Accurate data in primary and secondary schools are sketchy. Picciano and Seaman (2007, 2009, 2010) conducted a series of national studies on the extent and nature of online learning in American K–12 schools. They extrapolated that by 2016 as many as six million K–12 (mostly secondary) students would be enrolled in online or blended learning courses (Picciano & Seaman, 2009). However, since the above extrapolation, state legislatures have been accelerating the promotion of online learning in their public schools. Most states have provided support for some form of virtual schooling at the K–12 levels. The Florida Virtual School, for example, is among the most successful, with enrollments in excess of 100,000 students per year. Several states have established requirements stating that every high school student take at least one online course in order to graduate. As a result of this activity the six million–student enrollment figure cited above may be a low estimate.

Clearly, online and blended learning approaches are becoming commonplace in education throughout the world. These phenomena also represent a whole new area of research that examines a variety of issues related to learning effectiveness, student and faculty attitudes, access, workload, and cost benefits. There are a number of journals, such as *The Internet and Higher Education* (IHE), *Online Learning* (formerly the *Journal of Asynchronous Learning Networks*, or *JALN*), *The International Review of Research in Open and Distance Learning*, and the *Journal of Online Learning and Teaching* (JOLT), that devote themselves exclusively to issues and research related to the various modes of online instruction. A plethora of studies have thus been published that seek to explore the best practices, effectiveness, satisfaction, and challenges of teaching and learning online. For example, an extensive search of databases and citations for a meta-analysis project returned 1,132 abstracts on student outcomes in online and blended learning for the years 1996 to 2008 (U.S. ED, 2010). Although these abstracts only reflected research in student outcomes, there are numerous other studies on faculty satisfaction, student access, policy issues, and cost-benefit analysis in online and blended learning environments. In addition to formally published studies, numerous unpublished evaluations that are not indexed in public databases have been conducted by college and school administrators seeking to determine the effectiveness of online modalities in their own institutions. However, even with all of this activity, a good deal more research needs to be done. For example, in the area of K–12 education, there is a dearth of quality research in this area (U.S. ED, 2010). Even in higher education, because of the controversies that raise questions about the quality of online learning, "research-based guidance regarding effective online learning practices and their implementation in different contexts is strongly needed" (Means, Bakia, & Murphy, 2014, p.6).

Purpose

The purpose of this book is to examine various perspectives, issues, and methods for conducting research in online and blended learning environments. It provides in-depth examinations of the perspectives and issues that anyone considering research in online or blended learning will find insightful as they plan their own inquiries. This book is grounded in educational research theory and practice and would be of assistance to both the theory-based researcher and the evaluator investigating her/his own courses and programs. A comprehensive treatment has been undertaken that provides useful information on research paradigms, methods, and methodologies, which should be considered in designing and conducting studies in these areas. Lastly, examples of the most respected research in the field enhance each chapter's presentation.

Pedagogical Frontiers

The title of this book, *Conducting Research in Online and Blended Learning Environments: New Pedagogical Frontiers*, was chosen because it was the authors' conviction that online technology has opened up new possibilities for how teachers teach and how students learn. Online technology allows teaching and learning literally to occur at anytime and anyplace, and no longer shackles one to the time and place constraints of a physical classroom. Critical aspects of instruction, such as media-infused content, group interaction, reflective practice, simulation, and assessment, are augmented with online technology. A course discussion never ends, students must prepare to interact with colleagues in online forums where all can and are expected to contribute, and facilitated collaborative learning is commonplace. The new technologies have opened up many "frontiers" for pedagogues to explore as they convert or redesign their courses.

Another important aspect of the title is its emphasis on pedagogy and not technology. Even though we live in a technology-infused world, when it comes to teaching and learning, it is the pedagogy that should drive technology and not the other way around (Picciano, 2009). Faculty, with the assistance of instructional designers, are rethinking how they can use the technology to achieve their pedagogical goals and objectives. As a result, the 1990s and the first part of the 21st century have seen a plethora of new programs, courses, and course modules that approach teaching in ways that did not exist in the past. For example, a simple blog can extend course discussions for days, allowing for rich, reflective interactions that were rarely possible in the confines of a typical fifty-minute in-class period. Collaborative learning that was a logistical bane for many students can be initiated gracefully using wiki software that allows for ongoing online interaction, group project development, and media-infused presentations. More complex instructional activities involving gaming, simulations, and multi-user virtual environments challenge faculty, instructional designers, and students in ways never possible in a brick and mortar environment. Furthermore, these technology-based approaches can be used as standalones in fully online courses or can be blended with traditional class materials.

All of this pedagogical development has also unleashed the need for the careful evaluation of its benefits. A fundamental aspect of instructional design, and what many consider the crucial culminating step, is evaluation (Gagne, 1977; Dick, Carey, & Carey, 2011; Kemp, 1985). Unfortunately, this last crucial step is not always conducted, or conducted in ways that are much too brief and informal. For decades, faculty were basically on their own to develop courses and rarely took the time to formally evaluate their techniques and innovations. With the exception of faculty in schools of education, very few college faculty were familiar with the pedagogical theories behind instruction. However, as more of them became involved with technology, they were exposed to formal instructional design techniques and theories, and came to appreciate the importance of evaluation. In addition, the interest in evaluation led to a greater interest in formal research based on pedagogical theory and model-building. As indicated earlier in this chapter, thousands of studies have now been conducted examining all aspects of pedagogy in technology, and especially the newer online environments.

Online learning environments have also expanded interest in instructional design as a career and an area of professional research. Enrollments in graduate instructional technology and design programs have swelled as the demand for professionals in this area has increased. Instructional design has evolved to the point where many colleges and school districts have created departments and centers that now employ staffs to assist faculty with their course and program development needs. These departments were not common twenty years ago, or were modestly funded so that their impact was minimal. As part of their initial training and ongoing professional development, instructional designers are increasingly conducting research on the work they do and studying their techniques and approaches. In many cases, they are partnering with the faculty with whom they work. Centers on the scholarship of teaching have mushroomed to support these efforts. As a result of this activity, substantive new knowledge has been added to the knowledge base of pedagogical principles and applications. It is the hope of the authors that this book will be of assistance to those faculty, aspiring and veteran instructional designers, and researchers who are contemplating studying online and blended learning.

Definition of Terms

A basic rule of research is to carefully define key terms to minimize ambiguity on the part of readers. For this book, it is important that several key terms be defined as early as possible. If we start with the title, *Conducting Research in Online and Blended Learning Environments: New Pedagogical Frontiers*, four key terms (pedagogy, research, online learning, and blended learning) are included, for which definitions are provided below.

Pedagogy

Pedagogy refers simply to the art or science of teaching. It considers especially the instructional methods used in a course or learning module. Students in teacher education programs typically will take coursework that examines pedagogical principles and theories developed by the likes of Lev Vygotsky, Jean Piaget, John Dewey, and Robert Gagne. Many of these theories focus on the cognitive and social development of the learners. However, when applied to adult learning, Malcolm Knowles's theory of andragogy frequently comes into play. Knowles distinguished pedagogical theory as focused mostly on children and young people's learning, which is different than how adults learn. He posited that adults bring to the instruction process extensive life experiences that need to be considered in instructional design. Assumptions and insights based on the adult learner's knowledge and interests are used to develop meaningful instructional activities (Knowles, Holton, & Swanson, 2011). Since online and blended learning have become so commonplace in higher education, andragogical as well as pedagogical principles are assumed that come under the umbrella of pedagogy.

Education Research

The word research derives from the French *rechercher*, which means "to travel through" or "to search for carefully." Educational research is the seeking or searching for knowledge within the field of education. The formal definition of educational research is a careful, systematic investigation of any aspect of education. As professionals, educators should seek to increase their knowledge and improve their understanding of their profession: the teacher about teaching and learning, the administrator about leadership and school reform, the counselor about the social and psychological needs of students, the instructional designer about course design. The search for knowledge can be formal or informal and includes observation, gathering and analysis of performance data, individual case studies, and tightly controlled experiments. The search can be conducted by individual teachers, graduate students, professors in schools of education, or well-funded research organizations. The bottom line is that research helps us understand the education profession. Done for one's individual growth, it can be less formal and can rely on daily experiences, observations, and interactions. When shared with other professionals or when presented to one's colleagues for their feedback and constructive criticism, it needs to be more formal. Indeed, if education is to be considered a profession with paradigms for building knowledge and understanding, the use of systematic methodologies is critical. For the purposes of this book, all types of inquiry are respected; however, the more formal definition of education research that requires a systematic method(s) for collecting and analyzing data and reporting findings is highly recommended.

Online Learning

It would be an understatement to say that there is some confusion related to a definition of online learning. "Online" generally refers to a digital data communications network, the Internet and its smaller private cousins, intranets, being primary examples. Online learning in its simplest and most popular definition refers to any instruction delivered over a digital communications network. However, this definition needs clarification and refinement. First, online learning is not the same as distance learning or distance education. Distance learning (or education) has a long history using various instructional technologies such as paper manuals, radio, televised courses, and videocassettes, none of which rely on Internet technology. The British Open University is arguably one of the most successful distance learning organizations in the world, and yet many of its courses are not based on online technology.

Second, within the online environment, other terms such as "fully online," "virtual courses," "e-learning," "asynchronous learning," "distributed learning," "web-facilitated," and "web-enhanced learning" abound and contribute to confusion among many educators. Problems of definition are not new, especially when dealing with rapidly evolving technologies. However, some order is needed in this changing sea of terms. For the purposes of this book, and in the broadest sense, online learning is the preferred term for any instruction delivered over the Internet. However, a distinction will be made based on the amount of instruction delivered online, as compared to in person. Allen and Seaman (2014) have conducted eleven national studies on the extent and nature of online learning, and defined an online course as one where most or all of the content is delivered online. They more specifically defined such a course as having at least 80% of face-to-face seat time being replaced by online activity. This book will generally follow Allen and Seaman's definition. It is also our opinion that this definition, or similar, is fairly well accepted among many education researchers. However, it is also understood that a specific percentage (i.e., 80%) is confining, and it is understood that flexibility is needed.

Blended Learning

Blended learning is not one thing but comes in many different flavors, styles, and applications. It means different things to different people. The word "blended" implies a mixture more so than simply a combination of components. When a picture is pasted above a paragraph of text, a presentation is created that may be more informative to the viewer or reader, but the picture and text remain intact and can be individually discerned. However, when two cans of different colored paints are mixed, the new paint will look different from either of the original colors. In fact, if the new paint is mixed well, neither of the original colors will continue to be apparent. Similar situations exist in blended learning. The mix can be a simple separation of part of a course into an online component. For instance, a course that meets for three weekly contact hours might meet two hours in a traditional classroom while the equivalent of one hour is conducted online. The two modalities for this course are carefully separated, and although they may overlap, they can still be differentiated. In other forms of blended courses and programs the modalities are not so easily distinguishable. Consider an online program that offers three online courses in a semester that all students are required to take. The courses meet for three consecutive five-week sessions. However, students do a collaborative fifteen-week project that overlaps the courses. The students are expected to maintain regular communication with one another through email and group discussion boards. They are also required to meet face-to-face once a month on Saturdays, when course materials from the online courses are further presented and discussed, and some sessions are devoted to group project work. These activities begin to blur the modalities in a new mixture or blend where the individual parts are not as discernable as they once were. Add to this the increasing popularity of integrating video conferencing, podcasting, YouTube videos, wikis, blogs, and other media into classwork, and the definition of blended learning becomes very fluid.

In 2004, the Alfred P. Sloan Foundation funded an invitation-only workshop on blended learning. An important aspect of this workshop was to develop a working definition of the term "blended learning." The participants in this workshop had difficulty formulating a simple definition of blended learning, and the discussion alternated between a broad and a narrow definition. Gary Miller (2005), associate vice president for outreach and former executive director of the World Campus at Penn State University, described a lengthy process at his university which resulted in a definition containing five variations of "blended learning" environments. In the broadest sense, blended learning can be defined or conceptualized as a wide variety of technology/media integrated with conventional, face-to-face classroom activities (see Figure 1.1). However, several workshop participants wanted to focus on a narrower definition that centered on an online component that replaced seat time in the conventional classroom. The issue of a broad or narrow definition was discussed extensively, and the two core elements (online and face-to-face instruction) were deemed critical to blended learning. One year later, in 2005, at a second invitation-only workshop, the following definition of blended learning was adopted by the participants:

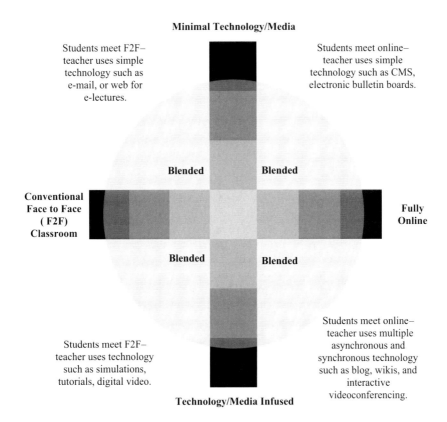

Figure 1.1 Conceptual Model of Blended Learning

Source: Picciano, A. G. (2009). Blending with purpose: The multimodal model. *Journal of the Research Center for Educational Technology, 5*(1). Kent, OH: Kent State University. Retrieved from www.rcetj.org/index.php/rcetj/article/view/11 [Accessed October 1, 2014].

1. Courses that integrate online with traditional face-to-face class activities in a planned, pedagogically valuable manner, and
2. Where a portion (institutionally defined) of face-to-face time is replaced by online activity

(Laster et al., 2005)

This definition serves as a guideline and should not be viewed as an absolute, limiting declaration. While it was developed to refer specifically to courses, it can also apply to entire academic programs. Several variations or models of blended learning have evolved since the above definition was presented. An excellent review of these is provided by Graham, Henrie, and Gibbons (2014) and is highly recommended for further information.

The Education Research Process

In the section above, on a definition of education research, the statement was made that for purposes of this book all types of inquiry are respected; however, the more formal definition of education research that requires a systematic method(s) for collecting and analyzing data and reporting findings is highly recommended. Formal education research derives in part from the classical or scientific method of conducting research that consists of four steps:

1. Defining a problem
2. Stating a main question or hypothesis
3. Collecting relevant data
4. Analyzing the data to answer the question or test the hypothesis

Paralleling the scientific method (see Figure 1.2), the educational research process consists of the following:

1. **Identifying a problem**—The researcher selects a topic in which she or he is genuinely interested and then tries to establish why the problem is important and worthy of research.
2. **Clarifying the problem**—The researcher reviews the research literature to determine what is known and what still needs to be known about the problem.
3. **Formulating a hypothesis or research question**
4. **Developing a methodology**—The researcher selects an appropriate research methodology and implements procedures for collecting, summarizing, and analyzing data.
5. **Reporting the findings**—Based on data analysis, the researcher presents a clear statement of the findings.
6. **Drawing conclusions**—Using the hypotheses or research questions as the guide, the researcher forms conclusions based on the findings.

The education research process is presented as an overall guide for conducting research and for clarifying the nature of a definition of formal education research. However, the authors of this book recognize that there are other research processes used in qualitative research, exploratory research, and big data analysis that do not

Scientific Method	Educational Research Process
Defining a problem	Identifying a problem
Stating a hypothesis or main question	Clarifying the problem
Collecting relevant data	Stating a hypothesis or research question
Analyzing the data to answer the question or to test the hypothesis	Developing a methodology
	Reporting the findings
	Drawing conclusions

Figure 1.2 Comparison of the Scientific Method and the Educational Research Process

necessarily follow the education research process described above. Be assured that these approaches are respected and are most appropriate for conducting research in online and blended learning. As will be seen in the following chapters, there is much important work that has been done with these methodologies.

The Chapters

This book is organized so that each chapter will examine a specific aspect of education research as applied to online and blended learning. Each chapter attempts to provide a self-contained treatment of a topic so that a reader can read and reread a chapter that is of specific interest. As a result, there is some overlap of the material covered throughout the book. However, this was done on purpose for the convenience of readers who may be interested in one specific aspect of education research in online and blended learning. For a broad review of the field of education research in online and blended learning, readers are very much encouraged to read the entire book and then select a chapter(s) for rereading as appropriate.

Each chapter will also include examples of the "best research" conducted in online and blended learning to provide the reader with ideas and insights into good practice. For example, Chapter 5 on survey research refers to the work of Allen and Seaman. Chapter 9 on the scholarship of teaching and learning refers to the work at the University of Central Florida. It is hoped that readers will glean ideas about research issues from these "best research" pieces as they plan their own study's methodology or method.

Chapter 2 provides an overview of paradigms, methodologies, and methods appropriate for designing research projects focused on issues related to online and blended learning. A three-tier conceptual framework for conducting research is presented.

Chapter 3 introduces the reader to various types and purposes of the literature review. It also introduces technology tools and strategies for more quickly identifying literature that is important to a particular scholarly inquiry. It concludes with a general process for conducting a literature review.

Chapter 4 looks at meta-analysis as a research technique that has been used for studying many issues in the social sciences, including the effects and impact of instructional technology. A meta-analysis is a study wherein a set of statistical procedures is used to summarize and synthesize the results of a number of independently conducted research studies. The chapter emphasizes that the underlying rationale for conducting a meta-analysis is the need or desire to synthesize findings across many studies into a common metric.

Chapter 5 presents survey research as one of the most popular methods for collecting data in the social sciences. This flexible means of data collection can be used with various sample sizes, from very small to very large, and can be used as the basis of a standalone study, or integrated with other methods including qualitative studies, inferential studies, correlation research, and comparative research. It has been used extensively in online and blended learning research.

In Chapter 6, Chuck Dziuban reminds us that the remarkable growth of online and blended learning throughout the world reinforces the need for improved data analysis methods. Newer and more effective computing options make it possible to provide useful information to a broad range of interested parties, such as policymakers, faculty, students, and the public at large. However, these options require careful considerations of the underlying concepts associated with data analysis.

Tony Picciano reviews the popularity of qualitative research in conducting education research, including the study of online and blended learning environments in Chapter 7. Qualitative research is a broad category of inquiry that uses a number of different methods and tools to assist in data collection and analysis, including case studies, ethnography, grounded theory, discourse analysis, and phenomenology.

In Chapter 8, Charles Graham introduces the reader to case study research as a flexible methodology that can be applied in a wide variety of contexts. He views it as ideal for studying educational contexts, including online and blended learning.

Patsy Moskal provides the reader with an overview of the scholarship of teaching and learning in Chapter 9. She reminds us that it is not a new concept but has evolved over decades, as faculty have become more involved with trying new teaching practices, instructional methods, and technologies in their classrooms in an effort to better reach students and effectively improve their instruction. She concludes that the scholarship of teaching and learning involves more than trying new things for the faculty member; it requires systematically researching the changes to instruction as a result of any modification they may have made to be able to determine and document what worked and what did not work.

Chapter 10 describes the importance of longitudinal research. The power of this method of evaluation is in its inherent ability to examine trends through repeated snapshots in time, or even following a cohort as they complete a module, course, or program in a given period of time. The repeated nature of longitudinal evaluation allows for potentially more precise findings, and the repeated nature of data collection helps provide an opportunity for iterative improvements to be made in instruction and data analysis, over the evolution of an initiative.

Chapter 11 focuses on a phenomenon that has created a considerable interest in the areas of online and blended learning research, namely the construct of big data. At its core big data has given us the ability to find important patterns and relationships that simply are not possible with smaller sample sizes.

Chapter 12 comments on the current trends in assessment of student outcomes in online and blended learning environments. Chuck Dziuban observes that students in these environments have to come to understand the importance of regular and meaningful feedback about their academic performance. Openly, they express their view that effective teaching must be embedded in benchmarks describing how they are progressing through their courses and programs. One side effect of the heightened interactivity in this type of learning has been a shift away from the assessment methods of the past, and a movement toward processes that are more contextual and relevant to what will be expected of students once they complete their studies.

Chapter 13 provides an extensive review of where we have been and where we are going in online and blended learning research. It is a fitting conclusion to the key ideas presented in this book.

References

Allen, I.E., & Seaman, J. (2014). *Grade change: Tracking online learning education in the United States*. Needham, MA: Babson Survey Research Group. Retrieved from www.onlinelearningsurvey. com/reports/gradechange.pdf [Accessed June 6, 2014].

Dick, W., Carey, L., & Carey, J. (2011). *The systematic design of instruction* (7th ed.). New York: Pearson.

Gagne, R. M. (1977). *Conditions of learning*. New York: Holt, Rinehart, & Winston.

Graham, C. R., Henrie, C. R., & Gibbons, A. S. (2014). Developing models and theory for blended learning research. In Picciano, A. G., Dziuban, C. D., & Graham, C. R. *Blended learning: Research perspectives, vol. 2* (pp. 13–33). New York: Routledge/Taylor & Francis.

Kemp, J. (1985). *The instructional design process*. New York: Harper & Row.

Knowles, M., Holton, E. F., & Swanson, R. A. (2011). *The adult learner* (7th ed.). New York: Taylor & Francis.

Laster, S., Otte, G., Picciano, A. G., & Sorg, S. (2005, April 18). *Redefining blended learning*. Presentation at the 2005 Sloan-C Workshop on Blended Learning, Chicago, IL.

Means, B., Bakia, M., & Murphy, R. (2014). *Learning online: What research tells us whether, when, and how*. New York: Routledge/Taylor & Francis Group.

Miller, G. (2005, June 30). *Blended learning and Sloan-C*. Posting to the official website of the 2005 Sloan-C summer workshop held in Victoria, BC.

Picciano, A. G. (2009). Blending with purpose: The multimodal model. *Journal of the Research Center for Educational Technology, 5*(1), 4–14. Kent, OH: Kent State University.

Picciano, A. G., & Seaman, J. (2007). K-12 online learning: A survey of U.S. school district administrators. *Journal of Asynchronous Learning Networks, 11*(3), 11–37. Needham, MA: The Sloan Consortium. Retrieved from www.sloan-c.org/publications/jaln/v11n3/v11n3_3piccianoseaman_member.asp [Accessed October 3, 2013].

Picciano, A. G., & Seaman, J. (2009). *K–12 online learning: A 2008 follow-up of the survey of U.S. school district administrators*. Needham, MA: The Sloan Consortium. Retrieved from www.sloan-c. org/publications/survey/pdf/k-12_online_learning_2008.pdf [Accessed October 3, 2013].

Picciano, A. G., & Seaman, J. (2010). *Class connections: High school reform and the role of online learning*. Boston: Babson College Survey Research Group. Retrieved from www3.babson.edu/Newsroom/Releases/online-high-school-learning.cfm [Accessed October 3, 2013].

U.S. Department of Education (U.S. ED), Office of Planning, Evaluation, and Policy Development (2010). *Evaluation of evidence-based practices in online learning: A meta-analysis and review of online learning studies*. Washington, DC. Retrieved from www2.ed.gov/rschstat/eval/tech/evidence-based-practices/finalreport.pdf [Accessed October 10, 2013].

Chapter 2

Paradigms, Methodologies, Methods, and the Role of Theory in Online and Blended Learning Research

Anthony G. Picciano

Studies of instructional practices such as online learning and blended learning lend themselves to the consideration of integrating research and practice. Research can take many forms in terms of scope, foci, and methods of analysis, and can be conducted from a "distance" with little interaction between the researchers and the instructional activities. For example, a study of the perceptions of school administrators on the use of online learning can be accomplished by sending a survey to a national sample of school principals. Although the ability of the researchers to locate themselves within the schools represented in the survey will be minimal (or nonexistent), the scale of this type of research can provide valuable data across different types of school districts (urban, rural, suburban), across regions of the country, and across levels of instruction (primary, middle, secondary).

On the other hand, a participating instructor in a "scholarship of teaching" program at a college might conduct research on the use of online technology in a single course offered over the period of one semester in a very different manner. This instructor might survey the students to determine their perceptions of the success of the course, or interview them to uncover nuance and subtlety not readily apparent in normal course activities. The instructor might have access to official student records, including student demographics, GPAs, and areas of concentration, to use in the study analysis; he/she would also have transcripts of an online discussion board or blog as documentation of the interactions and exchanges that took place during a class. In sum, the instructor has access and insight into data that can provide a deeper analysis than the data generally available in a study with a much larger scope.

In this chapter, large-scale as well as small-scale projects are acknowledged as important contributions to the online and blended learning research base. Most pertinent to the discussion in this chapter is the desirability of integrating sound and appropriate research approaches into the research on online and blended learning.

The chapter provides an overview of paradigms, methodologies, and methods appropriate for designing research projects focused on issues related to online and blended learning. A three-tier conceptual framework (see Figure 2.1) for conducting research will be presented that includes:

1. Paradigms
2. Methodologies
3. Methods

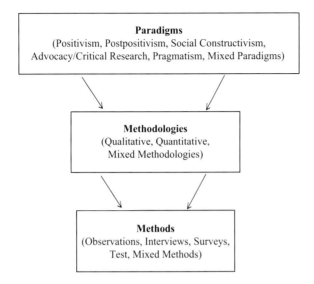

Figure 2.1 Three-Tier Conceptual Framework for Conducting Research

Overarching paradigms such as positivism, postpositivism, social constructivism/interpretivism, advocacy/critical research, and pragmatism will be discussed first. Second, quantitative, qualitative, and mixed methodologies will be examined. And within the third tier, various methods including surveys, experiments, observations, interviews, and content analysis tools will be introduced. The role of theory will also be examined, looking especially at social theory which is ideally suited for studying complex, highly interactive phenomena such as teaching and learning. The chapter will conclude with a recommendation that researchers remain open to considering all of the options presented in the framework, in that all are appropriate, and can be used, for studying online and blended learning. The challenge for the researcher will be to select the right options to fit the inquiry at hand.

Paradigms

A paradigm is a philosophical or theoretical framework within which theories, laws, generalizations, and the research performed in support of them are formulated. Other terms are sometimes used for paradigm. Creswell (2013), in a textbook on research design, uses the term "worldview." Crotty (1998) uses the term "epistemology." For purposes of this discussion, the word paradigm will be used. A paradigm influences the way research is conducted and the way knowledge is studied and interpreted. It establishes the aim, motivation, and expectations for the research. In conducting research, choices of methodologies, methods, and design should follow only after a paradigm has been established. In fact, without establishing a paradigm as the first step, there is little basis for subsequent choices regarding methodology and methods. A standardized taxonomy of research paradigms in the social sciences does not exist. Like the word paradigm itself, different terms have been used to describe similar paradigms, some of which overlap and can be the source of confusion. Among the most popular paradigms in social science research are positivism, postpositivism, constructivism, interpretivism, transformation, emancipation, advocacy, critical research, pragmatism, and deconstructivism. In the following sections, several popular paradigms will be briefly examined.

Positivism

Positivism views the universe as operating according to rational principles that can be studied empirically and quantified. Determinism is generally accepted as a guiding positivist tenet and accepts the existence of absolute truths that relate to causes and effects. Positivism can be seen in the ancient world (Aristotle) and was promoted during the Enlightenment by Francis Bacon, Rene Descartes, and John Locke. Positivistic approaches were first used widely by researchers and philosophers studying the natural world and were later adopted by social scientists. Positivism for the most part follows the scientific method and aims to test theories and hypotheses through observation and measurement. However, the fit of positivism with the social sciences has not always been graceful, and rather the subject of much debate. As succinctly stated by Pring (2000), the language of atoms and particles is not the same as the language of intensely complex human interactions such as teaching and learning. While many scientists accept a natural world order where cause and effect variables can be controlled and quantified, the social world is a far more ambiguous one, where many variables interact and intervene in ways that make it difficult, if not impossible, to achieve conclusive findings. As a result, a movement away from positivism evolved in the middle of the 20th century into what came to be called postpositivism.

Postpositivism

Postpositivism has been a source of confusion with regard to its relationship to positivism. Creswell (2013) sees postpositivism as a refinement that tempers the positivist working with theory, hypotheses, and measurement. He is reluctant in asserting that there are all-encompassing principles governing the social world. However, Trochim (2006) commented, "I don't mean a slight adjustment to or revision of the positivist position—postpositivism is a wholesale rejection of the central tenets of positivism." In 2006, Mackensie and Knipe commented on this confusion:

> Postpositivists work from the assumption that any piece of research is influenced by a number of well-developed theories apart from, and as well as, the one which is being tested (Cook & Campbell, 1979, p.24). Also, since theories are held to be provisional and new understandings may challenge the whole theoretical framework (Kuhn, 1962). In contrast, O'Leary (2004), provides a definition of postpositivism which aligns in some sense with the constructivist paradigm claiming that postpositivists see the world as ambiguous, variable and multiple in its realities—"what might be the truth for one person or cultural group may not be the 'truth' for another" (p.6). O'Leary (2004) suggests that postpositivism is intuitive and holistic, inductive and exploratory with findings that are qualitative in nature (pp.6–7). This definition of postpositivism seems to be in conflict with the more widely used definition provided by Mertens

(2005). Positivists and postpositivist research is most commonly aligned with quantitative methods of data collection and analysis.

(Mackensie & Knipe, 2006)

In sum, postpositivists see the limitations of the world order. They may approach research deterministically and seek cause and effect, but they understand that these are subject to change and are not absolute. They assume that findings may only be applicable to the situation at hand and are open to revision and reinterpretation in other environments. While tending to the quantitative, they also use qualitative methodologies.

Social Constructivism/Interpretivism

The social constructivist/interpretivist paradigm sees the world as socially constructed (Mertens, 2005). Realities are in the minds of the beholders and subject to multiple interpretations. Social constructivism/interpretivism posits that both researchers and subjects' views of the situation being studied are critical to the inquiry. In contrast to positivists and postpositivists, social constructivists do not always begin with a theory; rather they inductively develop a theory or pattern of meanings throughout the research process. Social constructivist/interpretivist researchers must understand their own subjectivity in conducting their inquiries. Creswell (2013) emphasizes that social constructivists understand that their own personal, cultural, and historical experiences shape their interpretations of the situations under study. Furthermore, in this paradigm the context of the research situation plays a critical role in shaping the interpretation, and hence no attempt can be made to generalize beyond the setting under study. While largely supporting qualitative methodologies, quantitative data may also be used to support or expand the analysis. Lincoln and Guba (1985) describe social constructivism as a naturalistic inquiry that is not antiquantitative and in fact can utilize quantitative data when appropriate.

Advocacy/Critical Research

Advocacy/critical research emerged in the 1980s with researchers who believed that social constructivism did not do enough to address the issues of social justice and the causes of marginalized individuals (Creswell, 2013). Drawing from the philosophies of Marx and Engels, and more recently from Freire, this paradigm advocates for political action to address social issues such as poverty, domination, and inequality. Freire, especially, saw advocacy/critical research as a tool to lift colonized populations out of their suppressed conditions. In conducting advocacy/critical research, subjects of the inquiry are seen as collaborators who help design the study, assist in data collection, and participate in the analysis. Participatory action research (PAR), for example, is a common manifestation of the paradigm. Quantitative, qualitative, and mixed methodologies can be used equally well with this paradigm.

Pragmatism

Pragmatism emanates from the work of a number of individuals, although John Dewey is considered a prime mover in its development. Dewey espoused finding solutions that work in education. Pragmatism draws on other paradigms, if needed, but does not get bound by philosophical or theoretical entanglements. Pragmatists are free to design research that best meets the needs of the questions at hand. Like social constructivism, it tends to be more context based and is not interested in finding absolute truths. It supports quantitative, qualitative, and mixed methodologies equally. Evaluation studies of instructional programs and processes frequently fall within the pragmatic paradigm.

The above descriptions do not constitute an all-inclusive discussion, but serve to provide an overview of the more popular paradigms. Readers should also be aware that paradigms overlap and studies can, in fact, be multiparadigmatic. Taylor and Medina (2013) comment that rather than standing alone as individual paradigms for framing the design of a researcher's inquiry, the newer paradigms can serve as referents. In other words, research can be designed by combining methods that apply to two or more of the paradigms. For example, it is not uncommon for a research study to combine methods from the social constructivist and critical paradigms to create a "critical auto/ethnography." This multiparadigmatic approach can prove powerful and should be considered where appropriate.

Methodologies

Methodologies are strategies that provide direction and a plan for researchers as they prepare and conduct their inquiries (Creswell, 2013). These methodologies can essentially be characterized as quantitative, qualitative, or mixed. The debates among the proponents of these methodologies, especially the first two, have been long and at times rancorous. Pring (2000) proposes that the debate between quantitative and qualitative methodologies is the age-old debate between mind and body. The quantitative represents the objective, real-world, body traditions, while the qualitative represents the socially constructed mental or mind traditions. However, the real world, or the world of common sense, cannot be captured by one or the other, and indeed there must be an overlapping of the two. Hence the call for, or at least a consideration of, mixed methods where appropriate. Pring argues that a qualitative investigation can clear the ground for the quantitative—and the quantitative can be suggestive of differences to be explored in a more interpretive (qualitative) mode. Qualitative research relies on meanings, concepts, contexts, descriptions, and settings, while quantitative research relies on measurements and counts (Berg, 2004). Qualitative research requires seeing, hearing, and perhaps touching and experiencing activities in natural environments. Quantitative research requires a distancing from the object of study, while the sorting, counting, and analysis of numerical data are done away from their sources.

Qualitative Methodologies

There are a number of qualitative methodologies. In this chapter, several of the more popular will be discussed, including case study, ethnography, grounded theory, discourse analysis, and phenomenology. These approaches may overlap one another and frequently do. For instance, a case study may be approached ethnographically. Brief descriptions of each of these methodologies are presented here in order to provide a basic understanding rather than an in-depth examination, which is not possible in a single chapter.

Case Study

Case study research is descriptive research that involves describing and interpreting events, conditions, or situations. The purpose of a case study is to examine in detail a specific activity, event, organization, or person(s). Case study is a very flexible methodology that comes in many different forms, including descriptive, exploratory, longitudinal, and multisite. The choice of object in a case study analysis is at the discretion of the researcher and can be a single school district, a school, a class, or an individual student. It is particularly popular among researchers examining online or blended learning in a single course or program.

Ethnography

Ethnography stems from the Greek "ethnos," meaning people, tribes, or nations, and "graphy," meaning writing. Ethnographic research is the writing about people in their natural or social setting. It is a form of descriptive research and is also referred to as "observational research" and "naturalistic inquiry." Among the social sciences, it has been especially popular in cultural anthropology because of the work of Margaret Mead and other noted anthropologists. Ethnography is well suited for research in instructional technology because so much of what is done in education is based on human interaction in natural and social settings such as schools, classrooms, and online environments.

Grounded Theory

Grounded theory is an inductive methodology that attempts to derive a theory from an activity, process, or interaction and is *grounded* in the views of the participants. It is sometimes referred to as "the discovery" of theory from data (Glaser & Strauss, 1967). Grounded theory is an iterative process that compares and refines findings with multiple observations.

Discourse Analysis

Discourse analysis examines how language is used in speech, written texts, and in context. It concerns itself with the use of language in an ongoing *discourse* continued over a number of sentences. It examines carefully the interactions of the generator of the discourse with the receiver of the discourse in a specific situational context. In online environments, it is ideally suited for examining interactions on discussion boards, blogs, and wikis.

Phenomenology

Phenomenology aims to describe the *essence and commonality* of a phenomenon by viewing it through the eyes of participants. It attempts to discover how the phenomenon actually is experienced, and usually involves a small number of subjects who are interviewed and observed as they participate in the phenomenon. It is not to be confused with the closely associated phenomenographic methodology which is used to investigate and describe *the qualitatively different ways* in which people experience, understand, see, and relate to phenomenon in the natural world.

Quantitative Methodologies

Quantitative methodologies include descriptive studies, correlation research, experimental research and quasi-experimental research. These methodologies rely on a careful collection of numerical data from subjects involved in a process or program. The development of computer technology in the past fifty years has enabled quantitative researchers to collect and analyze large amounts of data that can be stored and maintained for decades, if necessary.

Descriptive Study

The quantitative descriptive study uses numerical data to describe and interpret events, conditions, or situations. Among the more popular statistical measures used in a descriptive case study are frequency distributions, means, standard deviations, and cross tabulations. A quantitative descriptive study is concerned with describing a given population or phenomenon. However, if done well it can provide the foundation for a more extensive inferential study that serves as the basis for generalization. The potential is realized when the small base descriptive study is extended or replicated with a larger random sample, allowing the researcher to suggest that the findings be extended to the larger population. A quantitative descriptive study is especially effective when comparing subpopulations such as students, groups, different schools, or different academic programs. Comparative descriptive studies are popular among many educational researchers and especially government funding agencies.

Correlational Research

Correlational research uses numerical data to explore the relationship between two or more variables. The exploration provides insight into the nature of the variables themselves, as well as an understanding of their relationships. Furthermore, if the relationships are substantial and consistent, the findings enable the researcher to make certain predictions about the variables. The purpose of correlational research therefore is to describe relationships and predict future events based on these relationships. A correlational study may be designed to meet one or both of these purposes. In a correlational study designed to predict events related to two variables, one variable is identified as the predictor, or independent variable, while the other variable is identified as the criterion, or dependent variable. The value of the predictor or independent variable is used to predict the value of the criterion or dependent variable.

The fundamental statistical measure used in correlation is a coefficient that varies between -1.00 and $+1.00$. There are a number of different methods and formulae for calculating this coefficient, depending upon the type of data being analyzed. One of the more commonly used is the Pearson product moment correlation coefficient, which requires two sets of values that represent continuous, interval data such as standardized test scores and grade point averages. A negative coefficient (less than 0) indicates an inverse correlation; that is, as one variable changes (increases or decreases), the other changes in the opposite direction. A positive coefficient (greater than 0) indicates that as one variable changes, the other changes in the same direction. A coefficient of 0 indicates that there is no relationship between the variables.

It is important to remember that when doing correlational studies, a relationship does not necessarily indicate causality. There can be substantive correlations between two variables without one variable causing the other to happen. For example, if one were to study the relationship between student participation in extracurricular activities and student performance, one might find a high correlation; but participation in extracurricular activities does not cause high performance. Other variables related to participation in extracurricular activities, such as self-esteem and a positive attitude toward school, may in fact cause highly participative students to work harder and therefore to perform well.

Experimental Research

The purpose of experimental research is to study cause (independent variable) and effect (dependent variable) relationships between two or more variables, where the causal variable can be manipulated. In a classic example of a true experiment in education, two groups of students that are similar in key characteristics are randomly selected; one group (experimental) is taught for a period of time using a new technique or treatment, and a second group (control or placebo) is taught using a traditional technique. At the conclusion of the experiment, the two groups are tested to determine if there is a difference in their achievement. The teaching technique represents the causal or independent variable, and student achievement is the effect or dependent variable. The causal variable in this example has been manipulated by assigning students to groups in which different teaching methods are used. In analyzing the test results, if student achievement was greater in the experimental group, then the researcher can claim that the new teaching technique (treatment) was the cause. This basic experimental research model has been utilized many times in studies involving instructional technology.

Although the technique appears to be relatively simple, many researchers encounter a number of issues that make it difficult for them to conduct this type of experiment. For instance, one important question might be: Do we really want to experiment with the learning of children? Suppose the experiment outlined above was conducted on two fourth grade mathematics classes, and suppose rather than improving achievement, the achievement was significantly lower for the experimental group. Who is responsible for the significantly lower achievement of these children, and how do the researchers remediate the situation? This situation represents a major concern that applies to experimental research, as opposed to other methods where variables are not manipulated.

Quasi-Experimental Research

As a result of concerns with experimental research, researchers have developed a variety of quasi-experimental techniques that preserve elements of the experimental approach while allowing some practical deviations. For example, random sampling is not always possible, especially in the natural setting. Students are assigned to classes or to particular teachers for a number of sound educational reasons. Since conducting a random sample experiment might be disruptive or possibly harmful, many school administrators would be reluctant to grant permission to do so. As a result, a number of designs employing experimental methods were developed that do not depend upon random sampling. They are less rigorous than true experimental designs, but may be more practical to conduct in the field.

Mixed Methodologies

Just as it is possible to have multiparadigmatic approaches to research, the same is true for methodologies. In fact, there is an increased interest in mixing qualitative and quantitative methodologies. The tools of each methodology can be used to provide a more complete description and analysis of the subject of the study. For example, the methods of a quantitative descriptive study can be integrated into a qualitative case study and vice versa. In addition, other specialized methodologies, such as participatory action research (PAR) that actively involves subjects in data collection and analysis, are very conducive to mixing quantitative and qualitative methodologies.

Methods

Many methods are available to the educational researcher for collecting data. Visits to school settings to observe instruction, structured interviews with educators, examination of student records on school databases, surveys, and test instruments are all appropriate, depending on the nature of the study. The researcher decides how to collect data based on the research methodology selected to study the problem. An ethnographic study of student behavior in a class usually requires a visit(s) to the natural setting or classroom. A correlational study of the relationship between participation on online discussion boards/blogs and academic achievement would require accessing student records in databases for test scores, grade point averages, graduation rates, or other achievement data. Because a number of options usually exist, a researcher should plan ahead, organize, and then select or design an appropriate tool for collecting data. In the following paragraphs, several popular data collection methods are presented. They will also be discussed in more detail in later chapters that are devoted to examples of online and blended learning research.

Direct Observation

Some research methods, such as ethnography and forms of descriptive study, require observation of activities in a school or other natural setting. The observation may be conducted in person or by video recording.

In-person observations allow an activity to be scanned extensively for relevant behaviors and context. Observers are trained to take careful notes as they look and listen for subtle comments, clues, and nuances, such as facial expressions or inflection and tone of voice. Video requires camera and other equipment to be set up to record an activity. One benefit of video is that the recorded file can be observed over and over again. A video can also be shared with experts who were not present during the original recording, in order to receive their comments and advice. However, having a camera or other equipment visible might lead some individuals "to play to the camera" and not act as they normally do.

When conducting observations in person, the researcher must decide whether the observer is or is not an active participant (i.e., participant observer) in an activity and prepare accordingly. If the purpose of the observation is to record behaviors as objectively and completely as possible with little or no interaction, then the observer must be trained to keep his or her presence to a minimum. However, if the observer is to participate and assume a role in an activity, then the observer must be trained to act the role. For example, an observer might assume the role of a team-teacher in a class and so must be trained to be a teacher for the duration of the observation.

Observations, whenever possible, are conducted over a period of time. Accurate depictions require the observer to see and hear activities at multiple times. It is not unusual for observations, particularly those involving an educational activity, to go on for a semester, a year, or longer.

In addition to in-person or video observation of learning, researchers in online and blended learning environments have at their disposal student and instructor interactions on discussion boards, blogs, wikis, and other permanent records of course activities that can be reviewed and studied. These are invaluable sources of information and will be discussed in more detail in later chapters.

Structured Interviews

Structured interviews are carefully scripted tools for collecting data, wherein the researcher meets with and asks questions of an individual(s). Interviews can be conducted one-on-one, or they can be conducted with a group of subjects (i.e., focus group). The structured interview is well organized, and all questions are developed in advance and written as part of a script that the researcher or interviewer follows. The interview script contains the identification of the interviewee, where the interview is being conducted, short answer questions (either fill in the blank or multiple choice), and open-ended questions that allow the responder to explain how or why something exists or occurs. Open-ended questions allow the interviewer to pursue a line of questioning and to follow up with additional questions when the interviewee has mentioned something interesting or provocative. One good technique for designing a structured interview is to start with broad, general questions and move on to more direct, specific questions depending upon the responses.

Structured interviews are very effective data collection tools when the interviewer is adept at questioning, can make an interviewee feel comfortable, and is able to prompt honest responses. By the same token, structured interviews can be problematic if the interviewer is not adept or objective. Another major concern is prompting an interviewee to respond in a particular way; this is especially pertinent when interviewing children. Whether the subjects are children or adults, questions must be carefully worded to minimize leading the interviewee. For example, an interview of students concerning the benefits of blogging as part of a course activity might start with one of the following neutral questions: "How do you feel about blogging in this course" or "do you enjoy blogging in this course?" Questions designed to provoke should be minimized. For example: "Have you heard that some students flame at one another during online class discussions" or "do you know of anyone who thinks that online discussions are a waste of time?"

Structured interviews take time to conduct properly, and for this reason the researcher must carefully select the interviewees. Unless there is substantial funding for a research project, a small sample of interviewees will be selected to represent a larger population. If a larger sample is selected and more than one interviewer is used, then the interviewers need to be trained to be consistent in their line of questioning. A good technique in designing a structured interview is to field-test it several times with a very small group of representative interviewees to determine if there are any problems with the wording of questions or any other aspect of the interview. Structured interviews should also be designed to repeat key or important questions in slightly different forms to determine if the interviewees are consistent in their responses. If the interviewees allow it, making an audiotape of each interview will provide a simple mechanism for reviewing notes and responses.

Surveys

While observations and structured interviews are appropriate data collection tools for small populations, financially and logistically it is difficult or impossible to use them for studies requiring a large number of subjects. Survey research is one of the most popular tools for collecting data on large samples. It can be used for a number of different research methodologies, including descriptive studies, correlation research, and comparative research. Some well-respected experts consider survey research as a unique methodology rather than as a data collection tool (Wiersma, 2000). The art of conducting a good survey has a number of design considerations and will be discussed in more detail in Chapter 5.

Test Instruments

Test instruments are used to collect data for certain educational research topics and problems. For instance, student achievement is an area of study that frequently requires testing. While some researchers consider developing their own test instruments, this is not always necessary. Many excellent test instruments in a wide variety of topics have been developed, and deciding which of these instruments may be appropriate is an option that should be considered by the researcher.

Test instruments are available from commercial vendors, colleges and universities, and test organizations. *Tests in Print* is probably the best source for locating an appropriate test instrument. This multivolume reference is published by the Buros Institute of Mental Measurement and contains reviews of thousands of test instruments. Another popular source is the ERIC/ETS test locator website, which is available online at http://ericae.net/testcol.htm. This database also contains thousands of descriptions of test instruments and publishers. It is updated regularly by the Educational Testing Service (ETS).

Using Multiple Methods

While not all research is conducive to a combination approach, certain topics or methodologies, especially descriptive research, provide opportunities for researchers to combine two or more methods. For example, research on the use of online learning in schools may be done through surveys sent to a large sample of school administrators. After the surveys have been collected and the initial data analyzed, structured interviews of a smaller sample of administrators may be used to follow up on certain aspects of the survey results needing clarification, such as teacher training or curriculum development. In this example, the structured interviews are used to enhance the survey results and provide a more complete description or picture. As with methodologies, combining research methods takes advantage of having multiple tools at the researcher's disposal.

The Role of Theory

A discussion of the role of theory in education research easily fills volumes. While it is not the purpose of this section to review this extensive literature, the role of theory is fundamental to research and must be addressed. Simply put, a study conducted within a theoretical framework can contribute significantly to the knowledge base that exists on a phenomenon, topic, or issue. Theory allows the researcher to identify significant variables, to relate and assimilate findings to a larger body of research, and to identify areas for additional research.

For this discussion, theory is defined as the general principles or ideas that relate to a particular subject. The purpose of theory is to propose the answers to basic questions associated with a phenomenon. Graham, Henrie, and Gibbons (2013) reviewed this issue and recommend a three-part taxonomy first proposed by Gibbons and Bunderson (2005), which establishes theories that:

1. *Explore*—Answer "what exists?" and attempt to define and categorize
2. *Explain*—Answer "why does this happen?" and look for causality and correlation, and work with variables and relationships
3. *Design*—Answer "how do I achieve this outcome?" and describe interventions for reaching targeted outcomes and operational principles

Associated with theory is the term "model." As noted by Graham, Henrie, and Gibbons (2013), the terms are used interchangeably and generally refer to the same concept.

Theories for Education Research

Theories used in education research emanate from a number of disciplines and perspectives, depending upon the topic being studied. Education by its nature is interdisciplinary, and therefore its research bases can be approached pedagogically, psychologically, economically, politically, and socially. Among the most popular are social theories that are used to describe and explain social phenomena such as teaching, learning, school administration, and professional development. For example, the constructivist work of Vygotsky (1978) posits that learning, in essence, is problem solving and that the social construction of solutions to problems is the basis of the learning process. Vygotsky described the learning process as the establishment of a "zone of proximal development" in which the teacher, the learner, and a problem to be solved exist. The teacher provides an environment in which the learner can assemble or construct with others the knowledge necessary to solve the problem. John Dewey (1915) likewise saw learning as a series of practical social experiences in which learners learn by doing, collaborating, and reflecting with others. Seymour Papert (1980), in designing the Logo programming language, drew from Piaget (1952) the concept of creating social, interactive, technology-based microworlds or communities where children solve problems under the guidance of a teacher by working with a computer to examine social issues, mathematical and science equations, or case studies. Papert's approach can be applied to the design of any instructional technology application. The concept of community, as used in the term "communities of practice," has gained much popularity as a result of the work of Wenger and Lave (1991) in situated learning. Their position is that learning involves a deepening process situated in and derived from participation in a learning community of practice. Their work is very much in evidence in many studies related to learning communities. In sum, there exists a multitude of theoretical frameworks that have been and will continue to be applied to education research, including that which focuses on online and blended learning.

Theories Appropriate for Online and Blended Learning Research

Online and blended learning provide a plethora of opportunities to choose from a wide range of theories important to education researchers. The following examples serve to illustrate theory and research foci appropriate to online and blended learning environments.

Communities of Inquiry

The community of inquiry model developed by Garrison, Anderson, and Archer (2001), and derived from Dewey (1915) and Wenger and Lave (1991), has served as a framework for a large number of studies that examine the element of *presence* as it relates to cognition, social interaction, and teaching strategy. The concept of "presence," or a sense of being in a place and belonging to a group, is germane to studies of student interaction and engagement in an online or blended learning environment. Frequently comparisons are made between a student's physical presence in a face-to-face course and his/her presence in an online course where instruction is mediated by technology (discussion boards, wikis, blogs). These studies focus on whether students have a sense of belonging in the class and actively participate in the learning community. Observations are made about the extent to which students offer comments on material, ask and respond to questions, or form relationships with other students. Observations are also made about whether students feel alienation that might lead to attrition. In sum, this basic theory can provide a framework for a wide range of inquiries that focus on social aspects of instruction.

Bounded Rationality

The bounded rationality theory of Nobel laureate Herbert Simon (1957, 1982) has served as a framework for a wide range of research focused on administrative decision making. The essence of Simon's theory is that rational administrative processes have limits, because decision makers are limited or bounded by what they can possibly know about alternatives and the ramifications of their decisions. They may start with the rational process, but eventually they incorporate other factors based on experience and instinct in order to make decisions. Simon's theory is well respected internationally. The social theorist Pierre Bourdieu (2005), in discussing his theory of habitus, cites Simon and adds that the human mind is not only simply generically bounded but also socially bounded. With the advancement of learning analytics and big data as applied to online learning, Simon's theory of bounded rationality is most appropriate in studying the management of the online learning process. Online learning systems are now being developed that can generate a good deal of student transaction data, literally down to each keystroke. These systems are extending the limits of rational processes as conceived by Simon, and can be used to study student progress in a course to the point of developing predictive models to address issues such as retention and attrition. The use of learning analytics is fairly new, and a prime topic for research.

Learning Styles/Multiple Intelligences

The theoretical base on learning styles posits that individuals learn differently depending upon their propensities. Howard Gardner (1983) expanded the learning style theory to include intelligence by stating that the singular term "intelligence" has been too narrowly defined. He offered a theory of multiple intelligences (linguistic, mathematical, bodily-kinesthetic, spatial, musical, interpersonal, intrapersonal, naturalistic, and existential) that has been used extensively in studies of the development and effectiveness of curriculum material. Picciano (2009) built a "blending with purpose" multimodal model based on Gardner's theory of multiple intelligences that relates various pedagogical goals and objectives to instructional facilities that can be used in blended learning environments. Researchers interested in studying the effectiveness of combining various approaches and technological tools (i.e., wikis, blogs, multiuser virtual environments [MUVE], gaming) to meet the various learning styles of students in a blended course or program would find that Gardner and Picciano provide an appropriate theoretical framework.

Foucauldian Discourse Analysis

Discourse analysis, as defined by Michel Foucault, has two functions. One relates to the use of language as a key variable in explaining how social power is exercised. The second relates to the use of language, especially writing, as self-examination "to show oneself, make oneself seen, and make one's face appear before the other" (Foucault, 1997, p.243). Either or both of these functions of discourse are appropriate theoretical frameworks for studying the use of language in teaching and learning. The online environment, especially the asynchronous learning network model that is highly dependent on written exchanges on discussion boards and blogs, is a fertile area for research based on Foucauldian discourse analysis. Unlike the traditional face-to-face classroom where the recording of oral exchanges is not common, the recording of online exchanges between students and instructors and students and students is not only common but automatic. These exchanges are permanently recorded in course management systems and allow researchers access to a treasure trove of discourse data on student and instructor use of language during the social dynamics of the class. In addition, in most online environments all students are free to comment extensively on the topic of discussion. This is not likely in a traditional classroom where, because of time constraints, not all of the students are able to comment, and those who are able are restricted in terms of how much they can say. The online environment presents a unique opportunity, only available in the past by providing video recording equipment and staffing, for researchers to examine language fully in terms of social power and as a form of self-evaluation and expression.

Hegelian Dialectic and Technological Change

The Hegelian dialectic is a major theoretical framework for studying the effects of social change. The essential elements of the dialectic (thesis, antithesis, synthesis) resonate with change related to technology. In *Technopoly*, Neil Postman (1993) applied the dialectic to the effects of technological change on society. He referred to the mechanical clock, the printing press, and the telescope as examples of major technologies that changed the way people lived. These technologies did not destroy or remake social institutions, but rather changed them. He applied this same concept to digital technology, computers, data communications, and multimedia that have changed modern society and its institutions, including education. Postman wrote *Technopoly* before the large-scale use of the Internet, but surely his thoughts have significant application to online and web-based technology. Online and blended learning represent changes that schools and colleges are adopting in response to changes brought on by digital technologies. The ways in which these institutions have developed hardware and software infrastructures, academic programs, and administrative and student support services in order to integrate digital technology into their culture and operations can be studied within the dialectic theoretical framework formulated by Hegel and adapted by Postman. Research has been done in these areas, but much more is needed, especially at the institutional level.

In conclusion, scholars who wish to examine some facet of online or blended learning have at their disposal a variety of options (paradigms, methodologies, methods, and theories) when planning and developing a research project. The challenge is to select the combination of approaches that will best serve the inquiry. The chapters that follow will provide more detail on the topics presented above.

References

Berg, B. L. (2004). *Qualitative research methods* (5th ed.). Boston: Pearson Education.

Bourdieu, P. (2005). *The social structures of the economy*. Boston: Polity Press.

Cook, T., & Campbell, D. (1979). *Quasi-experimentation: Design and analysis issues for field settings*. Houghton Mifflin: Boston.

Creswell, J. W. (2013). *Research design: Qualitative, quantitative, and mixed methods approaches* (4th ed.). Thousand Oaks, CA: Sage.

Crotty, M. (1998). *The foundations of social research: Meaning and perspective in the research process*. London: Sage.

Dewey, J. (1915). *Democracy in education*. New York: Reprinted by Dover Publications (2004).

Foucault, M. (1997). Writing the self. In Davidson, A. (ed) *Foucault and his interlocutors* (pp. 234–247). Chicago: University of Chicago Press.

Garnder, H. (1983). *Frames of mind. The theory of multiple intelligences*. New York: Basic Books.

Garrison, R., Anderson, T., & Archer, W. (2001). Critical inquiry in a text-based environment: Computer conferencing in higher education. *American Journal of Distance Education, 15*(1), 7–23.

Gibbons, A. S., & Bunderson, C. V. (2005). Explore, explain, design. In Leondard, K. K. (ed) *Encyclopedia of social measurement* (pp. 927–938). New York: Elsevier.

Glaser, B., & Strauss, A. (1967). *The discovery of grounded theory: Strategies for qualitative research.* New York: Aldin Publishing.

Graham, C. R., Henrie, C. R., & Gibbons, A. S. (2013). Developing models and theory for blended learning research. In Picciano, A. G., Dziuban, C. D., & Graham, C. R. (eds) *Blended learning: Research perspectives, vol. 2* (pp. 13–33). New York: Routledge/Taylor Francis Group.

Khun, T. (1962). *The structure of scientific revolution.* Chicago: University of Chicago Press.

Lincoln, Y. S., & Guba, E. G. (1985). *Naturalistic inquiry.* Beverly Hills: Sage.

Mackensie, N., & Knipe, S. (2006). Research dilemmas: Paradigms, methods and methodology. *Issues In Educational Research, 16.* Retrieved from www.iier.org.au/iier16/mackenzie.html. Accessed: June 12, 2014.

Mertens, D. M. (2005). *Research methods in education and psychology: Integrating diversity with quantitative and qualitative approaches* (2nd ed.). Thousand Oaks: Sage.

O'Leary, Z. (2004). *The essential guide to doing research.* London: Sage.

Papert, S. (1980). *Mindstorms: Children, computers, and powerful ideas.* New York: Basic Books.

Piaget, J. (1952). *The origins of intelligence in children.* New York: Norton.

Picciano, A. G. (2009). Blending with purpose: The multimodal model. *Journal of the Research Center for Educational Technology, 5*(1). Kent, OH: Kent State University. Retrieved from www.rcetj.org/index.php/rcetj/article/view/11 [Accessed July 5, 2014].

Postman, N. (1993). *Technopoly: The surrender of culture to technology.* New York: Vintage Books.

Pring, R. (2000). *Philosophy of educational research.* London: Continuum.

Simon, H. (1957). *Administrative behavior.* New York: Macmillan.

Simon H. (1982). *Models of bounded rationality.* Cambridge, MA: MIT Press.

Taylor, P. C., & Medina, M.N.D. (2013). Educational research paradigms: From positivism to multiparadigmatic. *The Journal of Meaning-Centered Education, 1*(2). Retrieved from www.meaningcentered.org/journal/volume-01/educational-research-paradigms-from-positivism-to-multiparadigmatic [Accessed July 30, 2014].

Trochim, W. (2006). *Research methods knowledge base.* Stamford, CT: Cengage Publishing. Retrieved from www.socialresearchmethods.net/kb/positvsm.php [Accessed July 12, 2014].

Vygotsky, L. (1978). *Mind in society: The development of higher psychological processes.* Cambridge, MA: Harvard University Press.

Wenger, E., & Lave, J. (1991). *Situated learning: Legitimate peripheral participation.* London: Cambridge University Press.

Wiersma, W. (2000). *Research Methods in Education* (7th ed.). Boston: Allyn and Bacon.

Chapter 3

Reviewing the Literature When There Is So Much of It

Charles R. Graham

Introduction

A thorough literature review provides a solid foundation for any research endeavor, and is the way we situate our work in the context of what others have done. It is useful to think of journals and conferences as the communication medium in which a scholarly community is developed. A wise scholar shared this analogy that helps us to understand the role that existing literature plays within a knowledge creation community.

> **Analogy:** Imagine that you have been invited to a party with many distinguished guests. As you walk around, you notice small groups of individuals clustered in different parts of the room engaged in conversations. Consider what the reaction would be to the following scenarios.
>
> - Scenario 1—You walk up to one of the groups and without bothering to understand what is being discussed, you blurt out what is on your mind.
> - Scenario 2—You walk up to one of the groups and quietly listen to the conversation for a few minutes. Then, during a brief lull in the conversation, you make a comment that builds on the flow of conversation.
>   (adapted from David Whetten, personal communication)

This analogy has a parallel in the scholarly research community. Just as the interaction in scenario 1 might be viewed as socially inept and self-absorbed, researchers who do not understand and contextualize their research with what has happened in the past run the risk of their research not fitting into the current scholarly conversation. A literature review enables the researcher to identify with confidence where the scholarly conversations are going and where the areas for meaningful contribution are.

A challenge with research in an emerging area such as online and blended learning is that the conversations are not taking place in one central location; they are distributed across many disciplines and scholarly communities. For example, a recent analysis of the top-cited blended learning literature identified that there are actually a wide range of scholarly communities talking about blended learning, including medicine and nursing, business, engineering, political science, teacher education, biology, statistics, and English (Halverson, Graham, Spring, & Drysdale, 2012). The conversations in these different communities are very likely at different stages of development, but this does not mean that they cannot and should not learn from each other. The distributed nature of the online and blended learning literature presents a challenge to researchers because it requires becoming familiar with research that may be outside their specialized domains. It also heightens the need for comprehensive literature reviews, so that research efforts are well informed and build the knowledge base more coherently, rather than expending energy to reinvent what has already been tried before.

This chapter will introduce the reader to various types and purposes of the literature review. It will also introduce some technology tools and strategies for more quickly identifying literature that is important to a particular scholarly inquiry. Finally, a general process for conducting a literature review will be shared, and examples within the blended learning domain will be analyzed at each stage of the process.

Types/Purposes of Literature Review

Scholars have articulated many reasons why researchers embark on a literature review (Knopf, 2006; Baumeister & Leary, 1997; Boote & Beile, 2005). Some of those reasons include:

- To summarize and synthesize the scope and findings in a body of research
- To identify gaps in the existing research to guide future research
- To set the context and rationale for current research
- To critically examine methods and arguments used by researchers
- To assist in developing and evaluating theory
- To understand the historical development of an idea or theory

A thorough review of the literature allows the researcher to understand the scholarly conversation that is going on before making a contribution. This helps to ensure that the contribution builds on the ongoing conversation. Typically, literature reviews take one of three forms, with the latter two being much more comprehensive and in-depth than the first:

1. A component of a research article
2. A chapter in a dissertation or thesis
3. A stand-alone review article.

It is beyond the scope of this chapter to provide you with the details for how to conduct a comprehensive, quality literature review. There are many good articles to help with this, including:

- **Boote & Beile, 2005**—a great synthesis of essential elements to a dissertation literature review. In particular, a valuable scoring rubric for quality literature reviews can be found on p. 8.
- **Knopf, 2006**—a short practical guide with pointers on how to do an effective literature review
- **Baumeister & Leary, 1997**—guidance on how to write narrative literature reviews, with a great explanation of many common mistakes
- **Bem, 1995**—guidance for writing a review article and how that differs from a dissertation literature review

The focus of the remainder of the chapter will be to highlight examples of the literature review process and to show how new digital tools can assist in efficiently reviewing a large literature base so that researchers can effectively identify research trends and problems to inform their research.

Tools for Identifying Relevant Research

There are no tools that eliminate the hard work required to do a good review of research literature. The core value of a good literature review is the critical synthesis that allows the reader to see patterns, understand research gaps, and make connections between ideas that were not readily visible. While this synthesis work is challenging and requires significant effort, there are tools that can help streamline the process by speeding up access to the most relevant literature and facilitating collaborative analysis of a body of literature. Table 3.1 introduces four categories of digital tools that can be used to identify relevant research. Examples of each of these tools are provided, with the strengths and limitations associated with using the tool.

Process for Conducting Literature Reviews

The beginning of any literature review process can feel quite daunting. Searches in online databases often yield thousands of results not organized in any meaningful way. The sheer volume of potential articles to review can be overwhelming. However, out of the thousands of potential articles there are usually a couple of dozen articles that will have the greatest influence on your thinking. Finding those articles as quickly as possible is the early task in your review, and technological tools can help you speed up the process.

Figure 3.1 shows a generalized process for conducting a literature review. A systematic process should be conducted for any comprehensive literature review. Experts in a field are often able to shortcut the process (especially for abbreviated literature reviews in research papers) because they have identified and archived relevant research over many years. Examples of this include Garrison and Arbaugh's (2007) review of research on the community of inquiry, a theoretical framework often used in blended learning research, and reviews done by Graham and Dziuban (Graham, 2014; Graham & Dziuban, 2008). Altmetrics and alerting tools identified in Table 3.1 can help you to identify the most current research relevant to your interests as it is published.

The following sections of this chapter will draw from portions of the blended learning literature reviews identified below as examples of the literature review process.

- Research in online and blended learning in the business disciplines: Key findings and possible future directions. (Arbaugh, et al. 2009)
- Analysis of research trends in dissertations and theses studying blended learning. (Drysdale, et al. 2013)
- An analysis of high impact scholarship and publication trends in blended learning. (Halverson, et al. 2012)
- A thematic analysis of the most highly cited scholarship in the first decade of blended learning research. (Halverson, et al. 2014)
- The undergraduate experience of blended e-learning: A review of UK literature and practice. (Sharpe, et al. 2006).

Table 3.1 Useful Digital Tools for Conducting a Literature Review

Tool/Description	Examples	Strengths/Limitations
Subject Databases: This is the most traditional tool used for finding literature.	• **ERIC**—A database for literature related to educational research. (http://eric.ed.gov/) • **EBSCO**—A database of databases. You can select several subject databases to search at the same time. (http://ebscohost.com/) • **Web of Knowledge (ISI)**—A database indexing many science and medial journals and fewer education journals. (http://webofknowledge.com)	+ Usually allows searches based on rich metadata, including title, abstract, keywords, etc. − Queries search content only and not metrics that indicate the impact or quality of the publication. − Limited by the number and types of journals indexed in the database.
Citation Count Tools: Increasingly, citation counts for articles and journals are being used as a way to determine the most influential research and researchers. Citation counts are typically reported using raw count numbers (for articles), impact factors (for journals), or the h-index (for researchers).	• **Web of Science (ISI)**—Counts citations between articles indexed in a given database. It also calculates an impact factor based on citation counts for journals and researchers. • **Google Scholar Citations (GSC)**—Provides citation counts specific to publications, as well as general metrics including h-index and i10-index for scholars and journals. • **Publish or Perish (PoP)**—Searches the Google Scholar database and allows you to sort the data based on the number of citation a manuscript has received. (www.harzing.com/pop.htm)	+ Allows sorting of publications, journals, or researchers by how often they have been cited by others. − Value is limited by the publications indexed within the database. ISI, for example, indexes less than half of education journals, so will be less comprehensive for that domain. Google Scholar indexes a greater variety of materials, such as books and conference presentations, which can be both a positive and sometimes a negative.
Altmetrics: Alternative metrics for measuring the relative influence of research beyond the citation count metrics. Altmetrics are often associated with social media for researchers and might include (1) the number of times that a full-text	• **Academia.edu**—Allows authors to see metrics about publications, such as number of views and downloads by world region. (http://academia.edu)	+ They allow researchers and others to see how an idea is being received much more quickly than citation counts that often take years to accumulate.

(Continued)

Table 3.1 (Continued)

Tool/Description	Examples	Strengths/Limitations
document is downloaded or viewed, (2) the number of times a manuscript or author is discussed in social media outlets and discussion comments, (3) the number of times that an article is bookmarked or saved using social bookmarking tools, and/or (4) the number of times that an article is recommended to peers.	• **Mendeley**—Allows researchers to upload papers and see metrics on others who have added your papers to their personal libraries. (www.mendeley.com) • **ResearchGate**—Allows researchers to see metrics related to how often other researchers interact with your content. Scores increase based on frequency of views and reputation of viewers. (www.researchgate.net)	– They have not become mainstream; therefore there are no standard metrics used across research tools. They typically require you to be part of a community of researchers and use a particular social media portal as in the examples provided, and so they may disproportionally advantage researchers who are technology or social media savvy.
Alerting Services: Research alerting services is also a way to become aware of the most recent research that is being published on a particular topic, within a particular journal, or by a given author. Most databases and journals allow researchers to create customized alerts. Some types of alerts that are possible to set up include alerts based on citing of a specified article, keywords that appear in new manuscripts, and table of contents for recently published journal issues.	• **Citation Alerts**—Allows the researcher to receive an email alert when a selected article is cited by new articles added to the database. Example: Web of Knowledge (http://wokinfo.com/products_tools/products/related/citationalerts/) • **Table of Content Alerts**—Allows the researcher to receive an email alert with the table of contents for a new issue of a designated journal. Example: Wiley Online (http://olabout.wiley.com/WileyCDA/Section/id-404511.html) • **Keyword Alerts**—Allows the researcher to receive an email alert when any new content with the specified search criteria is added to the database. Example: Google Scholar (http://scholar.google.com/intl/en-US/scholar/help.html#alerts)	+ Alerts are a great way to keep up on the most current publications related to your particular topic. – Alerts only tell you about what new things are being added to the database, and so must accompany a more comprehensive search of existing literature.

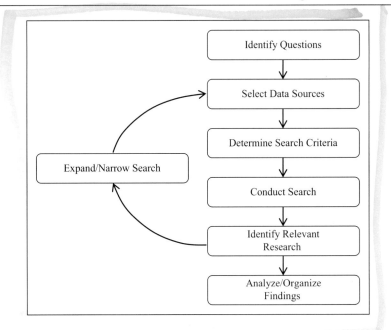

Figure 3.1 Generalized Literature Review Process

In addition to the five blended learning reviews cited, there are many good examples of distance education literature reviews available. Cavanaugh, Barbour, and Clark (2009); Davies, Howell, and Petrie (2010); and Lee, Driscoll, and Nelson (2007) are three good examples to review, because the authors have been fairly explicit about articulating the important details of the literature review process.

Identifying Research Questions

The first step of a literature review process is identifying questions that will focus the research. This can be done in question form or by identifying a purpose statement for the literature review (see examples of both in Table 3.2). Establishing appropriate questions at the beginning of the process will help to set bounds that focus the rest of the literature review process. Literature reviews that accompany empirical research should have built-in questions to guide the review. Unfocused, or lack of, research questions can lead to confusion and delays in the process.

Selecting Data Sources

The next step in the process is learning what databases you have access to and which ones will be most valuable in your search. An institutional librarian can be very helpful in sorting out specific details for any commercial subscription databases available through your institution. (Box 3.1 contains some definitions that may be helpful as you select databases to use in your search.) Some databases like EBSCO allow researchers to select and search across multiple databases with the same search. Other databases may be specific to one journal or to the journals distributed by a

Table 3.2 Examples of Guiding Questions from Literature Reviews

Source	Example
Halverson et al. (2014)	"Methodological trends: (1) What methodologies are being employed by the top-cited scholars? Topical trends: (2) What is the range and frequency of topics being explored in blended learning research? (3) What theories do these scholars draw on to support their study of blended learning?" (p. 20).
Arbaugh et al. (2009)	"To address these research and curricular concerns, we examine and assess the state of research of online and blended learning in the business disciplines with the intent of assessing the field and identifying opportunities for meaningful future research" (p.71).
Sharpe et al. (2006)	"The following research questions were derived from the aims to guide the review: a) How is the term 'blended learning' being used in higher education? b) What are the underlying rationales being used for blended e-learning? c) What monitoring and evaluation strategies are being adopted for ensuring and enhancing the quality of blended e-learning? d) What impact is blended e-learning having on the student experience? e) What are the success factors for blended e-learning?" (p.10).
Drysdale et al. (2013)	"Demographic trends: (1) How has the number of blended learning theses and dissertations changed over the past decade? (2) In what contexts (higher education, K-12, or corporate) is the blended learning research occurring? (3) At what organizational level—institution, program, course, or activity—are the blends taking place? Methodological trends: (1) What data analysis techniques are most commonly used in blended learning research? Topical trends: (1) What theories are used to frame research in blended learning? (2) What is the range and frequency of topics being explored in blended learning research?" (p.91).

specific publisher. Each database will differ in what metadata it keeps on the articles within the database and if Boolean operators can be used in the search.

The sources that you select will determine the quality and comprehensiveness of your review. Different databases provide different advantages and limitations. For example, an open access database like Google Scholar has an advantage in that it includes a lot of sources, including books, book chapters, and white paper publications. However, access to the broader range of publications may also be a limitation in trying to focus in on the most important journal publications. Additionally, Google Scholar has limited metadata fields to help in focusing a search.

**Box 3.1   Terms and Definitions for Understanding
             Database Searches**

Open-access database—This typically refers to a database that does not require a subscription to access and search its contents. Example: Google Scholar.

Indexed sources—This refers to the sources that are indexed or cataloged by the database. For example, the ERIC database catalogs a specific set of journals in the education domain, while there are other databases that catalog journals in nursing, business, engineering, etc. Google Scholar attempts to index all scholarly journals with metadata online.

Search terms—These are the words or phrases that the researcher wants to look for in searching the database. Examples: "blended learning," "hybrid course."

Metadata—Data that is kept in the database for each article. Examples include title, author, abstract, keywords, date published, etc. Typically the researcher chooses which metadata fields the search should include.

Full-text—Some databases actually have the full text of the article in the database.

Boolean operators—Boolean operators AND, OR, and NOT allow the researcher to create more complex searches. However, each database has its own syntax and rules for applying Boolean operators to a search. Example: search for "blended learning" AND "higher education."

As a part of your review you should be able to justify your selection of data sources and its reasonable coverage of the range of possible manuscripts that might have research important to your review. Oftentimes this is done by articulating "inclusion criteria" that outline the criteria for including or excluding certain data sources in the review. Table 3.3 contains some demonstrations of database selection and justifications from the example literature reviews. These examples show how inclusion criteria were identified based on categories such as database indexes, date, and content area. Additionally, some searches augmented the core data sources with recommendations from experts.

Determine Search Criteria

Selecting the search criteria, including keywords that will be used to delimit the search, is the next important step in the process. It is important to have a clear understanding of the terms you select, especially in doing reviews related to blended learning because of the range of definitions and associated ambiguities associated with the terms (Graham, 2014; Oliver & Trigwell, 2005). For example, Halverson et al. (2012) found that using the term "hybrid" alone in a search yielded a lot of

Table 3.3 Examples of Data Source Selection and Justification from Literature Reviews

Source	Example
Halverson et al. (2012)	"We utilized Harzing's Publish or Perish software program (2011), which retrieves and calculates academic citations from Google Scholar (see Figure 1). We sought an alternative to the ISI IF rating, which gives citation metrics for journals, not individual articles. ISI is also less able to provide a real-time search than Publish or Perish; as of 2010, Google Scholar had only a 9-day delay between article posting online and retrieval in Google Scholar (Chen, 2010). Finally, educational publications, and publications from the fields of distance and blended learning in particular, are not represented well in the ISI databases (West & Rich, in press). Thus Google Scholar overcomes many of the issues that plague the traditional IF and is a useful starting point for determining works with significant currency, resonance, timeliness, and influence in the field of blended learning" (p. 383).
Sharpe et al. (2006)	See section "Conduct Search" of the manuscript. They did the following to make their search as comprehensive as possible: • Systematically searched six databases • "Hand searched for relevant articles" in fourteen specifically identified journals • "Put out calls on the Heads of e-Learning Forum and Joint Information Systems Committee (JISC) e-Learning and Pedagogy Experts email distribution lists asking for suggestions for articles to include. We used our personal contacts to access unpublished literature. We also received submissions of papers in response to the project website" (pp. 10–11).
Drysdale et al. (2013)	"For this review, we collected all pertinent doctoral dissertations and masters' theses written through 2011 and submitted to ProQuest on or before April 3, 2012. We selected ProQuest because it receives 97.2% of all dissertations and theses from research universities in the United States and 87.2% of those from Canadian research universities (Davies et al., 2010)" (p. 91).
Arbaugh et al. (2009)	"An initial comprehensive search for peer-reviewed articles pertaining to 'on-line learning' in business courses that were published after January 1st, 2002 was conducted between September 2006 and September 2008. Databases examined in the review included ABI/Inform, Business Full Text, Business Source Elite, and Lexis/Nexis Business.... To supplement this review, articles on technology-mediated business and management education published before this time period cited in reviews by Arbaugh and Stelzer's (2003) and Salas, Kosarzycki, Burke, Fiore and Stone (2002) were included in this review. Finally, the primary journals for each business discipline, as identified in the journals database recently published in Academy of Management Learning & Education, were examined dating back to 2000 (Whetten, 2008)" (p. 72).

irrelevant results, because the word hybrid is commonly used in scientific research completely unrelated to education. So, the term had to be more narrowly specified to "hybrid learning," "hybrid instruction," and "hybrid course." Table 3.4 contains examples of how four reviews articulated their search terms.

Once the search terms have been selected, you will need to determine how to link the terms using Boolean operators, and you will need to determine what metadata to include in the search. The possibilities with both of these will be dependent on the capabilities of the database(s) you are searching. Using Boolean operators properly can save you a lot of time in the next steps. For example, consider the two options in Box 3.2. Each case will return a different set of results.

Table 3.4 Examples of Data Search Criteria from Literature Reviews

Source	Example
Arbaugh et al. (2009)	"Search terms for online • Blended • Mediated • Technology-mediated • Distance • On-line • Virtual • Web-based • Cyberspace • Computer based • Computer assisted • Distributed Search terms for learning • Education • Learning • Teaching • Instruction" (p.72)
Drysdale et al. (2013)	"Employing terms accepted in the literature on blended learning (Graham, 2006), we searched for manuscripts containing blend, hybrid, or mixed mode in the title or abstract, while limiting our search to manuscripts that were full-text and written in English. We further refined our search using Boolean operators to connect blend, hybrid, and mixed mode with educational terms (such as learning, environment, approach, method, instruction, course, program, and class) to create phrases pertinent to blended learning" (p.91).
Sharpe et al. (2006)	"Core terms ICT C&IT Educational technology E-learning / eLearning Blended learning Mixed mode learning Hybrid models of learning specifiers + pedagogy + student experience + learner experience + evaluation Virtual learning environment" (p.10).
Halverson et al. (2012)	We searched for publications about blended or hybrid learning from 2000 to 2011. We employed the following search terms: "blended learning," "blended instruction," "blended course," "blended environment," "blended class," "blended program," "hybrid learning," "hybrid instruction," "hybrid course," "hybrid environment," "hybrid class," and "hybrid program" (pp.383–384).

Box 3.2   Three Examples of Using Boolean Operators in a Search

CASE 1:
Search 1a—using the term "blended learning"
Search 1b—using the term "hybrid course"

CASE 2:
Search 2—using the terms "blended learning" OR "hybrid course"

CASE 3:
Search 3—using the terms "blended learning" AND "hybrid course"

Cases 1 and 2 will include all the same papers, but papers that use both terms will be represented twice in the combined results from Search 1a and 1b. Case 3 will return the fewest and may miss important research that uses only one term or the other.

Finally, the metadata search fields you choose will have implications for the results. For example, a search of the title field only will return a smaller number of papers than a search of the title and abstract; these in turn will return fewer items than a full text search. At the same time, a search of the title only will likely yield more focused results, because the term "blended learning" might be used in the full text of the paper without the focus of the research being related to blended learning.

Conduct Search

Conducting the search is a pretty straightforward step in the process. It can be helpful if you are aware of an article or two that you know the search could catch, so when you actually conduct the search you can double check the technical accuracy of setting up the search. Additionally, it is a wise practice to begin by limiting the search more narrowly in the beginning (with focused search terms and limited search fields) and then expanding the search out later in the process if needed. This allows you to find more directly relevant articles early on, because they are more likely to use keywords and terms in the title and abstract.

Identify Relevant Research

Once the search is complete, the hard work of sifting through the results for what is relevant begins. Because of space limitations, authors do not always include the protocol for sifting through the search results for what is relevant and what isn't. In the examples available in Table 3.5, Sharpe, Benfield, Roberts, and Francis (2006) were the most detailed in their criteria. Halverson et al. (2012) also explain their process of using citation count as a mechanism for sifting through to the research that has been identified by other researchers as the most relevant.

Table 3.5 Examples of Identifying Relevant Research in Literature Reviews

Source	Example
Arbaugh et al. (2009)	"This protocol identified 182 articles that examined online and/or blended learning in business and management education from the years 2000 through 2008" (p.72).
Drysdale et al. (2013)	"Our final search resulted in 263 manuscripts. Each manuscript was reviewed by two researchers to determine that blended learning was studied, not simply mentioned. An independent third rater negotiated any discrepancies in determining relevancy. Of the 263 manuscripts, 205 were deemed relevant to our study" (p.91).
Sharpe et al. (2006)	This study had eight criteria that they used to determine which of the articles their search identified were relevant to the review (see pp. 12–13 of manuscript). Parts of two criteria are shown here: "As the review aimed to be representative of the UK undergraduate experience, we favoured those studies which drew on recent data and excluded those drawing on data prior to 2000" (p.12). "We favoured evaluations that were triangulated i.e., that made use of data from a variety of times, methods and sources" (p.13).
Halverson et al. (2012)	"The initial search resulted in excess of 9,500 titles on 'blended'; the 'hybrid' results were in excess of 16,500 retrievals. All retrievals with zero citations were immediately discarded, as were non-English publications and conference proceedings" (p.384). "As a result of not narrowing the disciplines searched, we retrieved many publications that did not relate to 'blended' or 'hybrid' in our intended sense: . . . We discarded publications that did not fit in our stated definition of blended learning, as well as those in which blended or hybrid learning was peripheral rather than central. . . . We next sorted retrievals into categories—article, chapter, book, or 'other'—and then ordered them by number of citations. From all the citations, we selected the top 50 articles, the top 25 edited book chapters, and the top 10 books for analysis in this study." (p. 384).

Expanding or Narrowing Search Results

While the steps up to this point have been presented as a linear process, in actuality they are not. There is often narrowing or expanding that goes on during the process in order for the authors to have confidence that they are not missing important research. It is common to begin the search process and realize that the search has returned thousands of articles—too many to reasonably sort through. At that point, the researcher must go back and (1) limit the data sources, (2) try to focus the research terms by making them more specific, and/or (3) narrowing the fields being searched (e.g., title only instead of full text). An example is provided in Table 3.6 of two iterations of this process carried out by Halverson et al. (2012).

Table 3.6 Examples of Narrowing and Expanding the Search from Halverson et al. (2012, p.384)

Narrowing—In this case search terms were changed to narrow the search to produce more relevant outcomes.	"As a result of not narrowing the disciplines searched, we retrieved many publications that did not relate to 'blended' or 'hybrid' in our intended sense: 'Blended learning systems combine face-to-face instruction with computer-mediated instruction' (Graham, 2006, p. 5). The hybrid search retrievals were especially cluttered with irrelevant titles such as, 'Hybrid Approach for Including Electronic and Nuclear Quantum Effects in Molecular Dynamics Simulations of Hydrogen Transfer Reactions in Enzymes' from The Journal of Chemical Physics."
Expanding—In this case researchers identified that significant newer publications were being eliminated from the search, and so they expanded the search to account for these.	"We recognized that our selection criteria system favored older publications that have had more time to accrue citations. We thus created lists for the five top cited articles from 2009 (two of which were already included in the top 50), 2010, and 2011. However, 2011 had only two relevant article retrievals; clearly, not enough time has passed for these articles to accrue citations, despite their merit."

Table 3.7 Examples of Identifying Relevant Research in Literature Reviews

Source	Example
Arbaugh et al. (2009)	Organized findings based on organizational disciplines in business (management, finance, accounting, marketing, information systems, operations/supply chain management, economics search). Additionally, an eighth category of findings from multidisciplinary/program-level studies was added.
Drysdale et al. (2013)	Organized by a priori categories for demographic trends and methodological trends. • Demographic (learner type = corporate, higher ed., K–12, unspecified; organizational level = activity, course, program, institution, unspecified) • Methodological (primary method = inferential statistics, descriptive statistics, qualitative, combined inferential statistics and qualitative, combined qualitative and descriptive statistics) Topical themes emerged from the coding of manuscripts in the literature review and included nine primary themes, each with subthemes.
Sharpe et al. (2006)	Organizing themes were guided by the research questions and included: • Definition and uses • Rationales • Evaluating and monitoring • The learner experience
Halverson et al. (2014)	Methodological themes included (empirical = descriptive, inferential, qualitative; nonempirical = review, model; combination = combined, gold star) Topical themes build on the work of Drysdale et al. (2013) and included ten primary themes, each with subthemes identified in the literature.

Analyze/Organize Findings

As researchers begin to identify relevant research they will begin to organize the research in a meaningful way. This is a creative yet systematic process. Sometimes researchers come to the table with a set of a priori codes or organization that they want to use as an organizing structure. Examples of this are three literature reviews that used the Online Learning Consortium's (formerly Sloan Consortium) five pillars (learning effectiveness, access, cost effectiveness, student satisfaction, and faculty satisfaction) as an organizing framework (Graham, 2014; Graham & Dziuban, 2008; Vignare, 2007). Additionally, the demographic and methodological codes identified by Drysdale in Table 3.7 are good examples of a priori codes applied in the review process. Other times the themes will emerge from the data, as in the examples in Table 3.7.

References

Arbaugh, J. B., Godfrey, M. R., Johnson, M., Pollack, B. L., Niendorf, B., & Wresch, W. (2009). Research in online and blended learning in the business disciplines: Key findings and possible future directions. *The Internet and Higher Education, 12*(2), 71–87. doi:10.1016/j.iheduc.2009.06.006

Arbaugh, J. B., & Stelzer, L. (2003). Learning and teaching via the web: What do we know? In DeFillipi, R. & Wankel, C. (eds) *Educating managers with tomorrow's technologies* (pp. 17–51). Greenwich, CT: Information Age Publishing.

Baumeister, R. F., & Leary, M. R. (1997). Writing narrative literature reviews. *Review of General Psychology, 1*(3), 311–320. doi:10.1016/S0899–3467(07)60142–6

Bem, D. J. (1995). Writing a review article for psychological bulletin. *Psychological Bulletin, 118*(2), 172–177.

Boote, D. N., & Beile, P. (2005). Scholars before researchers: On the centrality of the dissertation literature review in research preparation. *Educational Researcher, 34*(6), 3–15. doi:10.3102/0013189X034006003

Cavanaugh, C. S., Barbour, M. K., & Clark, T. (2009). Research and practice in K–12 online learning: A review of open access literature. *International Review of Research in Open and Distance Learning, 10*(1), 1–22.

Chen, X. (2010). Google Scholar's dramatic coverage improvement five years after debut. *Serials Review, 36*, 221–226. doi:10.1016/j.serrev.2010.08.002

Davies, R. S., Howell, S. L., & Petrie, J. A. (2010). A review of trends in distance education scholarship at research universities in North America, 1998–2007. *International Review of Research in Open and Distance Learning, 11*(3), 42–56.

Drysdale, J. S., Graham, C. R., Halverson, L. R., & Spring, K. J. (2013). Analysis of research trends in dissertations and theses studying blended learning. *Internet and Higher Education, 17*(1), 90–100. doi:10.1016/j.bbr2011.03.031

Garrison, D., & Arbaugh, J. (2007). Researching the community of inquiry framework: Review, issues, and future directions. *The Internet and Higher Education, 10*(3), 157–172. doi:10.1016/j.iheduc.2007.04.001

Graham, C. R. (2006). Blended learning systems: Definition, current trends, and future directions. In Bonk, C. J. & Graham, C. R. (eds) *The handbook of blended learning: Global perspectives, local designs* (pp. 3–21). San Francisco, CA: Pfeiffer.

Graham, C. R. (2013). Emerging practice and research in blended learning. In Moore, M. G. (ed) *Handbook of distance education* (3rd ed.) (pp. 333–350). New York: Routledge.

Graham, C. R. (2014). Emerging practice and research in blended learning. In Moore, M. G. (ed) *Handbook of distance education* (3rd ed.) (pp. 333–350). New York: Routledge.

Graham, C. R., & Dziuban, C. D. (2008). Blended learning environments. In Spector, J. M., Merrill, M. D., van Merrienboer, J.J.G., & Driscoll, M. P. (eds.) *Handbook of research on educational communications and technology, vol. 3* (3rd ed.) (pp. 269–276). Mahwah, NJ: Lawrence Earlbaum.

Halverson, L. R., Graham, C. R., Spring, K. J., & Drysdale, J. S. (2012). An analysis of high impact scholarship and publication trends in blended learning. *Distance Education, 33*(3), 381–413. doi :10.1080/01587919.2012.723166

Halverson, L. R., Graham, C. R., Spring, K. J., Drysdale, J. S., & Henrie, C. R. (2014). A thematic analysis of the most highly cited scholarship in the first decade of blended learning research. *Internet and Higher Education, 20*, 20–34. doi:10.1016/j.iheduc.2013.09.004

Knopf, J. W. (2006). Doing a literature review. *PS: Political Science & Politics, 39*(01), 127–132. doi:10.1017/S1049096506060264

Lee, Y., Driscoll, M. P., & Nelson, D. W. (2007). Trends in research: A content analysis of major journals. In Moore, M. G. (ed.) *Handbook of distance education* (2nd ed.) (pp. 31–41). Mahwah, NJ: Lawrence Earlbaum.

Oliver, M., & Trigwell, K. (2005). Can "blended learning" be redeemed? *E-Learning, 2*(1), 17–26. doi:10.2304/elea.2005.2.1.2

Salas, E., Kosarzycki, M. P., Burke, C. S., Fiore, S. M., & Stone, D. L. (2002). Emerging themes in distance learning research and practice: Some food for thought. *International Journal of Management Reviews, 4*, 135–153.

Sharpe, R., Benfield, G., Roberts, G., & Francis, R. (2006). The undergraduate experience of blended e-learning: A review of UK literature and practice. In *The higher education academy* (pp. 1–103). York, UK: Higher Education Academy. Retrieved from www.academia.edu/ 188000/ The_undergraduate_experience_of_blended_e-learning_a_review_of_UK_literature_ and_practice_undertaken_for_the_Higher_Education_Academy [Accessed April 22, 2015].

Vignare, K. (2007). Review of literature on blended learning: Using ALN to change the classroom—Will it work? In Picciano, A. G., & Dziuban, C. D. (eds.) *Blended learning: Research perspectives* (pp. 37–63). Needham, MA: Sloan Consortium.

Whetten, D. A. (2008). Introducing AMLEs educational research databases. *Academy of Management Learning & Education, 7*, 139–143.

Chapter 4

How Meta-analysis Can Inform Online and Blended Learning Research

Anthony G. Picciano

This chapter looks at meta-analysis, a research technique that has been used for studying many issues in the social sciences, including the effects and impact of instructional technology. A meta-analysis is a study wherein a set of statistical procedures is used to summarize and synthesize the results of a number of independently conducted research studies. The underlying rationale for conducting a meta-analysis is the need or desire to synthesize findings across many studies into a common metric.

The use of meta-analysis grew as the amount of research being conducted accelerated, especially in the social sciences, including education-related topics. Thousands of studies are conducted annually on just about every topic and issue that informs our understanding of what works and perhaps doesn't work in education endeavors. It is important to mention that the vast majority (as much as 90%) of the studies in education result in positive findings about the technique, strategy, or policy being examined (Hattie, 2009). Anyone who has done a literature review of an education topic understands the enormity of the task of reading, digesting, and trying to make sense of the findings of these many, many studies. Keeping track of the research techniques, populations, and findings from study to study is a time-consuming and frequently lonely task that requires the reviewer to read material over and over again. Specially designed computer software programs such as *Zotero* and *Endnote* are available to assist the reviewer in maintaining a file of findings, notes, citations, and URLs. However, making judgments as to the quality of the study and the points of view of the researchers has historically remained a largely human activity. As a result, a technique was needed to assist and improve upon this narrative form of literature review activity. The idea for meta-analysis was born. Unlike a narrative, meta-analysis takes a quantitative approach and makes use of statistical techniques in order to estimate a possible effect across multiple studies (Kock, 2009).

Gene Glass, a statistician and researcher working in educational psychology, is credited with coining the term "meta-analysis," and illustrated the use of this technique in an address to the American Educational Research Association in San Francisco in April 1976. Various types of statistical procedures were used prior to 1976 to integrate findings from multiple studies and, to a degree, resembled meta-analysis, but the technique and term is most associated with Glass's introduction in 1976. Writing twenty-five years later, Glass indicated that meta-analysis grew out of necessity in the early 1970s, since the volume of research in many fields was growing at such a rate that traditional narrative approaches to summarizing and integrating research were beginning to break down. He further indicated that

> I had learned to be very skeptical of statistical significance testing; I had learned that all research was imperfect in one respect or another (or, in other words, there are no "perfectly valid" studies nor any line that demarcates "valid" from "invalid" studies).
>
> (Glass, 2000)

However, he also cautioned researchers not to over rely on meta-analysis; it can give you the ". . . BIG FACT but don't ask for more sophisticated answers; they aren't there" (Glass, 2000).

Basic Design Considerations in Conducting a Meta-analysis

Before examining meta-analysis as used for online and blended learning, it will be beneficial to review some of the major considerations in its design. As part of a single chapter, it is impossible to do an in-depth review. Readers who are considering using meta-analysis are encouraged to look at several excellent texts and articles that cover the topic in more depth. Highly recommended are Kock (2009), Cooper and Hedges (1994), Rosenthal (1991), and Glass, McGraw, and Smith (1981).

The Major Phases of a Meta-analysis

As recommended by Coopers and Hedges (1994) and Kock (2009), the major phases of a meta-analysis are as follows:

1. Defining the problem to be analyzed
2. Data collection
3. Data screening and evaluation
4. Data analysis and interpretation
5. Report presentation

These phases are similar to other research designs, but incorporate several subtle differences that need to be considered.

The first phase is similar to most other designs and essentially requires defining a researchable problem. In a meta-analysis, it is critical to clearly identify the variables to be analyzed as early as possible.

In the second phase, the meta-analysts identify and collect primary empirical studies that fit the defined research problem. Furthermore, these primary studies need to be in a style and format in which basic statistical information can be evaluated for the variables that are to be extracted for the meta-analysis. Unlike other research, this phase might involve identifying hundreds or even thousands of studies.

In the third phase, the researcher screens and evaluates the primary empirical studies identified in phase two to determine whether or not their data can be extracted with sufficient accuracy as to be useful for a meta-analysis. This step is unique to meta-analysis.

In the fourth phase, the data is extracted and interpreted for each primary empirical study according to the common metric (e.g., effect size) that will be used in the meta-analysis. For example, if the meta-analysts have decided to use Cohen's d for calculating an effect size, then this has to be done for each primary empirical study and then an average must be taken for all the studies.

In the fifth and final phase, the results of the meta-analysis are reported, as they would be in any other study. Typical in the report phase is a summary table or appendix identifying all the studies that were used for doing the meta-analysis.

It should be obvious in considering these phases or steps that a meta-analysis is a significant undertaking requiring months or years of effort. Such an endeavor may perhaps be better carried out by a team of researchers rather than a single individual.

Effect Size

Any presentation of meta-analysis has to include a discussion of effect size, which is generally the most important statistical metric used in determining the significance of the findings. An effect size is a measure of the strength or magnitude of a phenomenon and can be applied to a variety of research designs, such as the relationships between two variables in a population, the differences in the outcomes between two or more groups, or a sample-based estimate of some quantity. In social science research, effect size has achieved a certain status. It is recommended by the American Psychological Association to be included, where appropriate, in all reports of quantitative findings.

In a meta-analysis, a frequently used technique is to calculate an average effect size that describes the results across all of the individual studies examined. For example, let's say the purpose of the meta-analysis is to examine the effect of a mode of instruction (online versus face-to-face) on student outcomes. Effect size could be used as a common metric and calculated for a number of variables in each study in the meta-analysis. An average effect size could then be calculated across all of the studies to indicate whether student outcomes differ depending upon mode of instruction. In selecting the studies to be included in the meta-analysis, it is absolutely necessary to select studies that provide the data on the basic variable(s) needed to calculate the effect size.

One frustrating aspect of effect size is that there is neither one accepted effect size metric nor one accepted calculation. Gene Glass mentioned that he and his colleagues used a variety of correlations, regression coefficients, proportions, and odds ratios in the early years of conducting meta-analyses (Glass, 2000). The calculation of the effect size is also dependent upon the types of studies to be included in the meta-analysis and hence the metrics available. For example, a popular and simple calculation of effect size is Cohen's d, which can be used when comparing the differences between two groups (experimental and control) and is calculated by taking the difference in the means of the two groups and dividing it by the pooled standard deviation. In conducting a meta-analysis of correlation studies involving Pearson product moment correlation coefficients, the size of the correlation effect can be calculated by squaring the Pearson coefficient (r) to get a coefficient of determination (r^2) that is a measure of the proportion of variance shared by the two variables. In addition to variation in the type of effect size calculated, there are no commonly accepted standards for establishing the magnitude of the effects. Cohen (1988), for instance, recommended that Cohen's $d = 0.2$ was small, $d = 0.5$ was medium, and $d = 0.8$ was large. Hattie (2009), in his review of eight hundred meta-analyses examining educational studies, recommended that $d = 0.2$ was small, $d = 0.4$ was medium, and $d = 0.6$ was large.

In designing the statistical approaches for a meta-analysis, there are many options available. Researchers are free to use statistical treatments that best meet their needs and that can be justified to the readers and reviewers of their work.

Concerns and Criticisms

There are a number of concerns, and perhaps criticisms, regarding meta-analysis as a research method. First, as mentioned earlier in this chapter, Gene Glass cautioned researchers not to read too much into the results of a meta-analysis. This technique might give you a quick big picture, but it is not necessarily useful for deep, sophisticated analysis (Glass, 2000). This brings into question the time, cost, and effort needed to do a meta-analysis. Kock (2009) stated that meta-analysis requires advanced sophistication in statistical methods that many education researchers do not possess. Add to this the necessarily extensive review and evaluation of appropriate studies to be included in a meta-analysis, and the researcher is embarking on a huge endeavor that might yield only very basic knowledge to our understanding of the problem studied. For this reason, most present-day meta-analyses are being undertaken by well-funded teams of researchers that possess advanced knowledge in data collection, technology, and statistical applications.

A second important criticism that has been addressed many times is that meta-analysis incorporates findings from studies that vary considerably in terms of their objectives, definitions of terms, measurement of variables, and sampling techniques. Critics argue that meta-analysis is aggregating results from research findings that were never meant to be aggregated. This criticism has frequently been referred to as "combining apples and oranges." There is some truth to this, especially as applied to instructional technology. Teaching and learning are complex human interactive processes dependent upon a host of variables unique to the instructional situation. Different disciplines, teaching styles, learning styles, and student readiness are just some of the variables that come into play during instruction. Teaching chemistry is not the same as teaching art history, which is not the same as teaching basic composition. Attempting to aggregate findings from such varied instructional situations may be problematic as well as questionable. Glass (2000) struggled with this criticism, and even he at times had doubts about the appropriateness of comparing disparate studies. In the end, however, he concluded that while studies might be different in some significant way, that does not preclude our need to compare them. Researchers are constantly comparing different studies for one purpose or another. The narrative review of the literature, a basic requirement of formal research (i.e., thesis or dissertation), is fundamentally a comparison of different studies. If comparison is appropriate in this endeavor, why not also for meta-analysis?

Hattie (2009) raised a third important concern; namely, that meta-analysis focuses too much on the past and not on the future. It is true that meta-analysis examines what has already occurred, but this is not uncommon in many areas of education and research. The development of policy and practice almost always involves looking at what has occurred in order to plan for the future. This becomes a problem only when one goes too far into the past as to be irrelevant. This can be an issue, particularly for researchers doing work in instructional technology. A fundamental aspect of technology is that it changes, and sometimes rather quickly. Studies using "current technology" in the 1980s were no longer current by the 1990s and surely are not current today. This is an implementation issue and not inherent in the basic meta-analysis approach. Meta-analysts must select studies for their research that are appropriate for the problems that they are studying. In addition to the nature, variables, and sampling populations, the date and period of each study should also be considered. This is important for all meta-analyses, but is even more of concern when exploring the effects of technology.

Lastly, and perhaps the most long-lasting concern about meta-analysis, is the inclusion of low-quality studies. Glass faced this issue in the 1970s, and it continues to today. Hans J. Eysenck (1984), a major proponent of randomized, controlled experiments, argued vehemently that if a study has a fundamental error(s) in its design or implementation, it makes no sense to carry over this error(s) into a meta-analysis. He was highly critical of including nonrandomized and quasi-experimental studies in meta-analysis, and referred to this practice as "garbage in, garbage out." Glass and other proponents of meta-analysis have refuted Eysenck and promote a more inclusive, "cast a wider net" approach that allows averaging and other statistical techniques to take care of the quality issue. Hattie (2009) recommends that all studies to be included in a meta-analysis should be reviewed and evaluated for their appropriateness, including the "quality" of the research. At the same time, some flexibility is in order, and meta-analysis need not be limited only to those studies of the randomized, controlled variety.

Before concluding this section, a brief consideration should be given to those individuals who have been the major proponents of meta-analysis. Alexander Kock (2009) expressed enthusiasm for this approach, and notes its growth in popularity over the past decade and considers it to be the wave of the future for handling syntheses of research findings. John Hattie (2009) invested fifteen years of research in examining more than eight hundred meta-analyses and concluded that they have a significant role to play in education research. Gene Glass, the individual most associated with meta-analysis, when asked in 2000 about its future over the next twenty-five years, responded: "If our efforts to research and improve education are to prosper, meta-analysis will have to be replaced by more useful and more accurate ways of synthesizing research findings" (Glass, 2000).

Glass predicted that the synthesis of research would depend upon data archives that can be used to access, synthesize, and report on a variety of research questions and issues. He commented specifically that the Internet and its massive data storage and access capability is the vehicle that will make these data archives viable. There is some truth in what Glass said, but we are not there yet. In the meantime, meta-analysis remains one of the best techniques we have for synthesizing large numbers of studies on a particular research issue.

Meta-analysis and Instructional Technology

Computer technology, including online and blended learning, has been one of the hottest research topics in education for decades. There are many reasons for this, but essential to its popularity is the fact that technology is a moving target. Its changeability at times disrupts the playing field of best practices in education. The computer-assisted instruction of the 1960s and 1970s is not the simulation software and games developed in the 1980s and 1990s, and is not the Internet-based online learning programs of the 2000s. Furthermore, new technology does not always gracefully fit in with other education processes. It can require extensive funding for hardware, software, staffing, and facilities, and at times it requires teachers and other staff to retool their approaches to teaching and learning. The Internet and World Wide Web, introduced in the 1990s, have evolved into ubiquitous entities that impact everything we do, including how we teach and learn. Online and blended learning are becoming commonplace, and the need to study and evaluate their effectiveness grows. Meta-analysis can play a significant role in helping to understand their effectiveness.

The Grand Debate—Medium Versus Message

James Kulik and his associates at the University of Michigan were among the first researchers to conduct extensive reviews of the effects of technology on instruction. Using Glass's techniques, they conducted a series of meta-analyses in the 1970s and 1980s of hundreds of studies dealing with the effects of technology at different grade levels (elementary, secondary, college, and adult). Their general conclusion was that computer-based education had a beneficial effect on academic achievement, although it was not uniformly true at all grade levels and all subject areas (Kulik, 1984; Kulik, Bangert, & Williams, 1983; Kulik, Kulik, & Bangert-Downs, 1984; Kulik, Kulik, & Cohen, 1980; Kulik, Kulik, & Schwab, 1986).

Richard E. Clark (1983, 1985, 1989) refuted these findings by questioning the research controls used in most of the studies included in the Kulik meta-analyses. Clark made the same "garbage in, garbage out" argument offered by Hans J. Eysenck. Clark, however, went further and proposed that technology, or any medium, was basically a vehicle carrying an instructional substance and that real improvement in achievement only comes with improving the substance, not the vehicle. Unlike Marshall McLuhan's thesis that the "medium is the message," Clark posited that in education the message or content is the substance that matters. Clark's position has been challenged over the years by a number of researchers, such as Robert Kozma (1991, 1994a, 1994b) and Jack Koumi (1994), who see the medium as integral to the delivery of instruction. The two differing opinions on this issue remain to this day, and the "great debate" continues. As an indication of the ongoing nature and importance of this debate, a search of "Clark vs. Kozma" on Google provides over a million URLs, many of which refer to websites and blogs created in the past several years. Any researcher contemplating the examination of the effects of technology on learning would be well served by reading and rereading the articles by Clark, Kozma, and Koumi cited above. They provide valuable insight into the issues.

For our purposes, the basis for the debate was ignited by the meta-analyses conducted by Kulik and his colleagues, which synthesized much of the previous research on the issue. Since the Kulik work, thousands of studies, including meta-analyses, have been conducted on the same issue as the nature of the technology or medium (i.e., computer-assisted instruction, simulation software, online learning, etc.) keeps changing.

Meta-analysis for Online and Blended Learning

John Hattie was interested in student achievement, and in the early 1990s he started reviewing meta-analyses that dealt with the issue. Fifteen years later he had read and evaluated over eight hundred meta-analyses, some of which were conducted in the 1970s, and published his findings. Of his sample, over eighty meta-analyses representing almost 5,000 studies dealt with the effects of technology on student achievement. Hattie (2009) concluded that, based on the number of studies and meta-analyses, research on the effects of technology is perhaps most popular in the area of student achievement. Online and blended learning are relatively recent phenomena, having gained popularity as teaching modalities with the advent of the Internet in the 1990s. Despite their relatively recent emergence, the amount of research as judged by the number of studies is impressive.

In 2007, the United States Department of Education (U.S. ED) contracted with SRI International to conduct a meta-analysis of the effects of online learning on student achievement. Barbara Means, the lead researcher for this project, acknowledged that the work was done by a large team of staff members at SRI and named more than twenty individuals. The project was completed and a report prepared in 2009 and revised in 2010. As part of its work, the project team conducted a systematic search of the research literature published from 1996 through July 2008 and identified more than a thousand empirical studies of online learning. Their work provides an excellent case study of meta-analysis research examining the effects of online and blended learning. In the next few pages, some of the details of this work will be provided as an exemplar. Anyone contemplating a meta-analysis on this topic would do well to study the work of Barbara Means and her associates. The actual report is over ninety pages. An abstract is provided in Box 4.1.

Box 4.1   Abstract of the U.S. Department of Education Report (2010): *Evaluation of evidence-based practices in online learning: A meta-analysis and review of online learning studies*

A systematic search of the research literature from 1996 through July 2008 identified more than a thousand empirical studies of online learning. Analysts screened these studies to find those that (a) contrasted an online to a face-to-face condition, (b) measured student learning outcomes, (c) used a rigorous research design, and (d) provided adequate information to calculate an effect size. As a result of this screening, 50 independent effects were identified that could be subjected to meta-analysis. The meta-analysis found that, on average, students in online learning conditions performed modestly better than those receiving face-to-face instruction. The difference between student outcomes for online and face-to-face classes—measured as the difference between treatment and control means, divided by the pooled standard deviation—was larger in those studies contrasting conditions that blended elements of online and face-to-face instruction with conditions taught entirely face-to-face. Analysts noted that these blended

(Continued)

conditions often included additional learning time and instructional elements not received by students in control conditions. This finding suggests that the positive effects associated with blended learning should not be attributed to the media, per se. An unexpected finding was the small number of rigorous published studies contrasting online and face-to-face learning conditions for K–12 students. In light of this small corpus, caution is required in generalizing to the K–12 population because the results are derived for the most part from studies in other settings (e.g., medical training, higher education).

This study is available as a free download at www2.ed.gov/rschstat/eval/tech/evidence-based-practices/finalreport.pdf.

Overall Design Considerations

The first two sentences of the abstract of the U.S. ED meta-analysis provide critical information as to the overall approach taken:

A systematic search of the research literature from 1996 through July 2008 identified more than a thousand empirical studies of online learning. Analysts screened these studies to find those that:

(a)   contrasted an online to a face-to-face condition,
(b)   measured student learning outcomes,
(c)   used a rigorous research design, and
(d)   provided adequate information to calculate an effect size.

(U.S. ED., 2010, p. 1)

Items (a) and (b) clearly identify the two major variables that are the object of analysis—namely, modality of learning and student learning outcomes. Other variables such as student satisfaction, faculty satisfaction, and cost benefits are not included and are not of concern to this analysis. Because of the effort involved, meta-analyses usually concentrate on a limited number of variables. Item c respects some of the criticisms of meta-analyses that include poorly designed studies (i.e., garbage in, garbage out). Item d is critical to the selection of studies to include in the meta-analysis and refers to whether or not a study provides sufficient information to calculate an effect size. Minimally this would include means and standard deviations of the study groupings (i.e., control and experiment).

Definition of Terms

In all studies, it is critical for a researcher(s) to define his/her terms, especially as related to key variables. In the U.S. ED meta-analysis, there was much attention paid to what to include as online learning:

For this review, *online learning* is defined as learning that takes place partially or entirely over the Internet. This definition excludes purely print-based correspondence education, broadcast television or radio, videoconferencing, videocassettes, and stand-alone educational software programs that do not have a significant Internet-based instructional component. In contrast to previous meta-analyses, this review distinguishes between two purposes for online learning:

a. learning conducted totally online as a substitute or *alternative* to face-to-face learning,
b. online learning components that are combined or *blended* (sometimes called "hybrid") with face-to-face instruction to provide learning *enhancement*.

(U.S. ED., 2010, p. 9)

These definitions are most appropriate. It is crucial to differentiate fully online from blended learning because the two modalities can be radically different. Fully online is straightforward to a degree, but blended learning is nebulous at best and can mean different things in different situations. For instance, some schools would distinguish blended courses, where some portion of face-to-face seat time is replaced by the online components, from courses that simply enhance a course where a full complement of instruction is provided in face-to-face mode. Other issues of definition can arise when considering the amount of time spent in the face-to-face mode versus the online mode. The nature of the online mode, whether done fully or blended, is also open to possibilities depending upon whether it is instructor led, programmed instruction, drill and practice, simulations, gaming, collaborative writing project, etc. At the present time, any meta-analysis that has online and blended learning as a focus requires a serious consideration of definitions of the terms and careful decisions regarding what to include or exclude.

Screening for Usable Studies

Locating and screening studies that might meet the data criteria are the most time-consuming aspects of conducting a meta-analysis. Regarding work with technology and education, so many studies have been conducted that screening them for quality and appropriate data can easily become a huge undertaking. This was definitely the case with the U.S. ED meta-analysis. Below is an excerpt from the meta-analysis describing the screening process:

The initial electronic database searches . . . yielded 1,132 articles. Citation information and abstracts of these studies were examined to ascertain whether they met the following three initial inclusion criteria:

1. *Does the study address online learning as this review defines it?*
2. *Does the study appear to use a controlled design (experimental/ quasi-experimental design)?*
3. *Does the study report data on student achievement or another learning outcome?*

At this early stage, analysts gave studies "the benefit of the doubt," retaining those that were not clearly outside the inclusion criteria on the basis of their citations and abstracts. As a result of this screening, 316 articles were

retained and 816 articles were excluded. During this initial screen, 45 percent of the excluded articles were removed primarily because they did not
have a controlled design. Twenty-six percent of excluded articles were eliminated because they did not report learning outcomes for treatment and control
groups. Twenty-three percent were eliminated because their intervention did
not qualify as online learning, given the definition used for this meta-analysis
and review. The remaining six percent of excluded studies posed other difficulties such as being written in a language other than English ...

[During the next phase of the screening process] 99 studies [were exam-
ined] to obtain the data for calculating effect size from 45 studies. Fifty-four
studies did not report sufficient data to support calculating effect size.

(U.S. ED., 2010, pp. 11–12)

To summarize, the project started with a screening of 1,132 studies, of which
forty-five were fully usable for extracting effect sizes. The amount of effort that
went into the screening is not unusual, especially when dealing with an area of
research as popular as instructional technology. Researchers contemplating doing
meta-analysis in this area should consider whether they have the time and resources
to undertake the screening of possible studies.

Findings

The most important aspect of the U.S. ED meta-analysis is unquestionably the
findings. The overall finding of the meta-analysis is that classes with online learning (whether taught completely online or blended) on average produce stronger
student learning outcomes than do classes with solely face-to-face instruction. The
mean effect size for all fifty contrasts was +0.20, $p < .001$ (U.S. ED., 2010, p. 18).
It is important to keep in mind that an effect size of +0.20 is considered small, but
is nonetheless positive. However, the researchers for the meta-analysis went a step
further by separating the findings for fully online versus blended learning. To quote:

The conceptual framework for this study, which distinguishes between purely
online and blended forms of instruction, calls for creating subsets of the effect
estimates to address two more nuanced research questions:

1. *How does the effectiveness of online learning compare with that of face to-face in-
    struction?*

Looking only at the 27 Category 1 effects that compared a purely online
condition with face-to-face instruction, analysts found a mean effect of +0.05,
$p =.46$.

This finding is similar to that of previous summaries of distance learning
(generally from pre-Internet studies), in finding that instruction conducted
entirely online is as effective as classroom instruction but no better.

2. *Does supplementing face-to-face instruction with online instruction enhance learning?*

For the 23 Category 2 contrasts that compared blended conditions of online
plus face-to face learning with face-to-face instruction alone, the mean effect

size of +0.35 was significant ($p < .0001$). Blends of online and face-to-face instruction, on average, had stronger learning outcomes than did face-to-face instruction alone.

A test of the difference between Category 1 and Category 2 studies found that the mean effect size was larger for contrasts pitting blended learning against face-to-face instruction ($g+ = +0.35$) than for those of purely online versus face-to-face instruction ($g+ = +0.05$); the difference between the two subsets of studies was statistically significant ($Q = 8.37, p < .01$).

(U.S. ED., 2010, p. 12)

The effect size comparing blended learning and face-to-face instruction is far stronger at +0.35 and makes this finding far more significant. The researchers comment later in the study that some of the difference in the effects of blended learning might be attributed to more time on task than in fully online or face-to-face instruction.

In the discussion of the findings, there is an important recognition of the work of Richard Clark, who was referenced earlier in this chapter:

Clark (1983) has cautioned against interpreting studies of instruction in different media as demonstrating an effect for a given medium inasmuch as conditions may vary with respect to a whole set of instructor and content variables. That caution applies well to the findings of this meta-analysis, which should not be construed as demonstrating that online learning is superior as a medium. Rather, it is the combination of elements in the treatment conditions, which are likely to include additional learning time and materials as well as additional opportunities for collaboration, that has proven effective. The meta-analysis findings do not support simply putting an existing course online, but they do support redesigning instruction to incorporate additional learning opportunities online.

(U.S. ED., 2010, p. 51)

The Need for Further Meta-analyses

The U.S. ED meta-analysis established important baseline data for any other researcher planning to study the effects of online and blended learning. Its findings will be cited over and over again for years to come. However, it also illustrated that there is so much more research needed. For researchers interested in student outcomes, there continues to be a need for more comprehensive study. Since 2010, when the U.S. ED meta-analysis was published, there have been significant developments in online and blended learning. For example, consider the advances in mobile computing, learning analytics, credit recovery programs at the K–12 level, or massive open online courses (MOOCs) in colleges and universities. Meta-analyses in online and blended learning are also needed in areas other than student outcomes. Student access to learning, faculty satisfaction and attitudes, student satisfaction, and cost benefits are prime topics for study. Researchers contemplating doing meta-analyses can feel confident that if done well, their findings will be received with great interest and appreciation by researchers, policymakers, and practitioners alike.

References

Clark, R. (1983). Reconsidering research on learning from media. *Review of Educational Research, 53*(4), 445–459.

Clark, R. (1985). Evidence for confounding in computer-based instruction studies. *Educational Communications and Technology Journal, 33*(4), 249–262.

Clark, R. (1989). Current progress and future directions for research in instructional technology. *Educational Technology Research and Development, 37*(1), 57–66.

Cohen, J. (1988). *Statistical power analysis* (2nd ed.). Hillsdale, NJ: Erlbaum Associates.

Cooper, H. M., & Hedges, L. V. (1994). Research synthesis as a scientific enterprise. In Cooper, H. M., & Hedges, L. V. (eds) *The handbook of research synthesis* (pp. 3–14). New York: Russell Sage Foundation.

Eysenck, H. J. (1984). Meta-analysis: An abuse of research integration. *Journal of Special Education, 18*(1), 41–59.

Glass, G. (2000). *Meta-analysis at 25*. Unpublished paper, Arizona State University. Retrieved from www.gvglass.info/papers/meta25.html [Accessed August 6, 2014].

Glass, G. V., McGaw, B., & Smith, M. L. (1981). *Meta-analysis in social research*. Beverly Hills: Sage Publications.

Hattie, J. (2009). *Visible learning: A synthesis of over 800 meta-analyses relating to achievement*. London: Routledge/Taylor & Francis Group.

Kock, A. (2009). *A guideline to meta-analysis*. Berlin: Technische Universität Berlin. Retrieved from www.tim.tuberlin.de/fileadmin/fg101/TIM_Working_Paper_Series/Volume_2/TIM_WPS_Kock_2009.pdf [Accessed August 8, 2014].

Koumi, J. (1994). Media comparison and deployment: A practitioner's view. *British Journal of Educational Technology, 25*(1), 41–57.

Kozma, R. (1991). Learning with media. *Review of Educational Research, 61*(2), 179–211.

Kozma, R. (1994a). Will media influence learning? Reframing the debate. *Educational Technology Research and Development, 42*(2), 7–19.

Kozma, R. (1994b). A reply: Media and methods. *Educational Technology Research and Development, 42*(3), 11–14.

Kulik, J. A. (1984). Evaluating the effects of teaching with computers. In Campbell, G., & Fein, G. (eds) *Microcomputers in early education* (pp. 88–101). Reston, VA: Reston.

Kulik, J. A., Bangert, R., & Williams, G. (1983). Effects of computer-based teaching on secondary students. *Journal of Educational Psychology, 75*(1), 19–26.

Kulik, J. A., Kulik, C., & Bangert-Downs, R. (1984). Effectiveness of computer-based education in elementary schools. *Computers in Human Behavior, 1*(1), 59–74.

Kulik, J. A., Kulik, C., & Cohen, P. (1980). Effectiveness of computer-based college teaching: A meta-analysis of findings. *Review of Educational Research, 2*(2), 525–544.

Kulik, J. A., Kulik, C., & Schwab, B. (1986). The effectiveness of computer-based adult education: A meta-analysis. *Journal of Educational Computing Research, 2*(2), 235–252.

Rosenthal, R. (1991). *Meta-analytic procedures for social research*. Newbury Park: Sage Publications.

U.S. Department of Education (U.S. ED), Office of Planning, Evaluation, and Policy Development (2010). *Evaluation of evidence-based practices in online learning: A meta-analysis and review of online learning studies*. Washington, DC. Retrieved from www2.ed.gov/rschstat/eval/tech/evidence-based-practices/finalreport.pdf [Accessed August 7, 2014].

Chapter 5

Models of Survey Research

Anthony G. Picciano

The survey is one of the most popular methods for collecting data in the social sciences. This flexible means of data collection can be used with various sample sizes—from very small to very large—and can be used as the basis of a stand-alone study or integrated with other methods, including qualitative studies, inferential studies, correlation research, and comparative research. While some well-respected experts consider survey research a unique method in and of itself, others see it only as a tool to be used for data collection (Wiersma, 2000). Of all the research methods, survey research is perhaps the most familiar to the general public because it is used for many purposes by the mass media and other organizations. During election cycles, news agencies conduct dozens of surveys to determine which candidates are leading in their contests. Policy experts regularly conduct surveys to get the "pulse" of the public on a variety of issues. Market research depends upon surveying to determine the interest, tastes, and attitudes of targeted populations.

Survey research has advanced well beyond the printed, mailed instrument with a prestamped return envelope. Surveys are used in conjunction with interviews conducted in person, in group sessions, or on the telephone. With the ubiquity of the Internet, survey researchers are also taking advantage of electronic data collection facilities, such as *Survey Monkey*. As a result, survey research has evolved into the most commonly used method in the social sciences for studying a variety of phenomena, including education processes. In this chapter, survey research is examined as a technique that has been used extensively for studying the effects and impact of online and blended learning.

Basic Definitions and Design Considerations for Conducting Survey Research

Definition

The simplest definition of survey research is a method of sociological investigation that uses questions in written or verbal form to collect information about how people think and act. Typically it uses surveys

> to answer questions that have been raised, to solve problems that have been posed or observed, to assess needs and set goals, to determine whether or not specific objectives have been met, to establish base lines against which

future comparisons can be made, to analyze trends across time, and generally, to describe what exists, in what amount, and in what context.

(Isaac & Michael, 1997, p.136)

In contrast to survey research, a "survey" is simply a data collection tool for carrying out survey research. The term "survey instrument" is often used to distinguish the survey tool from the survey research that it is designed to support. A survey instrument is the means for gathering information about the characteristics, actions, or opinions of a group of people. It can also be used to assess needs, evaluate demand, and examine the impact of an approach, product, or technique.

Basic Design Considerations

It is not within the scope of this chapter to review the extensive literature on survey research methods. Entire books have been written on this subject. For an in-depth treatment, the reader may see any of the following excellent guides to survey research:

> Rea, L. M., & Parker, R. A. (2005). *Designing and conducting survey research: A comprehensive guide* (3rd ed.). San Francisco: Jossey-Bass.
> Alreck, P. L., & Settle, R. B. (2005 or latest). *The survey research handbook* (3rd ed.). New York: McGraw-Hill.
> Babbie, E. R. (1990 or latest). *Survey research methods* (2nd ed.). Stamford, CT: Cengage Learning Publishing Co.

However, for our purposes, a brief review of key concepts is in order. The art of conducting survey research includes the following steps:

- Design the instrument or questions
- Pilot test
- Select a sample
- Distribute the instrument or conduct interviews
- Follow up
- Record the data
- Analyze the results

Designing a survey instrument depends directly upon the problem or topic being studied and the target survey population. The design requires in-depth knowledge of the subject matter so that questions are accurate in content and easily understandable by the survey respondents. Consideration must be given to the reading level of target populations, especially in studies that involve subjects whose literacy skills are still developing (i.e., children, English language learners).

Simplicity of format is also an important aspect of survey design. Likert-type scales, popular in survey research, ask respondents to select a response from three to nine options in a consistent format. Depending on the questions, options might be:

Strongly Disagree	Disagree	No Opinion	Agree	Strongly Agree
Never	Rarely	Sometimes	Often	Always
Excellent	Very Good	Average	Fair	Poor

The Likert scale is named for Rensis Likert, who did a good deal of well-respected survey research on leadership and other aspects of organizational behavior at the University of Michigan. Likert's suggestions for wording questions on a survey include:

- Keep them short and direct.
- Include only one idea or concept per question.
- Avoid complex terms and difficult language.
- Make sure that the content is accurate.
- Make sure that all grammar is correct.
- Avoid leading the respondent to certain conclusions.

The above suggestions should be carefully considered since many potential respondents will not answer a survey if it looks overly complex, time consuming, or contains questions that are intimidating or confusing. Consistency in the question format significantly helps respondents understand how to respond to a survey.

Once a survey instrument has been developed, it should be piloted or field-tested on a small group of representative respondents. The pilot test should be designed to determine if any questions are difficult or confusing to answer. A time study should also be conducted to determine how long it takes to complete the survey, since the longer the survey, the lower the response rate. If the pilot test indicates minor or modest changes to the instrument, then these should be implemented immediately and preparation made to distribute the survey to a larger population. If major changes are required, the instrument should be pilot tested a second time, after these changes are made.

Selecting a sample will depend on the type of research to be conducted. In most cases, the survey population will be much smaller than the larger population that is the focus of the study. Random sampling is by far the most popular technique for selecting the smaller population for a survey. The process of selecting a random sample can be complex, but essentially requires that all the subjects in a population have an equal chance of being selected. One popular way to accomplish this is by assigning each potential subject a number, after which a computer sorts the numbers randomly, then selects every number at a certain interval (e.g., every fifth, tenth, or hundredth) depending on the desired size of the survey sample. Statistical software packages such as SPSS have built-in features for drawing random samples.

A stratified sample is a type of random sample that attempts to include representative proportions with certain characteristics (e.g., gender, ethnicity, income levels) of the larger population. This may be necessary because sometimes in generating a random sample, a disproportionate percentage of subjects with a particular characteristic (e.g., too many females, too many high-income families) are selected. The stratified sample corrects for any disproportion.

A convenience sample, also called an "accidental" sample or "man-in-the-street" sample, uses subjects that are convenient, close at hand, or easy to reach. For instance, undergraduates in colleges and universities are frequently asked by faculty to participate in surveys, as the students are readily available and generally willing to participate.

In considering how to select a sample, a decision must be made as to whether the survey will be administered once or several times. A cross-sectional study uses random sampling techniques if the sample is conducted once. Findings and conclusions are stated that apply to the survey population for that particular time.

In a longitudinal study, the researcher surveys a population over time, and the survey is administered several times. The researcher has the option of using a new random sample for each administration of the survey or following the original sample over time. In the latter case, a determination should be made of the sample's mobility and whether or not addresses or telephone numbers are likely to change during the period of the study.

Surveys are distributed in several ways. Mailings have historically been very popular. The costs for mailing are modest, the postal services are reliable, and respondents have a chance to peruse the instrument and determine if they wish to participate. If a survey is relatively short and the sample relatively small, a researcher may opt to use the telephone to contact potential respondents. This will likely be more costly and may require several attempts to contact respondents who are away from their phones. If the logistics are not too complicated and the sample not too large, face-to-face interviews can be conducted. In recent years, survey designers have been using the Internet to conduct surveys. This type of survey is relatively inexpensive, and its greatest benefit may be that the results are collected in electronic form and are available for immediate analysis. A drawback is that not everyone is connected to the Internet.

When conducting a survey, a major question is: What is an acceptable response rate? This is difficult to answer and will depend upon the nature of the survey. Many researchers working with stable populations and questions that are not considered overly sensitive will seek high (e.g., in excess of 50%) response rates. However, if the survey touches on sensitive issues (e.g., sexual practices, drug use) or the population is highly mobile (e.g., student dropouts), then lower response rates are to be expected. If there is any concern about a low response rate, a second or third follow-up distribution of the survey is appropriate.

If survey data have been collected using print, telephone, or face-to-face interviews, the results will need to be recorded and stored in an electronic (computer) form, assuming that the data will be analyzed, sorted, and reviewed using computer software tools rather than manually. Depending upon the size of the sample, this can be time consuming and error prone. Large research organizations usually employ professional data entry clerks to record survey results. To minimize errors, a well-designed survey will take recording the results into consideration by designing coding schemes that are simple and straightforward. A coding scheme refers to the final valid possibilities that can occur for an item on a survey. For instance, gender might appear on the survey as a check-off box that indicates "female" or "male." However, when the response to this question is recorded electronically, it may appear as a code, such as "1" or "2," or "F" or "M." The recoding of the code may or may not be done by someone intimately familiar with the study, and so the simpler the code, the fewer the errors. For most statistical analyses, a coding scheme that converts item responses into numbers rather than letters of the alphabet is highly recommended.

Once the data are converted into electronic form, they are ready to be analyzed. Survey analysis requires that a computer software program such as SAS or SPSS be used to sort and perform the appropriate statistical routines on the data. The two major types of statistical analysis performed on survey data are descriptive and inferential analyses. As the name implies, descriptive statistics are the basic measures used to describe survey data that have been collected, such as gender, age, income, etc. Examples of descriptive statistics for survey data include frequency distributions, measures of central tendency (mean, median, and mode), and measures of spread or dispersion, such as the range and standard deviation. Inferential statistics perform more robust analyses of survey data and are concerned with making larger inferences about social phenomena from a smaller sample. These can include associations between and among variables, such as cause-and-effect relationships. Examples of inferential statistics used in survey data analysis are t-tests that compare group averages, analyses of variance, correlation and regression, and advanced techniques such as factor analysis and cluster analysis.

Reliability and Validity

Some of the terminology associated with survey research is fairly straightforward. For instance, written survey instruments are referred to as questionnaires or test instruments. Verbal survey instruments are referred to as interviews. Other terms, such as "reliability" and "validity," are more complex, but are critical concepts for the researcher to understand and consider.

Reliability refers to the degree to which a survey instrument *consistently* measures what it is supposed to measure. Determining reliability usually involves administering the survey instrument to the same or similar sample two or more times and then comparing results using correlations which one would expect to be very high. "Cronbach's alpha" is a widely popular correlational technique to conduct reliability tests on survey instruments. It is particularly effective in assessing the consistency of items or questions on the instrument.

Validity refers to the degree to which a survey instrument measures what it is supposed to measure. There are several types of validity measures, including the following:

- "Content validity" considers whether the questions measure the content they were intended to measure.
- "Predictive validity" examines whether the responses are able to predict a criterion measure.
- "Concurrent validity" addresses the correlation of survey results with results from other sources.

Validity tests can be performed by correlating the results of one instrument with a similar measure that has already established its validity. For example, validity tests for making predictions, such as the use of Scholastic Aptitude Test (SAT) scores to predict college grade point average in the freshman year, might use correlation coefficients of the two measures (SAT scores and grade point averages) of a sample population to establish the predictive validity of the SAT. In some cases, where an appropriate measure to compare results of a test is not available, validity tests for content of subject matter might have to be done by a panel of experts who attest to the validity of the test.

In establishing reliability and validity of survey instruments, very high correlations (e.g., +.80 and above) are expected.

Sample Size

One of the most frequently asked questions when drawing a sample for survey research is "how many subjects are needed for the sample?" Some statisticians argue that the larger the sample, the better. Others argue that a well-drawn, small random sample is ideal. Regardless, the question comes up over and over again. A common approach to the problem is to calculate an appropriate sample size by determining the following:

1. **Population size**—How many total people are in the population being studied? If the population size is unknown, it can be approximated, or a formula based on standard deviations can be used.
2. **Confidence interval or margin of error**—The confidence interval determines how much higher or lower than the population mean you are willing to let your sample mean fall. If you've ever seen a political poll on the news, you've seen a confidence interval. It looks something like this: "55% of voters said yes to proposition A, with a margin of error of plus or minus 5%."
3. **Confidence level**—How confident do you want to be that the actual mean falls within your confidence interval? The most common confidence intervals are 95% confident and 99% confident.
4. **Standard deviation (SD)**—How much variance do you expect in your responses? Since the survey has not been administered yet, one doesn't know. Use .5, since this is a most forgiving number and ensures that your sample will be large enough.

With the above defined, a sample size can be calculated as follows:

Convert the confidence level to a z-score. The z-scores for the most common confidence levels are:

- 95%: z-score = 1.96
- 99%: z-score = 2.576

You can also use a z-score table.

The sample size equation is as follows:

sample size = ((z-score)^2 x SD x (1-SD)) / (confidence interval)^2
For an unknown population with a 95% confidence level, .5 standard deviation, and a confidence interval or margin of error of +/−5%.

$$((1.96)^2 \text{ x } .5(.5)) / (.05)^2$$

$$(3.8416 \text{ x } .25) / .0025$$

.9604 / .0025

384.16

385 respondents are needed

You can decrease your sample size by decreasing your confidence level (e.g., from 99% to 95%) or increasing your confidence interval (e.g., from a margin of error of +/−3 to +/−5). This will increase the chance for error in your sampling, but decrease the number needed in a sample.

There are a number of free, online sample size calculators available on the Internet. For example, see Creative Research Systems at www.surveysystem.com/sscalc.htm.

Concerns and Issues

As popular as survey research is, it is not without its detractors. George Beam, an associate professor of public administration at the University of Illinois, Chicago, in *The Problem with Survey Research*, makes a case against survey research as a primary source of reliable information. In this book, he argues that all survey research instruments produce unreliable and potentially inaccurate results. He reasons that researchers who rely on surveys only see answers to questions, and that it is impossible for them, or anyone else, to evaluate the results. They cannot know if the answers correspond to respondents' actual behaviors (objective phenomena) or to their true beliefs and opinions (subjective phenomena). He further reasons that reliable information can only be acquired by observation, experimentation, multiple sources of data, formal model building and testing, document analysis, and comparison (Beam, 2012). His points are well taken and should not be dismissed. Survey research, as all research methods, has certain weaknesses. Survey research is not meant to be a conclusive study of phenomena. Its purpose is to add to the knowledge that exists and to help guide future research. A survey administered to a group of individuals records their opinions at one particular moment in time and may not represent their attitudes at other times. Opinions change—look at election poll results that change from week to week as candidates are given the opportunity to express their opinions on issues. Nevertheless, survey research has its place in the social sciences as a technique that can be helpful in understanding human activities and opinions. Beam may be correct in stating that researchers should integrate survey research with other methodologies to maximize a study's results. While the same can be said for other research methods as well, there are several well-accepted issues with survey research that need to be discussed.

Cultural bias has long been an issue when utilizing survey instruments, especially those designed to test or assess achievement, aptitude, and attitudes. Race, ethnicity, and language play important roles in the way individuals see and perceive the world. This has to be recognized in the design of an instrument. Simple and direct questions are recommended. If the subjects represent diverse populations, the researcher would be wise to collect data on ethnicity to determine if there are significant differences in the responses. If there are, this has to be reported accordingly. Pilot testing a survey instrument can also uncover cultural biases and allow the researcher to refine the instrument if need be. In sum, questions need to adequately reflect the values, traditions, and beliefs of respondents, which in a diverse society may be different.

Related to cultural bias is the reading level of respondents. This is an obvious issue when dealing with younger populations of students who are still developing their reading skills, but it can also be a major issue for adult English language learners. Given the changing demographics in the United States, English language learners are representing larger percentages of the population, including students in primary, secondary, and postsecondary education. The wording of questions becomes significantly important and can adversely affect response rates and the accuracy of responses, especially if the subjects have problems understanding the questions. Again, instruments must be designed with subject populations in mind. Pilot testing will assist in refining questions, but in some cases interviewing might be a better option than conducting a survey.

As mentioned earlier in this chapter, sensitive topics affect response rates. It is well understood that many people will not respond to questions related to drinking alcohol, drug use, and sexual practices. Even what might be perceived as less sensitive topics, such as dropping a class or withdrawing from an academic program, might be too sensitive for some subjects to respond, particularly if reasons involve private family circumstances or financial problems. Researchers have to consider what a low response rate on a survey might mean to a study and plan accordingly, perhaps by drawing a larger sample.

Lastly, there is always a concern about the nonresponders, even if the overall response rate is acceptable. Survey researchers struggle with this issue over and over again because they are forced to speculate about the opinions and attitudes of the nonrespondents and how they might affect the accuracy of the data that were collected. Were questions too difficult? Did they not want to take the time to respond? Did they not like the wording of questions? Were they concerned about the confidentiality of their responses? All of these questions represent concerns that can affect the accuracy of findings and conclusions. An analysis of the characteristics of respondents and nonrespondents, if possible, might allow the researcher to make adjustments to findings if necessary. In addition, the administration of the survey instrument can be critical. For instance, subjects generally want to be assured of confidentiality. While few surveys can provide complete anonymity, where no identifying information is ever recorded to trace respondents with their responses, the steps taken by the researchers to preserve anonymity should be above reproach and stated clearly on the survey.

Survey Research in Online and Blended Learning

The Babson Survey Research Group has conducted an extensive amount of survey research on online and blended learning in American education (Box 5.1 provides a list of its online and blended learning research projects/reports, and all are available for free download). The findings from this body of research are used and cited regularly by national and international researchers, practitioners, and policymakers. For example, in 2008, Clayton Christensen, a professor at the Harvard Business School and the best-selling author of *The Innovator's Dilemma*, published a book with Michael Horn and Curtis Johnson entitled *Disrupting Class: How Innovation Will Change the Way the World Learns*. In this bestseller in the education and technology genre, Christensen, Horn, and Johnson presented a compelling rationale for changing education in a way that makes far greater use of online technology to provide more student-centered and individualized instruction. The book's call for change was cited by many educators as an important consideration for policymakers when looking at the future of American education. Among the most provocative aspects of this book are the predictions that approximately one-half of all high school courses will be online by the year 2019. In Chapter 4, Christensen et al. provide the bases for their predictions and, among other citations, refer to the Babson Survey Research Group study conducted by Picciano and Seaman in 2007. The survey research of the this study is considered to be among the most important research in online and blended learning. A fundamental question is: Why is this work so popular and well respected?

Box 5.1   Reports Based on Surveys of Online and Blended Learning Conducted by the Babson Survey Research Group

Sloan Series of National and Regional Surveys of Online Education
- *Going the Distance: Online Education in the United States, 2011*
- *Online Learning Trends in Private-Sector Colleges and Universities, 2011*
- *Class Differences: Online Education in the United States, 2010*
- *Learning on Demand: Online Education in the United States, 2009*
- *Staying the Course: Online Education in the United States, 2008*
- *Online Nation: Five Years of Growth in Online Learning*
- *Making the Grade: Online Education in the United States, 2006*
- *Making the Grade: Online Education in the United States, 2006 – Midwestern Edition*
- *Making the Grade: Online Education in the United States, 2006 – Southern Edition*
- *Growing by Degrees: Online Education in the United States, 2005*
- *Growing by Degrees: Online Education in the United States, 2005 – Southern Edition*
- *Entering the Mainstream: The Quality and Extent of Online Education in the United States, 2003 and 2004*
- *Sizing the Opportunity: The Quality and Extent of Online Education in the United States, 2002 and 2003*

Sloan K–12 Online Learning Survey Reports
- *Online Learning In Illinois High Schools: Has The Time Come?*
- *Class Connections: High School Reform and the Role of Online Learning*
- *K–12 Online Learning: A 2008 Follow-up of the Survey of U.S. School District Administrators*
- *K–12 Online Learning: A Survey of U.S. School District Administrators*

The Association of Public Land-Grant Universities/Sloan National Commission on Online Learning
- *Online Learning as a Strategic Asset, Volume II: The Paradox of Faculty Voices: Views and Experiences with Online Learning*

(Continued)

> - *Online Learning as a Strategic Asset: A Survey of APLU Presidents and Chancellors*
> - *Online Learning as a Strategic Asset: A Survey of NAFEO Presidents and Chancellors*
> - *Online Learning as a Strategic Asset: A Survey of AIHEC Tribal College and University*
>
> Reprinted with permission from Jeff Seaman. All of the above are available for download at www.onlinelearningsurvey.com/.

First, Jeff Seaman and A. Elaine Allen, who founded and lead the Babson Group, are experienced individuals who bring a wealth of research, statistical, and technological skills to their work. In addition, their research in online and blended learning has been well funded by several organizations, especially the Alfred P. Sloan Foundation. The combination of skill, experience, and funding can make for excellent research.

Second, their timing was most fortunate. Starting in the early 2000s, Seaman and Allen were ahead of the curve in tracking the development of online and blended learning. There was great interest in the new online technology and what it could do for education, but no other organization was collecting data on this phenomenon on a regular basis. The U.S. Department of Education was collecting data on a three-year cycle on distance learning in K–12 education but doing nothing in higher education. Also, the advances in online technology were occurring much too rapidly for data collected in three-year cycles. As a result, Babson had a waiting audience of scholars, media, and policymakers. Professional news outlets such as *Education Week* and *The Chronicle of Higher Education* published findings from their reports and frequently cite them in articles on instructional technology.

Third, and perhaps most important to their success, is the fact that the surveys are well designed and administered and the findings are well presented. Terms such as "online learning" and "blended learning" are clearly defined. Survey questions (see Figure 5.1 for an example) are straightforward and as consistent as possible in style and format. In addition to checking off answers, respondents are provided with the opportunity to make comments or explain the category "other." In terms of administration, techniques such as assuring respondents of anonymity are used. Response rates are generally very good and in some cases exceed 60% of the "known universe." This rate was achieved through multiple solicitations or mailings. Whenever possible, email and electronic data collection were used, but mailed paper surveys were also utilized to achieve acceptable response rates. Presentations of findings in the form of reports are clear and easily understood by scholars and general readers alike. Basic descriptive statistics (see Figure 5.2), such as frequency distributions, contingency tables, and means analyses, are commonly used. Bar charts and line graphs supplement the statistical presentations to increase understanding.

4. Regardless of whether or not your school is currently offering online or blended/hybrid courses, how much of a barrier are the following areas to offering or potentially offering fully online or blended/hybrid learning courses? Do not consider web-enhanced courses for this question.

	Not at all Important 1	2	3	Neutral 4	5	6	Very Important 7
Course development and/or purchasing costs.	O	O	O	O	O	O	O
Limited technological infrastructure to support distance education.	O	O	O	O	O	O	O
Concerns about course quality.	O	O	O	O	O	O	O
Restrictive federal, state, or local laws or policies.	O	O	O	O	O	O	O
The need for teacher training.	O	O	O	O	O	O	O
Concerns about receiving funding based on student attendance for online and/or blended/hybrid education courses.	O	O	O	O	O	O	O
Other (Specify below)	O	O	O	O	O	O	O

Figure 5.1 Sample Likert Questions from Babson Survey Research Group Survey of Illinois Principals

Lastly, Seaman and Allen had the foresight to seek funding to collect data for some of their projects on a longitudinal basis. For instance, the higher education surveys have been collected for ten years and a database established that can be added to with each subsequent administration of the survey. Furthermore, the U.S. Department of Education's Integrated Postsecondary Education Data System (IPEDS) was used to populate basic institutional characteristics on the database, thereby precluding an extensive initial data collection effort. The result is an extensive depository

	Total Enrollment	Annual Growth Rate Total Enrollment	Students Taking at Least One Online Course	Online Enrollment Increase over Previous Year	Annual Growth Rate Online Enrollment	Online Enrollment as a Percent of Total Enrollment
Fall 2002	16,611,710	NA	1,602,970	NA	NA	9.6%
Fall 2003	19,911,481	1.8%	1,971,397	368,427	23.0%	11.7%
Fall 2004	17,272,043	2.1%	2,329,783	358,386	18.2%	13.5%
Fall 2005	17,487,481	1.2%	3,180,050	850,267	36.5%	18.2%
Fall 2006	17,758,872	1.6%	3,488,381	308,331	9.7%	19.6%
Fall 2007	18,248,133	2.8%	3,938,111	449,730	12.9%	21.6%
Fall 2008	19,102,811	4.7%	4,616,353	668,242	16.9%	24.1%
Fall 2009	20,427,711	6.9%	5,579,022	972,669	21.1%	27.3%
Fall 2010	21,013,126	2.9%	6,142,280	563,258	10.1%	29.2%
Fall 2011	20,994,113	-0.1%	6,714,792	572,512	9.3%	32.0%

Figure 5.2 Sample Contingency Table/Cross-Tabulation from a Babson Survey Research Group Study of. Chief Academic Officers

Reprinted with permission from Jeff Seaman. Allen, I.E., & Seaman, J. (2013). *Changing course: Ten years of tracking online education in the United States.* Babson Park, MA: Babson Survey Research Group and Quahog Research Group, LLC.

of data on online and blended learning in higher education that is unmatched by any other organization.

In sum, the work of the Babson Survey Research Group represents a significant contribution to the scholarship on online and blended learning. Researchers contemplating study in this area would be wise to examine the techniques used for its survey design, administration, presentation, and data maintenance.

Conducting Survey Research on Online and Blended Learning

While becoming more commonplace, online and blended learning continues to attract a good deal of study and evaluation. Newer technologies such as learning analytics, gaming, and massive open online courses (MOOC) require new investigations and evaluations. Survey research has a place in this regard.

Scope of Survey Research

The Babson Survey Research Group provides significant baseline data on the state of online and blended learning nationally on the macrolevel. However, much of the survey research in this area is conducted on much smaller samples. Instructors studying the students in their courses, college administrators evaluating academic programs, instructional designers determining the effectiveness of professional development programs, and principal investigators determining the impact of online and blended learning within and across institutions have all contributed to the research base. In survey research, the size and availability of the population matters. Smaller sample sizes afford the researcher the ability to examine more closely the attitudes, opinions, and interactions of subjects. Written surveys can easily be enhanced by personal interviews to uncover nuances and subtleties not easily discerned with large samples.

When working with small samples such as students in a course, the class becomes a captive audience, and issues such as sampling size and response rates become much easier to resolve. Convenience samples and data from a course or institutional databases are readily available. This is true regardless of whether courses are conducted online, blended, or in face-to-face mode. However, the online and blended learning modes provide the opportunity to electronically capture a good deal more data, because large segments of lessons and class activities are automatically captured on learning management systems, discussion boards, blogs, and wikis. In a fully online course, much of the interaction between instructor and students is recorded and available. Every question the instructor asks, every answer a student offers, and every response on a quiz is available electronically. Students can also be surveyed or polled many times over the period of a course without much effort. Researchers interested in this level of survey research should take advantage of what the electronic media already provides. One word of caution: The subjects or students in these cases should not be subjected to intimidation by instructors or researchers to participate in a study or evaluation. Students should also be assured of anonymity and confidentiality.

Definition of Terms

All good researchers take the time to define and explain terms so that readers understand the nature of their work. In survey research this becomes critical to subjects and respondents as well. However, even in well-designed surveys with clear definitions of terms, problems can arise. For instance, earlier in this chapter, the work of the Babson Survey Research Group was cited as an exemplar of survey research. In discussions with Jeff Seaman, he candidly admits that collecting data on blended learning is a challenge. The reasons for this are varied, but one issue relates to a definition of terms. One school's "blended" course is another's "hybrid," and is still another's "web enhanced." In addition, there are not sufficient data controls in place in many colleges and universities to capture the data on courses that can be distinguished as "blended." As online technology becomes more commonplace in teaching and learning, instructors are blending online and face-to-face components as they wish, and in many cases without the knowledge of department chairs or other institutional administrators. Hence, some data are either unavailable or not necessarily accurate. As a result, large-scale survey research on blended learning across many institutions becomes difficult or prone to inaccuracy.

Response Rate Issues

The issue of response rate was presented briefly earlier in this chapter. As applied to survey research on online and blended learning, response rates can vary depending upon the subjects and the nature of the questions. The surveys administered by the Babson Survey Research Group had high response rates (sometime in excess of 60%) from senior administrators in the higher education community but somewhat lower rates in K–12 school districts. This may be so because many colleges and universities employ and maintain institutional research offices that routinely collect, maintain, and can provide a good deal of data on students, faculty, and other characteristics. This is not the case in K–12 schools, where survey requests are frequently handled by a general administrator or principal with many responsibilities. In addition, administrators in K–12 schools are under much more public scrutiny by the press and the media and are more cautious about responding to surveys and other data requests. Many of them will direct individuals requesting data to a publicly available "school report card," which rarely will have the kind of details needed for most surveys.

In smaller-scale survey research involving students and faculty, response rates will vary depending upon the nature of the questions. For example, most instructors using a convenience sample to survey students in a class can typically expect high response rates, assuming the questions are not overly personal or sensitive. Administrators conducting surveys of faculty participating in professional development likewise can expect excellent response rates. However, for certain populations, such as students who have dropped or withdrawn from a course, response rates will likely be much lower. These students may no longer feel connected to the institution, or they may not want to indicate their reasons for withdrawal, particularly if it involves financial, family, or other personal reasons. This is especially important when conducting research in online and blended learning, where dropout rates are much higher than in face-to-face classes. For instance, the MOOC courses that are being offered by colleges and universities typically have very high dropout rates, sometimes in excess of 90%.

The Need for Further Survey Research

Survey research has established itself as a most important methodology in the social sciences, including teaching and learning and the use of educational technology. As the technology changes, many new issues evolve that are worthy of study, whether at the macro- (across institutions) or microlevel (individual classes). Survey research can play an important role in examining these issues, whether conducted by itself or in conjunction with other research approaches. Mixed methods research is growing in popularity in the social sciences, and survey research in particular is proving flexible enough to integrate with other methods. Researchers contemplating doing survey research on online and blended learning can feel confident that many worthwhile research questions and issues are in need of study, and the results are eagerly sought by other researchers, policymakers, and practitioners.

References

Allen, I. E., & Seaman, J. (2013). *Changing course: Ten years of tracking online education in the United States*. Babson Park, MA: Babson Survey Research Group and Quahog Research Group, LLC.

Alreck, P. L., & Settle, R. B. (2005). *The survey research handbook* (3rd ed.). New York: McGraw-Hill.

Babbie, E. R. (1990). *Survey research methods* (2nd ed.). Stamford, CT: Cengage Learning Publishing Co.

Beam, G. (2012). *The problem with survey research*. Piscataway, NJ: Transaction Publishers.

Christensen, C. M., Horn, M. B., & Johnson, C. W. (2008). *Disrupting class: How innovation will change the way the world learns*. New York: McGraw-Hill.

Isaac, S., & Michael, W. B. (1997). *Handbook in research and evaluation: A collection of principles, methods, and strategies useful in the planning, design, and evaluation of studies in education and the behavioral sciences* (3rd ed.). San Diego: Educational and Industrial Testing Services.

Picciano, A. G., & Seaman, J. (2007). *K–12 online learning: A survey of U.S. school district administrators*. Needham, MA: The Babson Survey Research Group and The Sloan Consortium.

Rea, L. M., & Parker, R. A. (2005). *Designing and conducting survey research: A comprehensive guide* (3rd ed.). San Francisco: Jossey-Bass.

Wiersma, W. (2000). *Research methods in education* (7th ed.). Boston: Allyn and Bacon.

Chapter 6

Principles for Data Analysis in Online and Blended Learning Research

Charles D. Dziuban

The remarkable growth of online and blended learning throughout the world reinforces the need for improved data analysis methods. Fortunately, newer and more effective computing options make it possible to provide useful information to a broad range of constituencies, such as policymakers, faculty, students, and the public at large. However, data do not equal information, and as Silver (2012) cautions us, data do not have a voice of their own. We have to provide that voice in a manner that informs those who are trying to understand the contemporary educational environment. Because of this you will find yourself doing detective work (metaphorically) with data, trying to uncover what happened in your study. You will discover that there are many approaches to an acceptable solution because there is no single right answer. A great deal depends on the context of your research, the goals of the study, and the quality and amount of data that you are able to collect. Good research is iterative, with constant feedback loops that adjust your findings and even your original assumptions—it happens to us all the time. This is a formidable responsibility given the general public's mistrust of much of the information it encounters on a daily basis (Seife, 2010, 2014). Regularly, the authors are reminded of the quote from Mark Twain (1907)—"lies, damn lies, and statistics"—and the punch line from the old statistics joke—"how do you want it to turn out?"

Begin With a Self-Assessment

If you begin a study by collecting data and then looking around for a way to analyze them, you have gotten off to a shaky start. You should have your analysis strategies in mind before your study begins. If you do not give some prior thought to your analysis, it is highly likely that you will find yourself rummaging through textbooks, websites, or computer packages in an attempt to find procedures that might work for you. Many faculty members and students come into our offices with data in hand, hoping to find a "significant difference," and then leave crestfallen when that doesn't happen, believing that their study was a failure. Actually, they should have considered whether or not a significant difference was the most important element for a successful study. No significant difference, or a weak relationship, does not necessarily invalidate a study. In order to help you make an approximate determination of where you are in terms of analyzing data and interpreting results, we provide a self-analysis rubric. Table 6.1 is based on a mash-up of David Berliner's (1988) theory of expertise in pedagogy and the Interagency Language Roundtable (ILR)

Table 6.1 Self-Analysis Rubric

Stage I

Has limited intuitive understanding of the conceptual principles involved in data analysis

Wants context rules for data analysis

Generally unaware of the assumptions underlying various procedures

Sometimes confused by the results from the output of computing programs

Conforms to whatever procedures he/she is told to follow or has researched

Lacks understanding of important concepts, such as sampling distributions and estimators

Tends to ask questions such as "how large does my sample have to be?"

Tends to cut and paste results from printouts and do things such as reporting correlations to four decimal places.

Stage II

Develops some strategic and conceptual understating of data analysis procedures

Makes some decisions based on previous experience

Discerns that a particular data analysis strategy is not producing the desired results

Understands how analysis strategies play out across contexts

Prepares data and runs the analysis on his/her own

Understands that everything on the printout may not be relevant to his/her needs

Is able to explain the results to colleagues

Does not necessarily accept "significance" as the ultimate criterion for success

Stage III

Reads and generally understands analysis methods in journal articles

Proficient in understanding which assumptions are important and which ones are not for a particular procedure

Understands sampling distributions and relationships among analysis procedures

Sets priorities for his/her analysis strategies; i.e., "if I get this outcome A, I will try this procedure B"

Articulates goals for his/her analysis

Explains his/her results with a good deal of fluency

Has insights into the idiosyncrasies of analysis procedures

Understands that concepts are vital and the computations are secondary

Stage IV

Uses the language of data analysis at most levels that are pertinent to professional needs

Uses experience and know-how as guiding factors in the analysis

Possesses a good grasp of analysis across contexts

(Continued)

Table 6.1   (Continued)

Recognizes relationships among procedures—for instance, a two-way chi square contingency test and the phi coefficient

Recognizes patterns in data analysis

Uses some intuition to guide the analysis process

Discerns among analysis options and evaluates the advantages and disadvantages of each

Accommodates questions about the analysis with relative ease

language proficiency rubric used by the United States Foreign Service Institute (Clark & Clifford, 1988).

We offer this protocol in the attempt to help you do a realistic self-assessment of where you might be with respect to the data analysis process. This approach follows the work of George Lakoff (1987) on prototype theory, where you identify the category that most typifies you. Interestingly, in these kinds of assessments (as with most rubrics) it is entirely possible that you belong to some degree in each one of the categories. For instance, you may be proficient in one procedure and a novice in another. Certainly this is true for the authors.

The Solution Is Just a Click Away

Today, advances in computing technology have freed us from the daunting computational drudgery that discouraged analyses in the past, currently enabling us to work with much larger data sets. At the same time we must be mindful of what Wurman, Leifer, Sume, and Whitehouse (2001) and Taleb (2007, 2012) cautioned; that we can be overwhelmed with the pure amount of data at our disposal and the many ways in which we are able to present them—sometimes in informative and sometimes in confusing manners. However, consider this quote from Ferguson and Takane's sixth edition of *Statistical Analysis in Education and Psychology*: "Since the first edition of this book in 1959, remarkable changes have occurred in computational methods. Also enormous changes are anticipated in the future as increasing computational power is incorporated into smaller computers at decreasing cost" (1989, p.14).

Enthusiasm for computing power was on the horizon when this classic textbook was published, but since then advances have far surpassed anything that we could have imagined. Open source, as well as proprietary, statistical packages abound, making useful results just a click way. Unfortunately, this is good news and bad news at the same time. The good news is that any analysis we can imagine is well within our reach. The bad news is that it is far too easy to run analyses on bad or incomplete data, or create solutions we do not fully understand. There isn't one of us, including the authors of this book, who hasn't found him/herself diving in too deeply and being in over one's head. Additionally, online and blended learning and the newfound computing power have placed considerable stress on the tried and true analyses that have served us well in the past. For instance, concepts such as statistical significance, relationship, prediction, and classification take on fundamentally different meanings in a world where data changes in its calibration from day to day, hour to hour, and in some cases minute to minute. Modern data are dynamic, and we must respond accordingly. In fact, modern computational power allows us to enter the realm of data mining, where we are able to build robust decision rules that do not necessarily depend on statistical assumptions. Because of this, we have opportunities to provide the kind of information that accurately tracks the impact of online and blended learning—information that is authentic, contextual, and reflective. A bit of concentrated effort can put us in control of the data at hand. Unfortunately, our purpose in this little chapter cannot be to teach statistics and data analysis, but rather to outline a set of principles and resources that point the way to meaningful analyses in the new educational world.

Computing Resources

There are a large number of data analysis packages available to the reader, some open source and others proprietary, all easily found on the Internet. A small sample is listed below in Table 6.2.

Of course, there are other, more general purpose platforms that can be used for data analysis, such as Microsoft Excel (Albright, Winston, & Zappe, 2009). In addition, several proprietary platforms have developed access options, in some cases free of cost and in other cases at greatly reduced pricing. Another example of the continuing evolution of computational options is that SPSS has made R computational routines available through its platform, thereby combining proprietary and open source data analysis options (IBM Corporation, 2013). One can go to the Internet for extensive discussion of the advantages and disadvantages of most computation packages, as well as heated debates about the merits of each one. However, except for extremely specialized analysis procedures, most programs have equivalent options that yield comparable results. Depending on your organization or university, some version of a statistical analysis platform is probably available, and, of course, researchers always have the open source options. The authors commonly download open source programs, experiment with them, and then make a decision about their viability. There is great value and learning that comes from simply tinkering with these programs. Very quickly the reader will get a good feel for whether or not a particular platform resonates with his or her skill level and format preference. A small word of caution: It is highly unlikely that

Table 6.2 Data Analysis Packages

Open Source	Proprietary
OpenStat4	MATHLAB
PAST	Minitab
PSPP	SAS
R	SPSS
SOFA	Stat
	STATISTICA

any of us will have need for all the options in any of these programs. The reality, even for the authors, is that we use these platforms for solving the problems we encounter. Further, it is unlikely that we will ever be completely familiar with all the options in SPSS, SAS, R, or OpenStat4, but if we have a need for an analysis, a solution will be available to us.

Variables Are the Key to Data Analysis

The two fundamental questions in online and blended learning data analysis are: "What questions am I trying to answer" and "what are the variables I have at hand?" Handling these questions is a very important first step. For instance, am I interested in student learning outcomes or simply success in class? These are two variables that measure quite different constructs. Am I interested in changes in student or faculty attitudes or satisfaction with teaching and learning? Do I wish to investigate changes in student access or how faculty members change their teaching techniques as a result of instructional technology? These are examples of more general research questions that do not necessarily deal with hypothesis testing in the statistical sense. Oftentimes important issues in research may not require conducting a formal hypothesis test. For better or worse, there seem to be an almost unlimited number of research questions in the area, some of which are quite challenging. For example, questions about the quality of online courses compared to face-to-face lessons have daunted us for years. Often, the best we can do is find a stand-in variable for quality, such as success rate, end-of-course examinations, performance rubrics, and other measures—either standardized or created by the instructor or investigator.

There are any number of good resources for understanding the nature and consequences of variables and scales—some classic and some modern (Glass & Stanly, 1970; Ferguson & Takane, 1989; Anderson & Finn, 1996; Norman, 2010; Howell, 2010; Lomax & Hahs-Vaughn, 2012; Urdan, 2010; Cohen & Lea, 2004; Huck, 2012; Salkind, 2004). In addition, there are a number of resources that can help investigators gain a better conceptual understanding of statistics and data analysis (Wheelan, 2013; Urdan, 2010; Vickers, 2010; Pyrczak, 2006; Utts & Heckard, 2011). Anderson and Finn (1996) provide a useful way to conceptualize measures in the form of variables—categorical and numerical. These resources provide excellent guidelines for determining which analysis procedures are appropriate in a given situation. Of course, there are many guides to procedures online as well. Examples of some resources are listed in Table 6.3.

Table 6.3 Data Analysis Resources

Institute for Digital Research and Education by UCLA
Choosing the Correct Statistical Test by University of Alabama
Decision Tree for Statistical Test by Muhlenberg College
Practical Assessment, Research & Evaluation (a peer-reviewed electronic journal)
SAGE Research Methods

Nominal Categorical Variables

Often, we deal with variables that are simply indicators for categories to which people or intuitions belong. For instance, three authors of this book are male and one is female, with two representing the University of Central Florida, one The City University of New York, and one Brigham Young University. Certainly we are familiar with similar variables of this nature—ethnicity, college, department, major, marital status, occupation, course modality designation, and so on. These categories can be extremely useful for disaggregating other scales or measures in one's data collection protocol. For instance, is there a difference in satisfaction with online learning between males and females or among students in blended, online, and face-to-face courses? There is no problem assigning numbers to these categories. However, those designations simply serve as markers for categorical classifications of group membership. Of course, in online and blended learning research indicators for course modality have been found to be of prime importance for comparative studies (Means, Toyama, Murphy, Bakia, & Jones, 2010).

Ordinal Categorical Variables

On some occasions categorical variables are collected in rank order. There are many possibilities for ordered variables in online and blended learning research: socio-economic status (high, medium, low), year in school (freshman, sophomore, etc.), motivation for taking a particular course (high, medium, low), instructor effective-ness (excellent, average, poor), and job satisfaction (satisfied, ambivalent, and dis-satisfied). The thing about rank-ordered variables is that they provide the researcher a bit more information on who or what is first, second, third, and so on. Certainly, ranking is important in contemporary society. We are all familiar with the NCAA football rankings that come out every Monday morning, or the rankings that get sports teams into the playoffs. Very often student achievement in online and blended courses, or some project completed for class, is evaluated with a carefully developed rubric of some kind. Essentially, this results in a rank ordering into categories rang-ing from excellent to poor. We offer two words of caution about ranks. First, there is really no specific distance between a rank of one and two—they are just ordered. One can easily find him/herself slipping into assuming that the ranks are equidis-tant. Second, there are a limited number of ordered categories that make sense. See, for instance, Silver's (2012) discussion of the *U.S. News and World Report* ranking of colleges and universities. We would be very hard-pressed to make a meaningful dis-tinction between two universities, one of which is ranked 170 and the other ranked 171. Consider Table 6.4 illustrating the percentage of students who assign an overall rating of excellent to various course modalities.

In reviewing this simple table, it becomes obvious that there are several options for interpreting the results. By ordering the percentages of excellent ratings for the five course modalities, we see that blended courses rank first and blended lecture capture courses rank fifth. The difference in percentages that causes first and fifth ranking is 8.9%. If we just presented the ranks you would not know that. Also in Table 6.4, you can see that face-to-face and online courses rank two and three, respectively. However, the difference that causes that rank order is 0.5%. For all practical purposes, online and face-to-face courses are in a dead heat for excellent

Table 6.4 Percentage and Number of Students Assigning Overall Excellent Ratings for Course Modalities

Course Modality	%	n	Rank
Blended	56.6	121,768	1
Face-to-face	53.8	108,046	2
Online	53.3	40,219	3
Lecture Capture	48.7	1,831	4
Blended Lecture Capture	47.8	9,998	5

ratings. In addition, the sample sizes vary greatly so that the percentage differences represent vastly different absolute numbers of students. As investigators we do have a responsibility to make some value judgments about the results that add context for those who view our data. A good research practice is to present the ranks and the underlying data on which the ranks were formed so the reader can better contextualize the results. There are a number of resources for rank order data. These fall under the classification of nonparametric, or distribution-free, procedures (Siegel & Castellan, 1988; Hollander & Wolfe, 1999; Gibbons & Chakraborti, 2003). Additional information on analyzing data using nonparametric statistics can be found from online resources such as *StatSoft*, an electronic statistics textbook from Statistica.

Interval Numerical Variables

Numerical variables carry more information than categorical variables (nominal or ordinal). Interval variables (scales) are constructed such that the units are equivalent all along the scale. For instance, on an IQ test the assumption is made that the distance between two individuals who have scores of 120 and 130 is equivalent to the distance between two individuals with scores of 100 and 110. However, we all learned in measurement 101 that because there is no meaningful zero point on the scale (zero IQ), the ratio of two numbers is not valid. The same is true for multiple-choice, end-of-course examinations. In theory, a student could get none of the items correct on the final examination, but that by no means indicates a complete lack of subject knowledge. This can get a bit tricky, but we would be reasonably safe in saying that a number of the scales we encounter, such as student satisfaction measures, course examination measures, and the Likert scale devices, if carefully constructed and validated, might be treated as interval scales. However, almost never do their score ratios make sense. Interestingly, the ratios of many discrete categorical variables can make sense. If one student takes thirty online courses and another student takes fifteen blended courses during their studies, the ratio can be useful as long as the context is fully explained. For instance, the student who enrolled in the larger number of online courses may have been in a completely online program where that was the only course mode option.

Variable Scales and Declassification

Once you have made some decision about the variables of interest in your study, it is important to give consideration to the best way you can build a scale for it. If we consider the previous section on variables, it should be clear that higher scales carry the most information. But consider this: You can always convert a higher-level scale (in terms of measurement) to one below it, but you cannot go from a lower scale to a higher one. For instance, the University of Central Florida assesses success in courses by using grades as an outcome measure. Although we compute grade point averages, it has been argued in many places that the best information we can get from grades is a rank ordering. Now suppose we wanted to compare the success rates across face-to-face, online, and blended courses. One option is to simply look at the grade distributions for the whole university across those modalities for undergraduate students. The problem is that not only do we want to assess whether or not grades are impacted by course modality, but we also know that grades reflect many other aspects of course and department besides modality—philosophy, rigor, gatekeeping tendencies, and many other things. For example, look at the grade distribution in Table 6.5 for an online, blended, and face-to-face class.

The percentages of the five grades vary greatly across the classes, so that these distributions might well reflect many of the other class characteristics as well as the modality of the classes. The question becomes: Will declassifying the grades some-how help us portray the data in a useful way? Of course the distribution problem cannot be eliminated by this process, but it can be reduced within the context of these data. If the grade distributions are declassified so C or better is success and any grade below a C is a nonsuccess, the impact of the original grade distributions can be reduced. In this instance, the highest success levels are found in blended and online classes (97%, 92%), with the lowest rate in face-to-face (79%). The consequence of a procedure such as this is a loss of specificity. However, the gain comes from a reduction of grade variability impacted by a multitude of class characteristics that have little to do with course modality. In many instances, declassification can be helpful with complex data by providing simpler and more straightforward results that various groups and individuals can incorporate into their decision-making process. Often straightforward and direct approaches are the best ways to provide information.

Prescreening Is Invaluable

Before comparative, correlational, predictive, or significance tests are carried out, it is always a good idea to get to know the data by taking its vital signs, much as a doctor does with an incoming patient. For instance, in the case of nominal or ordinal data, it is a good idea to compute the frequency distributions. This gives the investigator a good indication of the data's accuracy, the distributional characteristics, and whether or not there are errors to be found. The grade distributions in Table 6.5 gave the investigator a good sense of the grading characteristics of each class. This prescreening never fails to be helpful. Furthermore, for ordinal data it is informative to compute the median and semi-interquartile range for the data, giving the investigators an indication of the central tendency and variability in the data. For interval and ratio data, all students at the University of Central Florida are taught to

Table 6.5 Grade Distributions in Blended and Online Courses by Number of Students (n) and Respective Percentages

Course Modality	Grade	n	%
Blended	A	67	59
	B	31	28
	C	11	10
	D	2	2
	F	1	1
Online	A	18	18
	B	55	55
	C	19	19
	D	7	7
	F	1	1
Face-to-face	A	10	9
	B	24	22
	C	52	48
	D	15	14
	F	8	7
% of C or higher grades			
Blended	97		
Online	92		
Face-to-face	79		

compute the "moments" of their distributions—that is, the mean, standard deviation, skewness, and kurtosis for each variable under consideration. We cannot overestimate the importance and value of this prescreening procedure. Besides being the best way to find aberrant data, this process helps to identify outliers—those cases that may be so extreme that they will have an adverse impact on the generality of the results. In addition, there is simply no better way to understand the characteristics of your data set than by spending a bit of time carefully exploring and describing it. In the long run, this process will save time, costs, and resources that come from an erroneous finding. Understanding your data is critically important.

Making Sense Out of Statistical Hypothesis Testing

Russell (2001) popularized the use of statistical hypothesis tests to determine the effectiveness of online teaching and learning by publishing *The No Significant Difference Phenomenon*. In reviewing a large body of research studies, we find that educators implicitly accepted the notion that statistical hypothesis tests were a good indicator of online learning's success. Certainly this trend has continued over the past two decades—where researchers collect their data and apply a statistical test of some kind to determine if their results are "significant." However, the authors believe it is incumbent on the researcher to precisely understand what hypothesis is being tested when they run a procedure. Specifically, when a statistical hypothesis test is being conducted you are answering the following question: "What is the probability that I will observe the results in my sample if it is collected from a population in which the null hypothesis was true?" For each test that is completed there is a very specific hypothesis associated with the procedure. For instance, in reporting that there was a significant difference in final examination scores between an online and comparable face-to-face course at the .01 level of significance, we can say that we have reason to believe that that there was less than a .01 chance this could have come from the population where the null hypothesis is true. Therefore, we reject the null hypothesis. Modern computation has made making hypothesis decisions at the .05 and .01 levels simple, because virtually all analysis programs generate the complete sampling distribution for the test and give the investigator the exact probability that his or her sample came from a population where the null hypothesis was true.

However, the general research community working in the technology-mediated teaching and learning area has appeared to make two assumptions that are not true. The first is that a smaller p value indicates a more substantial difference and that statistical and practical significance are synonymous. Unfortunately, neither one of these assumptions is correct. A smaller p value simply indicates there is less chance that your sample came from a population in which the null hypothesis was true. This is an easy mistake to fall into, especially with computer programs able to give the exact probabilities, which in some cases are rounded to .000. Commonly, researchers run multiple tests and in one table report p values of .05, .01, and .001, tacitly implying that some of their correlations are more important than others. However, these p values speak only to the likelihood of the null hypothesis being true—in the case of correlations, that the value in the population is zero. When an investigator reports a significant correlation, the hypothesis test really has very little information about the strength of the relationship in the population. Therefore, it is entirely possible that a statistically significant correlation is of no practical value. William Hays very early and succinctly summarized the problem in this way:

> It is very easy for research psychologists, particularly young psychologists to become over concerned with statistical method. Sometimes the problem itself seems almost secondary to some elegant statistical method of data analysis. But overemphasizing the role of statistical significance in research is like confusing the paint brush with the painting. This form of statistical inference is a valuable tool in research but it is never the arbiter of good research.

(1973, pp.385–386)

Therefore, the researcher would be well advised to spend a little time understanding precisely what hypothesis is being tested for each procedure that he/she completes and then deciding whether or not that hypothesis test answers the research question in which he/she is interested. As you will see in the next section of this chapter, there are alternatives to the null hypothesis that may be tested.

Some Options for Using Statistical Hypothesis Testing in Online and Blended Research

The controversy over statistical hypothesis testing led the American Psychological Association (APA) to carefully review the entire process and recommend that investigators provide not only information about the statistical significance of their findings but additional information as well that would allow readers to assess the magnitude of the effect—the effect size recommendation (Orwin, 1983; Rosenthal, 1994; Fidler, 2010). Chapter 4 in this book on meta-analysis demonstrates the use of effect sizes in summarizing the results from several disparate studies. Various authors disagree about whether these effect sizes should be presented when the investigator reports that the null hypothesis is not rejected, but in general we recommend that investigators do it as a matter of course. This agrees with the APA position on effect size. Several resources for computing effect size can be found online. Further, the APA goes on to recommend that whenever possible, confidence intervals for that data should be presented as well. There are two reasons for doing this. First, the more information the researcher gives the reader, the better. Second, doing so will help with deciding what is or is not important in one context or another.

What Makes a Significant Difference?

The No Significant Difference Phenomenon (Russell, 2001) made the case that, in most instances, comparing student outcomes by the nominal variable class modality only showed trivial differences. Russell (2001) pursued this question, tallying the number of "significant findings," while another group conducted meta-analyses based on effect sizes (Means, Toyama, Murphy, Bakia, & Jones, 2010). However, Walster and Cleary (1970) provided a thoughtful perspective on data analysis when they suggested that statistical significance is best used as the basis for a decision-making rule, and not as an absolute determinant. They reemphasized that hypothesis testing answers the following question: "What are the chances that I will get my sample results when the null hypothesis is true in the population?" These significant tests are a function of three things:

1. Significance level (e.g., .05, .01, or some other value)
2. Sample size
3. Some effect size or degree of non-nullity as a mean difference. Usually, in the statistical literature, this difference is signified as delta (Δ).

Historically, the way most researchers conduct experimental and comparison studies is to arbitrarily pick a significance level, get the largest sample size obtainable, and run the study. The consequence of conducting studies in this way is that by arbitrarily picking a significance level and sample size, the difference that will be significant is predetermined. And certainly very large sample sizes cause rejection of the null hypothesis, even if the difference is trivial.

The point is that the analysis is much more meaningful if some thought and decision making go into the process prior to collecting and running any data. If the researcher can specify Δ_1, a difference that is of no interest or will not make a practical difference in his or her judgment, then the lower bound for the process has been established. Similarly, identification of Δ_2 a difference that will make a practical difference, causes the hypothesis testing procedure to take on a completely different perspective. This involves three steps:

1. Identify Δ_1 first—this is not important to me.
2. Identify Δ_2—this is important to me.
3. Pick a significance level you can live with—.05, .01, or something else.
4. Pick a sample size that will catch Δ_2 but not Δ_1. There are a number of resources available to help the researcher accomplish this (Murphy, Myors, & Wolach, 2008; Cohen, 2013; Liu, 2013; Kraemer & Thiemann, 1987; Aberson, 2010).

There are programs that require that the investigator provide this prior information, to protect him or her from calling a trivial difference significant and to provide the best opportunity for finding a difference that will be important in his/her judgment. However, this decision-making process cannot be accomplished by collecting data and automatically running it through an analysis program. Waiting for the program to tell you whether or not your results are significant does not optimize the potential information in your study. We need to provide careful reflection on the process and take full responsibility for our decisions. Statistical tests are a resource, not the final result. In the final analysis, any procedure will produce value if it can provide useful information to those trying to understand the impact of online and blended learning.

In concluding this chapter, we leave the reader with a set of principles that have served the authors well for many years.

1. When you have a choice, simple is really much more effective.
2. Effective progress is better made in small steps.
3. Statistical analysis is wonderful, but it is not everything.
4. High quality educational design makes a big difference.
5. Just because you can doesn't necessarily mean you should run a particular analysis.
6. If you get too sophisticated, people won't know what you are talking about—make your analysis relevant to your audience.

We have attempted to provide a thought experiment about how to approach analyzing data that you collect for determining impact and effectiveness of online and blended learning. To be clear, this is not an easy task and one that is evolving as we work on this book. The best we can hope for is to provide insights from many years of collective experience—and there is no substitute for experience. We are fond of a quote from C.S. Lewis: "Experience: that most brutal of teachers. But you learn, my God do you learn" (n.d.). However, that is not to say that you cannot do an effective job of data analysis without extensive experience—it just takes a bit of care. We recommend that you start by doing a realistic self-assessment of where you might be on the data analysis continuum. Then, work hard to identify the important variables in your study and how you will scale them. Once you have collected your data, spend whatever time you need to understand and describe it effectively. Should you plan to test statistical hypotheses, make sure that you thoroughly understand what is being tested. If you follow these simple steps you will be well on your way.

References

Aberson, C. L. (2010). *Applied power analysis for the behavioral sciences*. New York: Routledge.

Albright, S. C., Winston, W. L., & Zappe, C.J. (2009). *Data analysis and decision making with Micro-soft® Excel*. Mason, OH: South-Western Cengage Learning.

Anderson, T. W., & Finn, J. D. (1996). *The new statistical analysis of data*. New York: Springer.

Berliner, D. C. (1988, February). *The development of expertise in pedagogy*. Charles W. Hunt Memorial Lecture presented at the annual meeting of the American Association of Colleges for Teacher Education, New Orleans. Retrieved from http://files.eric.ed.gov/fulltext/ED298122.pdf [Accessed April 20, 2015].

Clark, J. L., & Clifford, R. T. (1988). The FSI/ILR/ACTFL proficiency scales and testing techniques. *Studies in Second Language Acquisition, 10*(2), 129–147.

Cohen, B. H., & Lea, R. B. (2004). *Essentials of statistics for the social and behavioral sciences*. Hoboken, NJ: John Wiley & Sons.

Cohen, J. (2013). *Statistical power analysis for the behavioral sciences*. Hillsdale, NJ: Lawrence Erlbaum Associates, Inc.

Ferguson, G. A., & Takane, Y. (1989). *Statistical analysis in psychology and education*. New York: McGraw-Hill Book Company.

Fidler, F. (2010, July). The American Psychological Association publication manual sixth edition: Implications for statistics education. In Reading, C. (ed) *Data and context in statistics education: Towards an evidence-based society (Proceedings of the 8th International Conference on Teaching Statistics)*. Ljubljana, NL: International Statistical Institute.

Gibbons, J. D., & Chakraborti, S. (2003). *Nonparametric statistical inference* (5th ed.). Boca Raton, FL: Taylor & Francis Group.

Glass, G.V., & Stanley, J. C. (1970). *Statistical methods in educational psychology*. Englewood Cliffs, NJ: Prentice-Hall, Inc.

Hays, W. L. (1973). *Statistics for the social sciences* (vol. 410). New York: Holt, Rinehart, and Winston.

Hollander, M., & Wolfe, D. A. (1999). *Nonparametric statistical methods* (2nd ed.). Hoboken, NJ: John Wiley & Sons.

Howell, D. C. (2010). *Fundamental statistics for the behavioral sciences* (7th ed.). Belmont, CA: Cengage Learning, Inc.

Huck, S. W. (2012). *Reading statistics and research* (6th ed.). Boston, MA: Pearson Allyn & Bacon.

IBM Corporation, SPSS Statistics (2013). *The power of IBM SPSS statistics and R together*. Retrieved from www.ibm.com/developerworks/community/files/form/anonymous/api/library/b5bb8a42-04d2-4503-93bb-dc45d7a145c2/document/0f1a7b3b-31eb-4b62-9c62-1daa4d163a13/media/WhitePaper-UsingRandStatisticsTogether.pdf [Accessed April 20, 2015].

Kraemer, H. C., & Thiemann, S. (1987). *How many subjects? Statistical power analysis in research*. Newbury Park, CA: Sage Publications, Inc.

Lakoff, G. (1987). *Women, fire, and dangerous things: What categories reveal about the mind*. Chicago, IL: University of Chicago Press.

Lewis, C. S. (n.d.). *C. S. Lewis quotes*. Retrieved from www.quoteswave.com/picture-quotes/259815 [Accessed April 20, 2015].

Liu, X. S. (2013). *Statistical power analysis for the social and behavioral sciences: Basic and advanced techniques*. New York: Routledge.

Lomax, R. G., & Hahs-Vaughn, D. L. (2012). *An introduction to statistical concepts*. New York: Routledge.

Means, B., Toyama, Y., Murphy, R., Bakia, M, & Jones, K. (2010). *Evaluation of evidence-based practices in online learning: A meta-analysis and review of online learning studies*. Washington, DC: U.S. Department of Education, Office Planning, Evaluation, and Policy Development.

Murphy, K. R., Myors, B., & Wolach, A. H. (2008). *Statistical power analysis: A simple and general model for traditional and modern hypothesis tests* (3rd ed.). New York: Routledge.

Norman, G. (2010). Likert scales, levels of measurement and the "laws" of statistics. *Advances in Health Sciences Education, 15*(5), 625–632.

Orwin, R. G. (1983). A fail-safe N for effect size in meta-analysis. *Journal of Educational Statistics, 8*(2), 157–159.

Pyrczak, F. (2006). *Making sense of statistics* (4th ed.). Glendale, CA: Pyrczak Publishing.

Rosenthal, R. (1994). Parametric measures of effect size. In Cooper, H., & Hedges, L.V. (eds) *The handbook of research synthesis* (pp. 231–244). New York: Sage.

Russell, T. L. (2001). *The no significant difference phenomenon*. Raleigh, NC: North Carolina State University.

Salkind, N. J. (2004). *Statistics for people who think they hate statistics* (2nd ed.). Thousand Oaks, CA: Sage.

Seife, C. (2010). *Proofiness: The dark arts of mathematical deception* (p. 62). New York: Viking.

Seife, C. (2014). *Virtual unreality*. New York: Penguin Group.

Siegel, S., & Castellan, N. J. (1988). *Nonparametric statistics for the behavioral sciences* (2nd ed.). New York: McGraw-Hill.

Silver, N. (2012). *The signal and the noise: Why so many predictions fail-but some don't*. New York: The Penguin Press.

Taleb, N. N. (2007). *The black swan: The impact of the highly improbable fragility*. New York: Random House, Inc.

Taleb, N. N. (2012). *Antifragile: Things that gain from disorder*. New York: Random House, Inc.

Twain, M. (1907). Chapters from my autobiography: XX. *The North American Review, 185*(618), 465–474.

Urdan, T. C. (2010). *Statistics in plain English* (3rd ed.). New York: Routledge.

Utts, J., & Heckard, R. (2011). *Mind on statistics* (4th ed.). Boston, MA: Cengage Learning.

Vickers, A. (2010). *What is a P-value anyway?: 34 stories to help you actually understand statistics*. Boston, MA: Addison-Wesley.

Walster, G. W., & Cleary, T. A. (1970). Statistical significance as a decision rule. *Sociological Methodology, 2*, 246–254.

Wheelan, C. (2013). *Naked statistics: Stripping the dread from the data*. New York: W. W. Norton & Company, Inc.

Wurman, R.S., Leifer, L., Sume, D., & Whitehouse, K. (2001). *Information anxiety 2* (vol. 6000). Indianapolis, IN: Que.

Chapter 7

Qualitative Research in Online and Blended Learning

Anthony G. Picciano

Closely associated with the social constructivist/interpretivist paradigm, qualitative research has emerged as a very popular methodology for education research, including the study of online and blended learning environments. Lincoln and Guba (1985) provide an extensive review of qualitative research that covers many of the reasons for its popularity, as well as its appropriateness in education research. Qualitative research is a broad category of inquiry that uses a number of different methods and tools to assist in data collection and analysis; these include case studies, ethnography, grounded theory, discourse analysis, and phenomenology, as well as a number of other specific approaches. Descriptions of each of these methodologies can be found in Chapter 2. The methodologies can overlap one another, and frequently do. For instance, you can have a case study that may use ethnographic techniques, or a phenomenology that may incorporate discourse analysis for data collection. In recent years, qualitative methods have also been integrated or "mixed" with quantitative methods to provide a more triangulated approach to studying education phenomena. For example, a qualitative study using discourse analysis may rely on quantitative methods for summarizing and comparing occurrences of coded or tagged words and phrases in one or more transcripts of data. A qualitative case study utilizing interviews of subjects might also use survey research to develop a broader sample of opinions about a topic that evolved originally from the interviews.

The Basic Tools of Qualitative Research

The basic tools of qualitative research include direct observation and structured interviews.

Lincoln and Guba (1985) stress the importance of direct observation within the natural setting in order to be able to record the nuance and subtlety of complex social interactions such as occur in many educational activities. The school or classroom frequently provides the natural settings for conducting observations, which may be conducted in person or by video recording. As mentioned in Chapter 2, in-person observations allow an activity to be scanned extensively for relevant behaviors and context. The researcher must decide whether the observer is an active participant (i.e., participant observer) in an activity, and prepare accordingly. If the purpose of the observation is to record behaviors as objectively and completely as possible with little or no interaction, then the observer must be trained to keep his or her presence to a minimum. However, if the observer is to participate and assume a role in an activity, then the observer must be trained to act the role. Observations, whenever possible, should be conducted over a period of time. Accurate depictions require the observer to see and hear activities at multiple times. It is not unusual for observations, particularly those involving an educational activity, to go on for a semester or a year or more.

Structured interviews are carefully scripted tools for collecting data, wherein the researcher meets with and asks questions of an individual(s). Interviews can be conducted one-on-one with subjects, or they can be conducted with a group of subjects (i.e., focus group). The structured interview should be well organized, and all questions should be developed in advance and written as part of a script that the researcher or interviewer follows. The interview script should contain identification of who is being interviewed and where the interview is being conducted, short answer questions (either fill in the blank or multiple choice), and open-ended questions that allow the responder to explain how or why something exists or occurs. Open-ended questions also allow the interviewer to pursue a line of questioning and follow up with additional questions when the interviewee has mentioned something interesting or provocative. A good technique for designing a structured interview is to start with broad, general questions and move on to more direct, specific questions, depending upon the responses. Structured interviews are very effective data collection tools when the interviewer is adept at questioning, can make an interviewee feel comfortable, and is able to prompt honest responses. Structured interviews take time to conduct properly, and for this reason the researcher must carefully select the interviewees. Unless there is substantial funding for a research project, a small sample of interviewees will be selected, who may or may not represent a larger population. If a larger sample is selected and more than one interviewer is used, then the interviewers need to be trained to be consistent in their line of questioning.

Online and Blended Learning: Prime Environments for Qualitative Research

Online and blended learning environments are excellent for conducting qualitative research. Fully online environments usually provide an extensive record of interactions in a course via the course or learning management system. Data such as student and instructor discourses on discussion boards, blogs, or wikis can be collected and analyzed either after the fact or during class exchanges. In blended environments, observing what occurs in a traditional, face-to-face class meeting versus online activities can yield provocative comparisons of the two instructional modalities. In sum, human (student and teacher) interactions with online material or each other are prime sources of data in the instructional process and provide a number of possibilities for conducting qualitative research in these environments.

Examples of Qualitative Research in Online and Blended Learning

Discourse Analysis

Discourse analysis examines how language is used in speech, written texts, and context. It concerns itself with the use of language in an ongoing discourse continued over a number of sentences. It carefully examines the interactions of the generator of the discourse with the receiver of the discourse in a specific situational context. In online environments, it is ideally suited for examining interactions on discussion boards, blogs, and wikis. For a thorough review of discourse analysis as a research method, the work of James Gee is highly recommended (Gee, 2010; Gee & Handford, 2013).

For conducting discourse analysis in instruction, Wegmann and Thompson (2014) provide a SCOPe (Self, Content, Others, Platform) model for studying student interactions in face-to-face and online (discussion board) environments, a popular research area. They also compare the processes for collecting discourse data in the two modalities (see Boxes 7.1 and 7.2). The processes in these two boxes are essentially the same, except for steps 2 and 3, where data collection is somewhat easier for the discussion board because the discourse is already in electronic form. They go on to present an extensive description of organizing and coding data according to the four SCOPe categories of interactions. There are other models that researchers can use, but Wegmann and Thompson have done a particularly good job of focusing discourse analysis on student interactions, a key component in face-to-face and online learning environments.

Box 7.1   Process to Conduct Discourse Analysis with Face-to-Face Instruction

1. Clearly define the research question and the population of students to be studied.
2. Audio-record a targeted oral class discussion.
3. Transcribe student text into two-columned chart (4" for first column, 2" for second column) with students' words of the left column and the right column blank.
4. Code student text fragments and moves (how students are using their language). After a list of moves is created, they may be collapsed together or divided into several different categories.
5. Repeat with additional rater(s), if possible. Check for inter-rater reliability.
6. Tabulate the kinds of moves that students used, keeping in mind the specific research question.
7. Revisit the research question.
8. Make note of patterns among and between students. The quantity, quality, and types of moves that are used the most frequently are analyzed according to the research question.
9. Compare results of the analysis with the research question.

Adapted from Wegmann, S. J., & Thompson, K. (2014). SCOPE-ing out interactions in blended environments. In Picciano, A. G., Dziuban, C. D., & Graham, C. R. (eds) *Blended learning: Research perspectives, vol. 2* (pp. 73–92). New York: Routledge/Taylor Francis Group.

Box 7.2   Process to Conduct Discourse Analysis with Asynchronous Discussion Board Posts

1. Clearly define the research question and the population of students to be studied.
2. Compile written discussion posts from all students.
3. Paste text into two-columned chart (4" for first column, 2" for second column) with students' words on the left column and the right column blank.
4. Code student text fragments and moves (how students are using their language). After a list of moves is created, they may be collapsed together or divided into several different categories.
5. Repeat with additional rater(s), if possible. Check for inter-rater reliability.
6. Tabulate the kinds of moves that students used, keeping in mind the specific research question.
7. Revisit the research question.
8. Make note of patterns among and between students. The quantity, quality, and types of moves that are used the most frequently are analyzed according to the research question.
9. Compare results of the analysis with the research question.

Adapted from Wegmann, S. J., & Thompson, K. (2014). SCOPE-ing out interactions in blended environments. In Picciano, A. G., Dziuban, C. D., & Graham, C. R. (eds) *Blended learning: Research perspectives, vol. 2* (pp. 73–92). New York: Routledge/Taylor Francis Group.

Box 7.3 provides the abstract of a study entitled "Building Understanding in Asynchronous Discussions: Examining Types of Online Discourse," by Seungyeon Han and Janette R. Hill (2006). The methodology was a qualitative case study using discourse analysis that focused on one master's-level course that was offered during a short (four-week) session. The participants consisted of the instructor (n = 1), two doctoral students as facilitators (n = 2), and K–12 teachers and school library media specialists as students (n = 23). At the time of the study, most students (n = 21) had experience (i.e., one or more courses) learning in an online environment. There were six different project groups, with two project groups paired as a discussion group. Consequently, there were three different discussion groups (n = 6–8 participants) using the discussion boards throughout the implementation of the course. Each group was assigned to a specific discussion forum with two discussion topics per week. The first author of this paper (Han) was one of the facilitators and supported student participants in completing individual and group projects and assisted with the discussion. She also had primary responsibility for data collection and analysis. The second author of this paper (Hill) was the major instructor and was primarily responsible for course design, implementation, and facilitation. One discussion group (n = 8) was selected for in-depth analysis of the learning process.

Box 7.3   Abstract of Han, S., & Hill, J.R. (2006)

Building understanding in asynchronous discussions: Examining types of online discourse

This study explored how students' learning is reflected in asynchronous online discussions. The study specifically examined how online discourse contributes to the learning process. In examining online group discussions using discourse analysis, five different types of discourse were identified: goal setting, reflection, connection, original reformulation, and re-direction.

With the different types of discourse, we explained how each message or a threaded message facilitated the discussion, particularly in terms of collaborative efforts to achieve the goal(s). The nature of each type of discourse was illustrated, including how different strategies were identified in the data and how different results of discussion were demonstrated in the data. We also describe the methodological issues related to the analysis of online discourse and discuss implications for research and practice.

Journal of Asynchronous Learning Networks, 10(4), 29–50. The full article is available as a free download (with login) at http://sloanconsortium.org/jaln/v10n4/building-understanding-asynchronous-discussions-examining-types-online-discourse.

During the implementation of the course (i.e., four weeks), this group generated one hundred seventy messages directly related to the content of the course. The first step in the process involved reading and interrogating (i.e., cross-examining the threads) all transcripts of the asynchronous discussion by both of the researchers.

As indicated in the abstract, the major finding was that five different types of discourse were identified:

- Goal setting
- Reflection
- Connection
- Original reformulation
- Redirection

The authors went on to illustrate each type of discourse, including how different strategies were identified in the data and how different results of discussion were demonstrated in the data. They also described the methodological issues related to the analysis of online discourse. This study is a fine example of a small-scale case study integrated with discourse analysis. Readers are encouraged to review the entire study (which is available at http://sloanconsortium.org/jaln/v10n4/building-understanding-asynchronous-discussions-examining-types-online-discourse) for more details.

Phenomenography

Phenomenography and phenomenology share the word "phenomenon," from the Greek meaning to shed light. Both are respected qualitative methodologies that can be used effectively in education research. Some researchers see the two as related, while others point out their differences (Larsson & Holmstrom, 2007). Phenomenography, with the suffix -graph, "denotes a research approach aiming at describing the different ways a group of people understand a phenomenon," whereas phenomenology, with the suffix -logos, "aims to clarify the structure and meaning of a phenomenon" (Larsson & Holmstrom, 2007). For a more thorough review of phenomenography as a research method, the work of Ference Marton is highly recommended (Marton, 1981; Marton & Booth, 1997). In this section, a study by Paige McDonald is presented to illustrate a phenomenographic approach to studying adult experiences in blended learning courses. The purpose of her study was to identify and describe three qualitatively different ways adult learners experienced blended learning in higher education. Box 7.4 provides a brief abstract of her study.

Box 7.4 Abstract of McDonald, P. (2014)

Variation in adult learners' experiences of blended learning in higher education

Blended learning is emerging as one model of choice in higher education. Yet, adult learners face unique challenges in higher education, so understanding the qualitatively different ways they currently experience blended courses is critical to successful adoption of blended learning in higher education. This chapter identifies and describes three different patterns representative of variation in adult learners' experiences of blended learning in higher education: Supplementary Learning, Interdependent Learning, and Adaptable Learning. Study findings have implications for course design, learner success, and faculty presence in blended courses and for future research in each of these areas.

In Picciano, A. G., Dziuban, C. D., & Graham, C. R. (eds) *Blended learning: Research perspectives, vol. 2* (pp. 215–234). New York: Routledge/Taylor Francis Group.

In her study, McDonald provides a detailed description of her methods. Interview data served as the primary data source for identifying variation in experiencing a phenomenon. Two in-depth, one-hour interviews with each participant during the progression of a blended course served as the primary data source. The first interview used information from a preinterview questionnaire to further explore participants' reasons for participating in a blended course. Additional questions explored experiences in current blended courses: activities, interactions with peers and faculty, interactions with technology, and the relationship between face-to-face and online sessions. The second interview posed questions about course experiences that had occurred since the first interview, relying upon similar questions. It also asked learners to define blended learning and to offer their opinions on participating in blended courses.

A preinterview questionnaire, document analysis, and observation were also used in data collection. The preinterview questionnaire facilitated selection of ten adult participants from four different blended courses. It queried the participant's age; current enrollment in a blended course; prior experience with face-to-face, online, and blended modes of delivery; preferred mode of delivery; comfort level with using technology in learning; goals within the current course; and relation of the current course to personal and professional goals.

Document analysis and observation increased researcher understanding of the contexts in which blended learning was experienced by participants and allowed for verification of identified patterns of experience. The researcher reviewed program guidelines for blended courses, instructors' syllabi, and course materials to gain awareness of the contexts in which study participants experienced blended learning. Observations of the face-to-face class sessions of the blended courses focused on variation in physical contexts, facilitation styles, use of technology in the classrooms, types of interaction present, and types of feedback provided. Online observations considered the degree to which faculty utilized online folders for posting materials, types of interactions present, types of feedback provided, and timing of interactions and responses to discussion questions.

In terms of findings, this study revealed three different patterns representative of the qualitatively different ways adult learners experience blended learning in higher education:

1. Supplementary learning—Where learners ascribed meaning to blended learning based on the experience of two separate structural components, a face-to-face and an online component.
2. Interdependent learning—Where learners ascribed meaning to blended learning based on the experience of a complimentary and interdependent relationship between the online and face-to-face components of blended courses.
3. Adaptable learning—Where learners assigned meaning to blended learning based upon their perception of its adaptable form. Conceptualizations of structure were most complex in this pattern. The self-as-learner was most heavily emphasized in descriptions related to this pattern; context and process were described in relation to their ability to meet the learner's needs and to support higher levels of learning.

Graphics were used to illustrate the three patterns in each of the four courses, as well as to compare the basic course components of context, process, and learner in each pattern. This was a well-done phenomenographic study that provided fine detail on its methods, as well as a clear presentation of its results.

Grounded Theory: Multi-institutional, Semistructured Interview Research

As seen in the previous two examples, qualitative studies frequently involve small sample sizes that focus on microlevel situations occurring within a course or a school. However, with proper funding qualitative research can be used effectively for macrolevel analyses across institutions. With a grant from the Australian Learning and Teaching Council (ALTC), Ryan, Tynan, Hinton, and Lamont-Mills (2012) undertook a study (see Box 7.5 for abstract) to examine workload issues at four

Australian universities. More specifically, the purpose of the study was to report on staff perceptions of increased workload and the strategies used to manage workload while maintaining quality, and to explore the implications of increased workload for the future of university teaching. Faculty workload in online environments has received a good deal of attention in the professional literature, and is evolving as a collective bargaining issue. However, the amount of actual research on the issue is sparse.

Box 7.5   Abstract of Australian Department of Education: Australian Teaching and Learning Council (2012)

Out of hours: Final report of the project e-teaching leadership: Planning and implementing a benefits-oriented costs model for technology enhanced learning

Workload issues associated with online and blended teaching has received little rigorous investigation in higher education environments. The study reported here, funded by a grant from the Australian Learning and Teaching Council, explored staff perceptions of increased workload attendant on teaching with digital technologies, the models used in institutions to allocate workload, and how staff used particular technologies to manage teaching hours. The chapter indicates that 'e-teaching' has become routine in Australian universities, and that the tasks associated with e-teaching have increased teaching hours, with large gains for student flexibility, at the cost of staff time.

Retrieved from https://eprints.usq.edu.au/21319/2/Tynan_Ryan_Hinton_Mills_LRTC_2012_PV.pdf [Accessed August 22, 2014]. A shorter version of this report is *Out of hours: Online and blended learning workload in Australian universities*, by Yoni Ryan, Belinda Tynan, and Andrea Lamont-Mills (2014). In Picciano, A. G., Dziuban, C. D., & Graham, C. R. (eds) *Blended learning: Research perspectives, vol. 2* (pp. 215–234). New York: Routledge/Taylor Francis Group.

Grounded theory is an inductive methodology that attempts to derive a theory from an activity, process, or interaction and is *grounded* in the views of the participants. Briefly, it attempts to discover theory from available data. As described in the Australian workload study, a grounded theory approach was used that allowed for the generation of data about the impact of technologies on workload when teaching online or blended courses. From an analysis of the interview data using deductive and inductive approaches, a series of propositions were developed (Ryan, Tynan, Hinton, & Lamont-Mills, 2012).

To collect data, semistructured interviews were conducted with a purposefully selected sample of twenty-five academic (faculty) and professional (support) staff at each of four universities: the University of New England (UNE), the Australian Catholic University (ACU), the University of Southern Queensland (USQ), and Central Queensland University (CQU). Three are predominantly distance education universities but with sizable on-campus numbers at several campuses, and ACU is primarily campus based, but nationally distributed, and is moving rapidly to online delivery to combine small class size numbers at the various campuses. Interviewees were selected on the basis that they had taught or were teaching in online and blended modes, with a wide range of years of experience, and differing levels of seniority. The one hundred interviews produced eighty-eight valid responses. A small number of these (three out of eighty-eight) who had taught but were now designated as support staff were included, to give some perspective on how academics were managing their online delivery. Descriptive themes were analyzed using N-Vivo, and subthemes were subsequently generated. A literature search was undertaken (of the research and "grey," or non–peer reviewed, literature, including education media such as *The Chronicle of Higher Education*) on workloads and costs associated with online-only and blended learning, drawing on U.S., Canadian, UK, and Australian studies. The research questions were as follows:

1. What research is available on how workload is allocated in online and blended learning environments through Workload Allocation Models (WAMs)?
2. How do staff perceive the validity of their institutional WAMs with respect to teaching time?
3. How do academic staff "manage" workload in online and blended teaching?

The study provides rich descriptions of their findings for each of the research questions. Here is a sample from the interviews:

> One of the things about online is that people see it as a personal service. You say—yes, there's the Blackboard discussions and so on. That means that every day you go into it and you service that Discussion group—every day. If I'm running a lecture group—like face-to-face stuff—I'm not servicing those classes every day. And then of course students decide—oh well, they're a bit diffident about putting up a stupid question, so they email you or ring you . . .
>
> (Ryan, Tynan, Hinton, & Lamont-Mills, 2012, p.78)

> I think it takes a lot longer for me to form a suitable reply online than it does for me to just spit out an answer. Because I spend a lot of time thinking "how should I say it? Have I said that OK? Is someone going to take that the wrong way?" And I'll spend half an hour on a five minute question.
>
> (Ryan, Tynan, Hinton, & Lamont-Mills, 2012, p.102)

> With 170 students, I'm probably spending in excess of 14 hours a week plus with the students, answering their queries. . . . I probably spend a good five to 10 hours the week before the semester starts.
>
> (Ryan, Tynan, Hinton, & Lamont-Mills, 2012, p.104)

These quotations provide insights into the nature of the extra workload that might be engendered when teaching an online course. The interview technique is perhaps most appropriate for collecting this type of descriptive data.

In general, the interviewees in this study overwhelmingly perceived their work-load allocation as not sufficiently accounting for the additional time required by teaching in fully online or blended modes. This study did not attempt to quantify additional work hours in "e-teaching," although one of the eighty-eight participants was prepared to estimate that blended learning added 20% to classroom instruction time, and another posited it consumed double a face-to-face workload. Nevertheless, the study provided important insights into perceived additional workload as a direct result of the new technology tasks and communication modalities in teaching.

Mixed Methods in a Participatory Action Research (PAR) Study

Action research usually studies an issue at the microlevel and focuses on the development, implementation, and testing of a new program, product, plan, or procedure. A major purpose of action research is to seek to improve performance and to solve practical problems (Picciano, 2004). Participatory action research (PAR) is a variation in which subjects of the study make recommendations for improving performance. It is a reflective process with multiple points of data collection, analysis, and adjustments to the object of the study as recommended by participants. PAR can use either qualitative or quantitative methods or both as determined by the subjects/participants involved in the study. Vaughan et al. (2014) conducted a PAR study that examined the development and implementation of a blended Bachelor of Education (teacher education) program at Mount Royal University in Calgary, Alberta, Canada (see the abstract in Box 7.6). This study specifically examined the field placement component of the program. Data were collected over an academic year, using surveys, focus groups, and a shareable Google document. Students enrolled in the program and faculty who taught in the program were the main participants.

Box 7.6   Abstract of Vaughan, N., LeBlanc, A., Zimmer, J., Naested, I., Nickel, J., Sikora, S., . . . & O'Connor, K. (2014)

To be or not to be: Student and faculty perceptions of engagement in a blended bachelor of education program

This study describes an action research study that evaluated the effectiveness of a blended Bachelor of Education Elementary Program at a Canadian university from a student and faculty perspective using the National Survey of Student Engagement (NSSE) framework. Data were collected via online surveys, focus groups, and the use of an editable *Google Doc*. The study participants provided recommendations for improving the blend of classroom and field-based learning experiences based on the five NSSE benchmarks.

In Picciano, A. G., Dziuban, C. D., & Graham, C. R. (eds) *Blended learning: Research perspectives, vol. 2* (pp. 104–121). New York: Routledge/Taylor Francis Group.

The methods section of the study contains good detail on the research plan and execution. All students enrolled in the program, as well as faculty who taught in the program, were invited to participate. Five (N = 5) of the six faculty and 86% of the students (N = 77) participated in the study. The data collection process began with an online survey during the first week of classes in September 2011. Baseline data included students' initial perceptions regarding their engagement in the B.Ed. program and their rationale for wanting to become a teacher. The investigators obtained survey questions from the Beginning College Survey of Student Engagement (BCSSE, 2011) and used the SurveyMonkey (www.surveymonkey.net) application to administer the survey online.

In March 2012, the investigators asked students to complete another online survey focused on their perceptions of engagement after having completed the first year of the B.Ed program. The investigators based the questions for this survey on the National Survey of Student Engagement (NSSE, 2011) and, once again, used SurveyMonkey to facilitate the online process. During this time, the investigators asked faculty members to complete a similar online survey that used questions from the Faculty Survey of Student Engagement (FSSE, 2011).

At the end of March 2012, data from the surveys were tabulated, collated, and posted on an editable Google document (http://tinyurl.com/bedfirstyearstudy). During the first two weeks of April 2012, students and faculty who had participated in the online surveys were invited to add comments and recommendations to this Google document. In addition, the investigators conducted a student focus group to discuss the survey results (N = 24) and held a departmental retreat to begin making plans to implement the recommendations generated from this action research study.

The authors of the study identified patterns, themes, and categories of analysis that emerged out of the data rather than having being imposed on them prior to data collection and analysis. Descriptive statistics (e.g., frequencies, means, and standard deviations) were calculated for the online survey items using MS Excel. Comments and recommendations from the student and faculty focus group sessions were added directly to the Google document. The authors compared the results from the BCSSE and NSSE student surveys and focus group to identify "disappointment gaps" between students' beginning and end of first year perceptions of engagement. Similarly, the authors compared the NSSE and FSSE survey and focus group results to highlight "misunderstanding gaps" between student and faculty perceptions of engagement at the end of the first year of the B.Ed program.

The results of this research focused on five categories of student engagement, including:

- Student interactions with faculty members
- Active and collaborative learning
- Level of academic challenge
- Enriching educational experiences
- Supportive campus environment

The findings were supported by an extensive number of tables tabulated from the surveys and excerpts from focus group discussions. Here is an excerpt from a focus group relating to "enriching educational experiences:"

Student focus group participants commented that the field placements and school tours were the highlight of their first year experience. "I really enjoyed the volunteer school experience. It reassured me that I was going into the right career. I also enjoyed the school tours as they helped me gain a better understanding of what the education system is heading towards, and what programs are out there to assist struggling students" (Student Focus Group Participant 2). They also indicated how important the *Google Doc* journal and *Google Site* portfolio were for "integrating my Mount Royal class and volunteer placement experiences and establishing a philosophy of education that I truly believe in" (Student Focus Group Participant 9).

(Vaughan et al., 2014, p.116)

The study also provides insights into issues that need action and should be addressed to improve the program. For example,

students also indicated, however, that time constraints were a major challenge to participation in these types of "out-of-class" activities . . . 75% of the students work more than 10 hours a week (more working hours than homework hours) and almost 20% spend at least this amount of time commuting to the university each week.

(Vaughan et al., 2014, p.117)

The study is an excellent example of an action research study that integrates quantitative and qualitative methods and is used in partnership by students, faculty, and administration to design, plan, and improve an academic program such as the Bachelor of Education program at Mt. Royal University.

The Need for More Qualitative Research

In a reference at the beginning of this chapter, Lincoln and Guba (1985) stressed the importance of direct observation in the natural setting as a method for recording the nuance and subtlety of complex social interactions as they occur in many educational activities. Qualitative research is a critical part of the agenda for research in online and blended learning environments, whether used alone or mixed with quantitative methods. It provides insights that help us understand and improve the dynamics for developing and implementing technology in education. In this regard, it plays a most important role in examining the human-intensive issues related to pedagogy, professional development, student services, and administrative processes. In a word, qualitative research is essential.

References

Beginning College Survey of Student Engagement (BCSSE) (2011). *Administering BCSSE.* Retrieved from http://bcsse.iub.edu/_/?cid=16 [Accessed August 1, 2014].

FSSE (2011). *Faculty survey of student engagement.* Retrieved from http://fsse.iub.edu/ [Accessed August 11, 2014].

Gee, J. (2010). *An introduction to discourse analysis: Theory and method* (3rd ed.). New York: Routledge.

Gee, J., & Handford, M. (2013). *The Routledge handbook of discourse analysis.* New York: Routledge.

Han, S., & Hill, J. R. (2006, December). Building understanding in asynchronous discussions: Examining types of online discourse. *Journal of Asynchronous Learning Networks, 10*(4). Retrieved from http://sloanconsortium.org/jaln/v10n4/building-understanding-asynchronous-discussions-examining-types-online-discourse [Accessed August 9, 2014].

Larsson, J., & Holmstrom, I. (2007). Phenomenographic or phenomenological analysis: Does it matter?. *International Journal of Qualitative Studies on Health and Well-being, 2*(1), 55–64. Retrieved from www.ijqhw.net/index.php/qhw/article/view/4945 [Accessed August 12, 2014].

Lincoln, Y. S., & Guba, E. G. (1985). *Naturalistic inquiry.* Beverly Hills: Sage.

Marton, F. (1981). Phenomenography–Describing conceptions of the world around us. *Instructional Science, 10,* 177–200.

Marton, F., & Booth, S. (1997). *Learning and awareness.* Mahwah, NJ: Lawrence Erlbaum Associates.

McDonald, P. (2014). Variation in adult learners' experiences of blended learning in higher education. In Picciano, A. G., Dziuban, C. D., & Graham, C. R. (eds) *Blended learning: Research perspectives, vol. 2* (pp. 215–234). New York: Routledge/Taylor Francis Group.

National Survey of Student Engagement (2011). *Fostering student engagement campus wide- annual report 2011.* Bloomington, IN: Center for Postsecondary Research.

Picciano, A. G. (2004). *Educational research primer.* London: Continuum.

Ryan, Y., Tynan, B., Hinton, L., & Lamont-Mills, A. (2012). *Out of hours: Final report of the project e-teaching leadership: Planning and implementing a benefits-oriented costs model for technology enhanced learning.* Strawberry Hills, AU: Australian Department of Education, Australian Teaching and Learning Council. Retrieved from https://eprints.usq.edu.au/21319/2/Tynan_Ryan_Hinton_Mills_LRTC_2012_PV.pdf [Accessed August 21, 2014].

Ryan, Y., Tynan, B., & Lamont-Mills, A. (2014). Out of hours: Online and blended learning workload in Australian universities. In Picciano, A. G., Dziuban, C. D., & Graham, C. R. (eds) *Blended learning: Research perspectives, vol. 2* (pp. 215–234). New York: Routledge/Taylor Francis Group.

Vaughan, N., LeBlanc, A., Zimmer, J., Naested, I., Nickel, J., Sikora, S., . . . & O'Connor, K. (2014). To be or not to be: Student and faculty perceptions of engagement in a blended bachelor of education program. In Picciano, A. G., Dziuban, C. D., & Graham, C. R. (eds) *Blended learning: Research perspectives, vol. 2* (pp. 104–121). New York: Routledge/Taylor Francis Group. A version of this study is available at https://docs.google.com/a/mtroyal.ca/document/d/1II91E3JI9oStL-h_JGf0nW031Pn6jnWs6sn3JITBRww/edit?pli=1.

Wegmann, S. J., & Thompson, K. (2014). SCOPE-ing out interactions in blended environments. In Picciano, A. G., Dziuban, C. D., & Graham, C. R. (eds) *Blended learning: Research perspectives, vol. 2* (pp. 73–92). New York: Routledge/Taylor Francis Group.

Chapter 8

Case Studies

An Authentic Research Method

Charles R. Graham

Introduction

Case studies are a common methodology used in blended and online learning research. The case study methodology is often chosen because it is a very flexible method that can be applied in a wide variety of contexts. It is a methodology that is often viewed as ideal for educational contexts because it doesn't require the manipulation or controlling of contextual variables. "The case study method allows the investigators to retain the holistic and meaningful characteristics of real-life events" (Yin, 2003a, p.2). Additionally, a case study methodology is often used because the researchers are interested in better understanding their own particular context, and they have access to data within their own context.

So what is case study research, and how might it be applied to study blended and online learning? This chapter will begin by briefly describing case study research and when it is ideal for a researcher to select this approach. The bulk of the chapter will focus on how to design case studies and the analysis of examples of case study research in the domain of blended learning.

It is beyond the scope of this chapter to provide comprehensive coverage of the topic of case study research. This chapter will provide an introduction and specific application examples in the blended learning domain. However, readers wishing to extend their knowledge of the topic might review the work of the following prominent case study researchers:

- **Robert K. Yin**—*Case Study Research: Design and Methods* (Yin, 2003a); *Applications of Case Study Research* (Yin, 2003b)
- **Robert E. Stake**—*The Art of Case Study Research* (Stake, 1995); *Multiple Case Study Analysis* (Stake, 2006)
- **Sharan B. Merriam**—*Qualitative Research and Case Study Applications in Education* (Merriam, 1998)

What is case study research?

> . . . the single most defining characteristic of case study research lies in delimiting the object of study, the case.
>
> (Merriam, 1998, p.27)

Miles and Huberman define a case as "a phenomenon of some sort occurring in a bounded context" (1994, p.25). Yin defines the case study as "an empirical inquiry that investigates a contemporary phenomenon within its real-life context, *especially when the boundaries between phenomenon and context are not clearly evident*" (2003a, p.13, emphasis added). The "bounded context," or case in which a phenomenon occurs, can be a person, a program, a school, a course, an activity, or any unit of analysis that has clear boundaries.

There are many different types of case studies. There is no commonly agreed upon taxonomy of case studies. In looking at the purpose of a case study, Stake (1995) distinguishes between "intrinsic" and "instrumental" case studies. The "intrinsic" case study is designed to better understand the particular case itself. For example, in the blended learning domain it might mean trying to understand how students are experiencing a particular blend being implemented in a specific course. The "instrumental" case study is designed to understand something more general, such as the phenomenon experienced in the case. For example, in the blended learning domain it might mean studying a specific blended learning classroom to try and better understand learner engagement in blended and online contexts.

Yin (2003a, 2003b) describes exploratory, descriptive, and explanatory categories of case studies. Exploratory studies are often done prior to having a focused research question, with the purpose of leading to more focused research. This kind of research, while valuable, may be overused and may have led to a perception that there is a lack of discipline and rigor in case study research. Descriptive case studies often address questions of "what," "who," "where," "how many," and "how much." Their purpose is not to prescribe but rather to provide a rich account or description of the case and associate phenomena. Finally, explanatory case studies address questions of "how" and "why."

Merriam (1998) outlines three types of qualitative case studies: "descriptive," "interpretive," and "evaluative." Descriptive case studies, according to Merriam, are not theoretical and seek to provide rich details about the phenomena being studied without generalizing to other cases and contexts. The interpretive case study takes the description a step farther into the theoretical realm. This may involve using the case study to challenge existing theoretical assumptions or even provide a basis for theory development. The evaluative case study adds a layer of researcher judgment to the description and explanation of the descriptive case study.

When to Use a Case Study Approach

> In general, case studies are the preferred strategy when "how" or "why" questions
> are being posed, when an investigator has little control over events . . .
>
> (Yin, 2003a, p.1)

There are many situations in which case study research may provide a strong option for investigating a phenomenon. The nature of the question the researcher is interested in asking is the first consideration. Yin (2003a) suggests that research questions that get at "how" or "why" questions are ideal for case study research. Additionally, inquiries that seek to describe in detail a context or phenomenon in order to increase understanding or dispel misconceptions might be good candidates for the case study. A second consideration for case study research involves contexts that are highly complex, especially if the context is difficult to control, as you might try for in experimental research. Case study research can be a good approach for these situations because it is a methodology that allows for investigating phenomena in authentic, unpredictable, real-life situations. In these real-life situations, case study research may also be "ideally suited to investigate outliers and other unusual phenomena" (Gall, Borg, & Gall, 1996, p.585). Finally, case study research is often more accessible to a lay reader than other types of research. Because case study research often deals with holistic descriptions and analyses of real-world contexts, a reader without advanced statistical or deep methodological training can still understand it and relate to the rich descriptions contained in it.

Process for Designing and Conducting Case Studies

> ... unlike experimental, survey, or historical research, case study does not claim any particular methods for data collection or data analysis.
>
> (Merriam, 1998, p.28)

Case study designs can involve a wide array of data collection and analysis methodologies. There are not specific methodologies required for case study research. Often, case studies involve the use of both qualitative and quantitative data. Figure 8.1 shows a generalized process for designing and conducting a case study. This chapter will describe each of the steps in the process and use examples from published blended learning research to help with understanding.

Table 8.1 identifies eight manuscripts that will be used as examples to illustrate different aspects of the case study methodology. These examples were chosen because they were (1) identified by the authors as case studies (except for Staker et al., 2011),[1] (2) they related directly to a blended learning context, (3) they

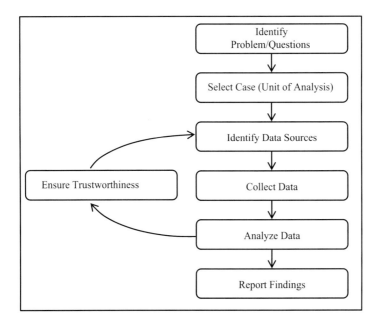

Figure 8.1 Generalized Process for Designing and Conducting a Case Study

Table 8.1 Examples of Case Studies in the Blended Learning Research Context

Case Study	Brief Description
Osguthorpe & Graham (2003)	One of the highly cited case studies in blended learning. This study constituted a special issue of the journal *Quarterly Review of Distance Education* and documented five divergent cases of blended learning. The lead article was a cross-case analysis synthesizing findings from the five individual case studies.
King & Arnold (2012)	This case study looks at how faculty who are teaching in blended learning contexts consider issues of design, communication, and motivation when implementing their courses. It was selected because its unit of analysis was the instructor.
Graham, Woodfield, & Harrison (2013) Porter, Graham, Spring, & Welch (2014)	These are two sequential case studies looking at the phenomenon of institutional adoption of blended learning. The Graham, Woodfield, and Harrison (2013) study was used to develop an institutional adoption framework. The Porter, Graham, Spring, and Welch (2014) follow-up study provides insight into a specific aspect of the adoption framework.
Graham & Robison (2007)	This study looked at the broad range of blended learning occurring at a specific institution of higher education. It used case examples of blended learning implementation to identify transforming, enhancing, and enabling blends.
Motteram (2006)	This case study looks at the use of a blended approach in the training of language teachers. It explores the connection between blended learning and important issues in the adult education literature, including deep and surface learning, communities of practice, and educational dialogue.
Dron, Seidel, & Litten (2004)	This case study describes the challenges with the design and implementation of a blended course. The study uses the theory of transactional distance as a lens for interpreting the experience (Moore, 2013).
Staker et al. (2011)	This manuscript presents forty cases (that they call profiles) of K–12 blended learning. The cases are used to develop several models of blended learning that are widely used in the K–12 context.

provided a diverse range of problems and approaches to case study research, and (4) they were familiar to the author. The examples selected span the range of different types of case studies identified earlier by Yin (2003a, 2003b) and Merriam (1998). The examples also highlight a range of different units of analysis, from the individual to the university, as well as different methods of data collection and analysis. Finally, there are widely different levels of methodological detail in the examples. Seeing this contrast will hopefully prompt greater inclusion of methodological specificity in future case studies around blended learning.

The following sections each highlight a part of the generalized process for designing and conducting a case study that is depicted in Figure 8.1.

Identify a Problem

The first step to any research endeavor is to identify a problem or research question for the inquiry to address. This is no different with case study research—the first step must involve identifying a meaningful problem to be investigated. There are many ways to come up with meaningful problems to address. Often, researchers will look close to home at challenges that they are facing in their own work contexts for problems that they want to better understand. Table 8.2 presents the problem being addressed in each of the eight case study examples (in the researchers' own words, where practical).

Two of the examples (Graham, Woodfield, & Harrison, 2013; Staker et al., 2011) had the explicit purpose of model development. The follow-up Graham, Woodfield, and Harrison (2014) study explored the model more deeply for institutions transitioning from stage 1 to stage 2 in the model. The Staker et al. manuscript uses the model as a way of categorizing blends. The ultimate purpose of these model development case studies was to be able to generalize to other cases. Other examples provided have a less explicit goal of being directly applied to other cases, even though the language in the King and Arnold (2012) questions is very broad, making it seem as if they are trying to generalize to all higher education faculty. Almost all the examples are descriptive in some way, with Dron, Seidel, and Litten (2004) using a specific theoretical lens to interpret the experiences within the case and Motteram (2006) having an evaluative twist to the research questions.

Select a Case (Unit of Analysis)

Selecting a unit of analysis is an important step in developing a case study. Table 8.3 provides information about the unit of analysis, number of cases, and sampling procedure used in each of our examples. It is best if the case study is explicit about identifying the unit of analysis rather than making the reader figure out what the unit is. The Staker et al. (2011) example does not explicitly define the boundaries of the unit of analysis. The reader can see that the case is sometimes a center, sometimes a school, and in all cases a service provider of blended learning. Most of the examples provided in Table 8.3 focus on a course or institution as the unit of analysis. The King and Arnold (2012) case stands alone in having faculty as the unit of analysis. The number of cases included in the analysis is also an important consideration. Notice that cases with the purpose of model development involve

Table 8.2 Problems that Each Case Study Example Attempted to Address

Source	Example
Osguthorpe & Graham (2003)	***Exploratory*** This study was done early in the evolution of blended learning, when there was very little understood or written about blending. Its purpose was to explore distinct types of blends, as well as the purposes or goals instructors articulated for implementing their unique blended approach.
King & Arnold (2012)	***Descriptive*** "We sought to gain an in-depth understanding of how faculty of higher education blended courses consider course design, communication, and motivation when planning and implementing courses. Using a collective case study approach, we sought to answer the following research question: How do higher education blended learning faculty take into account the factors of course design, communication and motivation when designing their courses?" (pp.46–47).
Graham, Woodfield, & Harrison (2013)	***Theory/Model Development*** 1. "Identify and provide details about issues that administrators should recognize in order to guide their institutions towards successful adoption and implementation of BL. 2. Identify some markers related to institutional strategy, structure, and support that would allow administrators to gauge their progress towards institutionalizing BL" (Graham et al., 2014, pp.8–9).
Porter, Graham, Spring, & Welch (2013)	1. "Identify institutional strategy, structure, and support markers that would allow administrators to determine their progress in transitioning from awareness and exploration of BL to adoption and early implementation. 2. Identify and provide details about issues administrators should address in order to successfully facilitate their institution's transition from awareness and exploration of BL to adoption and early implementation" (Porter et al., 2014, p.185).
Graham & Robison (2007)	***Descriptive*** 1. "How prevalent is blended learning at BYU? 2. How is blended learning changing instructional practices at BYU" (p.86)?
Motteram (2006)	***Evaluative*** "This research was designed to evaluate the experiences of these in-service teachers and to consider whether the module was achieving its aims in providing a valid experience for them. More broadly the study is concerned with whether blended learning is a useful and valid experience in adult education in general. The paper considers the following questions: 1. How have different groups appreciated the blended experience? 2. Why was it that for one particular group the online interaction seemed less successful? 3. What do these experiences tell us about the best way of conducting such activity? 4. Is such activity relevant for onsite learners" (p.18)?

(Continued)

Table 8.2   (Continued)

Source	Example
Dron, Seidel, & Litten (2004)	**Interpretive** "This paper describes a blended learning course which has attempted to apply Michael Moore's theory of transactional distance" (p.163).
Staker et al. (2011)	**Descriptive-Theory/Model Development** The researchers state their goals as: • "…objective is to study and describe the emergence of online learning in all its forms, in an effort to channel the disruptive trend toward greater quality" (p.4). • "offer[ing] a more intimate look at a small sample, with the intention to identify emerging models [of blended learning]" (p.3).

the largest number of cases, likely because it provides additional confidence in the model being developed.

Finally, it is important that case studies provide a clear description of the case selection process and a rationale for the selection. It is most common for a purposive selection methodology to be used in case studies. Patton (1990) identified a number of different types of purposive sampling methods. A few examples include:

- **Typical case**—Selecting cases that represent the typical or normal
- **Extreme or deviant case**—Selecting cases that represent the extremes or outliers
- **Intensity**—Selecting cases that represent a high level of the phenomenon of interest
- **Maximum variation**—Selecting cases that are as different as possible
- **Convenience**—Selecting cases primarily because the cost is low for accessing the case

Cases that are selected based on convenience or personal connection to the case have the lowest potential credibility, unless the researchers are able to provide a clear additional rationale for how the case is particularly well suited to address an important issue.

An important thing to note about this step in the generalized case study process is that it is important to clearly identify the unit of analysis and number and type of cases, as well as the type of selection procedure used. Far too many case studies lose credibility and value in the minds of the readers because they don't provide this important information about the study.

Identify Data Sources and Collect Data

Data used in case studies can be both quantitative and qualitative in nature. Table 8.4 shows some of the data sources identified by the example studies in this chapter. Data sources should be a good fit for the research questions being posed.

Table 8.3 Units of Analyses and Selecting/Sampling of Cases for Each Example Study

Source	Example
Osguthorpe & Graham (2003)	**Unit of analysis:** Course **Number of cases:** 5 **Selection/sampling:** Purposive—cases were selected to emphasize the diversity between topics, purposes, and approaches to blending.
King & Arnold (2012)	**Unit of analysis:** University faculty member **Number of cases:** 5 **Selection/sampling:** Purposive—selected from a pool of faculty based on whether they taught blended learning courses and responded to a survey.
Graham, Woodfield, & Harrison (2013)	**Unit of analysis:** University **Number of cases:** 6 **Selection/sampling:** Purposive—selected across a continuum, from being early in the adoption process to being mature adopters. Institutions were selected where the researchers had contacts.
Porter, Graham, Spring, & Welch (2014)	**Unit of analysis:** University **Number of cases:** 11 **Selection/sampling:** Purposive—selected institutions involved at the early stages of adoption and implementation of blended learning. All cases were part of a grant with the intent to transfer knowledge about blending from an institution with a long history of blended learning implementation.
Graham & Robison (2007)	**Unit of analysis:** University **Number of cases:** 1 **Selection/sampling:** Convenience sample selected primarily because it was the researchers' own institution.
Motteram (2006)	**Unit of analysis:** Module (or course) taught multiple times over a three-year period **Number of cases:** 1 **Selection/sampling:** Convenience sample selected because of involvement with the module.
Dron, Seidel, & Litten (2004)	**Unit of analysis:** Course **Number of cases:** 1 **Selection/sampling:** Convenience sample selected because the researchers were involved in the course development.
Staker et al. (2011)	**Unit of analysis:** K–12 institution (center, school, service provider) **Number of cases:** 40 **Selection/sampling:** Appears to be a convenience sample of K–12 providers of blended learning. No mention is made of sampling or selection procedure. Though the following is stated, "the 40 profiled organizations, although not a statistically representative sample of the U.S. market, provided a large enough data set to indicate strong patterns in the distribution of content providers and technology tools across the emerging blended-learning landscape" (p.161).

Table 8.4 Data Sources That Were Used in Each of the Example Case Studies

Source	Example
Osguthorpe & Graham (2003)	The lead article cited is a cross-case analysis and uses the five individual case studies as the primary sources of data. The data sources below are found across all five individual cases, with no one case using the same data. • Participant observation • Student surveys • Course evaluations • Instructor time surveys • Instructor interviews • Student focus groups • Student artifacts (assignments, projects) • Grades and other performance measures
King & Arnold (2012)	• **Survey**—Brief introductory survey • **Interviews**—One semistructured interview with each participant
Graham, Woodfield, & Harrison (2013) Porter, Graham, Spring, & Welch (2014)	• **Interviews** with key personnel at each institution • **Supplemental documents** provided by some interviewees
Graham & Robison (2007)	• **Survey** of university faculty • **Interviews** with seventy-two faculty across twelve colleges
Motteram (2006)	Data collected over three academic years (2000–2003) • **Open-ended questionnaire** given to module participants in 2000 and 2001 • **Focus groups** with module participants in 2002 and 2003 • **Participant messages** in online discussion forum in 2002 and 2003 • "For the purposes of this paper the questionnaires and focus group transcriptions were the main data used" (p.23).
Dron, Seidel, & Litten (2004)	• **Participant observation**—No explicit mention is made of data collected
Staker et al. (2011)	• No explicit mention of data collection methods other than: "All numbers reflect data from the 2010–11 school year unless otherwise indicated. Innosight Institute has created an online database to continue compiling public profiles of organizations that are delivering K–12 blended learning."

Common qualitative data sources include

- **Interviews**—These can be highly structured, where the exact questions are asked of each person and there is no deviation from the interview script, or semistructured, where the interviewer has wide latitude to explore ideas not explicitly written into the script.
- **Focus groups**—These are basically group interviews where the participants can interact with each other, as well as the interviewer who is facilitating the focus group.
- **Open-ended surveys**—Many surveys include open-ended questions that are rich in qualitative data regarding the case(s).
- **Observation**—Observation can include live observation, as well as delayed observation of activity via video or audio recording.
- **Discussion transcripts**—Research that involves online learning often includes data from online discussion boards, synchronous chat sessions, or even email conversations between participants.
- **Document analysis**—Documents often play an important role in a case study to provide context, as well as a source of data for coding. Examples of documents might include lesson plans, course syllabi and other materials, policy documents, etc.

When multiple, diverse sources of data are used in the case study, this is a form of triangulation called "data source triangulation," which can increase the richness of the case as well as the confidence of the readers in the trustworthiness of the findings.

Analyze Data

There are no data analysis methods that are unique to case studies. Any data analysis method can be used as part of the case study methodology. It is more typical for case studies to focus on qualitative data analysis methods, though many use both qualitative and quantitative forms of analysis. Table 8.5 contains a list of data analysis procedures for each of the case study examples in this chapter.

One common weakness in case studies is the underspecification of the analysis methods. You can see this challenge in several of the examples in this chapter. Often, qualitative methods involve some kind of open coding of the data to identify themes. Other times there are a priori themes from a previously established theory being used in the coding. It is important that the analysis methods be described in enough detail that a reader does not have questions about exactly what process the researchers went through. As a general practice, think about trying to communicate the methods of the study or training a peer who is going to help you finish the study. Are the analysis techniques articulated clearly enough to allow that to happen?

Ensure Trustworthiness

In quantitative research there are standards for establishing reliability and validity for the findings. Qualitative research has similar standards, with a focus on the "trustworthiness" of the findings. Trustworthiness is a term often used in qualitative research to

Table 8.5 Data Analysis Procedures in Each of the Case Study Examples

Source	Example
Osguthorpe & Graham (2003)	Each of the five individual case studies in the series has its own distinct methodology. The Osguthorpe and Graham article does a synthesis across the five cases. The data analysis procedures for the cross-case analysis were not clearly articulated in the manuscript. Readers must infer that the methodology involved an identification and coding of themes across the cases that addressed the following questions: • What was being blended? (three categories identified) • What are the goals? (six categories identified)
King & Arnold (2012)	"We indexed the interviews prior to data analysis. We each coded the survey responses and interview transcripts using an a priori coding scheme based on the three factors (communication, motivation, and course design) found to be important in the literature on blended courses. Table 2 provides a detailed description of the coding scheme. Throughout the coding process, we both observed that course design was composed of two separate processes, which were recoded into 'Course Preparation' and 'Course Design.' Course preparation included the professors' intentions for creating a blended course, the planning involved for the course (workshops or other resources used to develop the course), and the revision process for future courses. Course design discussed the actual layout of the course on the learning management system (LMS), which is a software program that can be used to administer course content via the Internet. Upon completion of the coding by each researcher, coding decisions were compared between researchers, and all discrepancies were discussed and reconciled before further analyzing the data. We grouped the codes into themes through a thematic analysis of the interview indices (Miles & Huberman, 1994). Particular attention was paid to the recoding of course preparation and design, as well as the intended purpose of components based on the professors' chosen design. We also conducted a thematic analysis of the survey responses to identify common tactics used in designing and teaching blended courses. Data belonging to established themes were compiled in a word-processed document" (p.49).
Graham, Woodfield, & Harrison (2013)	"The investigators used constant comparison methodology to do a thematic analysis, typically done by comparing data sets from particular cases: interviews, field notes, or documents. After reviewing the interview transcripts, they analyzed and compared the data to identify themes, patterns, and tentative categories regarding the stage of BL implementation (Lincoln & Guba, 1985)" (p.7).
Porter, Graham, Spring, & Welch (2014)	"The researchers reviewed, analyzed, and compared the data contained in the interview transcripts to identify themes, patterns, and tentative categories regarding the various issues regarding BL implementation (Lincoln & Guba, 1985). The authors sought to ensure trustworthiness of the qualitative inquiry by observing standards of credibility and transferability (Lincoln & Guba, 1985)" (p.188).

(Continued)

Table 8.5   (Continued)

Source	Example
Graham & Robison (2007)	"To address the first question regarding the prevalence of blended learning at BYU, we present descriptive statistics from the faculty survey on blended learning. Faculty adoption of blended learning is compared based on several demographic variables such as age, rank and status, and gender. Analysis was conducted to understand if certain demographics are more or less likely to implement blended learning strategies. The analysis of the qualitative case interviews uses a framework described by Graham (2006) to identify examples of transforming blends, enhancing blends, and enabling blends. Exemplars for each of these categories were drawn from the seventy-two faculty interviews described previously. Three main criteria were considered when selecting the case vignettes to present in this chapter: (1) the scope of the blend, (2) the purpose of the blend" (pp.88–89).
Motteram (2006)	"The data were processed by focusing on the research questions and considering whether the comments of the participants could tell us anything about the issues. Data were transferred to separate coding sheets so that all the comments on a particular question could be reviewed together and trends and issues highlighted" (p.23).
Dron, Seidel, & Litten (2004)	No explicit mention is made of analysis methods the researchers used.
Staker et al. (2011)	No explicit mention is made of analysis methods the researchers used.

communicate a standard of quality for the findings. Lincoln and Guba (1985) provide four general criteria for establishing the trustworthiness of qualitative research.

- **Credibility**—Similar to internal validity in quantitative research. It means that the findings are believable to critical consumers of the research, as well as to the participants in the research. Some common practices for establishing credibility include prolonged engagement, persistent observation, triangulation, peer debriefing, negative case analysis, progressive subjectivity checks, emic or folk perspectives of the participants, and member checking (see Williams, n.d.).
- **Transferability**—Similar to external validity in quantitative research. It means that the interpretation of the findings can be transferred or applied to other contexts different from the specific context of the study. Transferability is often established through a rich description of the study context (see Williams, n.d.).
- **Confirmability**—Similar to reliability in quantitative research. Confirmability is the degree to which the interpretations could be corroborated by others, including participants. An audit trail can be kept by researchers to allow independent auditors to see the process by which interpretations and conclusions were drawn (see Williams, n.d.).
- **Dependability**—Similar to objectivity in quantitative research. Dependability establishes if the researcher has been consistent in the application of the methods over time and not careless. A dependability audit can be used to document

the process and allow independent auditors to review the activities of the researchers (see Williams, n.d.).

Table 8.6 shows the attempts of the example studies in this chapter to establish trustworthiness. It is clear from these examples that this is an area that needs significant work in blended learning case studies, specifically, if not in case studies generally. As you can see, most case studies do not attempt to explicitly establish any kind of trustworthiness (or validity or reliability for quantitative data) of the interpretations and conclusions. In some cases implicit strategies are used, as in the Graham and Robison (2007) example, where strategies such as explaining researcher bias, rich description, and data source triangulation help establish trustworthiness of the findings.

Table 8.6 Explicit Attempts to Ensure Trustworthiness in the Case Study Examples

Source	Example
Osguthorpe & Graham (2003)	• No explicit mention of methods to ensure trustworthiness in the cross-case analysis
King & Arnold (2012)	• No explicit mention of methods to ensure trustworthiness
Graham, Woodfield, & Harrison (2013)	"During data analysis, the authors ensured trustworthiness of the qualitative inquiry by observing standards of credibility and transferability (Lincoln & Guba, 1985). To be credible, a study must be plausible to critical readers and approved by those providing data. The authors sustained credibility with triangulation, member checks, and peer debriefing. Triangulation was accomplished by referring to multiple sources of information, including pertinent literature, semi-structured interviews, and institutional documents. After information compilation, the authors engaged in member checking by asking interviewees to review and verify the accuracy of the authors' work. Further, the authors debriefed with disinterested peers by meeting to review data collection methods, analysis, and conclusions. The authors also sought to promote transferability, readers' ability to apply findings from one context to other contexts or settings. The authors sought to promote transferability by providing accurate institutional data (context), as well as rich descriptions of the themes and related institutional data" (Graham et al., 2013, p. 11).
Porter, Graham, Spring, & Welch (2014)	"To sustain credibility, the authors engaged in triangulation by referring to multiple sources of information, which included pertinent literature, semi-structured interviews, and institutional documents. After compiling relevant data, they employed member checking as they asked interviewees to review and verify the accuracy of the authors' work. In addition, the authors debriefed with peers to obtain and implement feedback regarding their research. To promote transferability the readers' ability to apply findings from one context to other contexts or settings researchers provided contexts by giving accurate institutional data and rich descriptions of the themes" (Porter et al., 2014, pp. 188–189).

(Continued)

Table 8.6   (Continued)

Source	Example
Graham & Robison (2007)	• No explicit mention of methods to ensure trustworthiness • Explaining researcher bias • Rich description • Data source triangulation
Motteram (2006)	• No explicit mention of methods to ensure trustworthiness • Rich description
Dron, Seidel, & Litten (2004)	• No explicit mention of methods to ensure trustworthiness • Rich description
Staker et al. (2011)	• No explicit mention of methods to ensure trustworthiness

Report Findings

The way the findings are organized and presented to the reader is one of the most important parts of a case study. Table 8.7 details how the example studies from this chapter have organized their findings. In many cases, the findings were organized by themes that came from an existing theory/model or were discovered in the research process. In other cases the findings were presented as more of a narrative representing participant experiences. The findings sections that are most successful are those that are able to provide a clear focus to the outcomes that address the research questions.

Table 8.7 Organization of Findings from the Case Study Examples

Source	Example
Osguthorpe & Graham (2003)	Each of the individual five cases focused findings on a rich description of the blended approach in action. Individual cases also presented findings (both qualitative and quantitative) about the student experiences in the blends. Findings from the cross-case analysis of five cases of blended learning were limited and consisted of identifying three categories of blending that address the question, "what is being blended?" Additionally, six categories were identified related to the goals for blending. The analysis explained the categories and identified where the five cases fit in terms of the categories.
King & Arnold (2012)	For each of the four "themes" taken from the research questions, researchers identified "code descriptions," using bullet points. Several paragraphs of prose were written for each theme, touching on many of the identified codes.
Graham, Woodfield, & Harrison (2013) Porter, Graham, Spring, & Welch (2014)	The outcome (findings) of the 2013 case study was the blended learning institutional adoption framework. The framework identified three broad themes (strategy, structure, and support), with subthemes under each. Indicators for each of the subcategories across three stages of adoption were identified. In addition to the framework that was presented in tabular form, the findings were organized by adoption stage, with examples of each theme for each stage of institutional adoption. Examples came from the six institutional cases in the 2013 study and the eleven institutional cases in the 2014 study.

(Continued)

Table 8.7   (Continued)

Source	Example
Graham & Robison (2007)	Numerical data in charts were presented that showed the prevalence of blended learning at the institution. Three categories of blends were identified (transforming, enhancing, enabling). Six vignettes from the data illustrating the blends and providing faculty perspectives were provided.
Motteram (2006)	The findings were organized into four sections, one for each of the research questions. Each section tried to directly address the research question using quotes and numerical data from the study.
Dron, Seidel, & Litten (2004)	The findings are a narrative of a single module/course and its evolution over time, using the theory of transactional distance (Moore, 2013) as a lens. Conclusions at the end of the paper are drawn as lessons learned from the experience.
Staker et al. (2011)	Descriptive data for each case, such as grades, enrollment, content provider, etc., is presented. Additionally, a visual representing how each case fits into the developed model of blended learning is provided. Narrative findings for each case were synthesized into four categories: • History and context—description of history and context of program • Blended model—description of blended model • Results—any results or data from the program • On the horizon—future plans A synthesis of the cases is presented with charts that show where cases fit relative to each other on the dimensions of content delivery, geographic location, and blended learning model.

Conclusions

Much of the current research related to blended and online learning takes the form of case studies. Bliuc, Goodyear, and Ellis note that "a large percentage of research into blended learning at universities takes the form of case-studies. These are much more common than the other categories of research ..." (2007, p.232). They further explain that "the field is relatively new and many researchers are still in exploratory mode: aiming to discover which are the more robust variables or constructs that explain successful experiences of face-to-face learning when it is combined with some technologically-supported learning" (p.232). Case studies can be a great way to explore blended and online learning and the salient variables. However, as we look at the case study research that focuses on blended and online learning, much of it lacks methodological specificity in terms of data analysis procedures and explicit efforts to address research quality through attending to issues of trustworthiness, validity, and reliability for quantitative methods. Case study research in blended and online learning may be strengthened by a focus on being explicit about the elements of a case study, as outlined in Figure 8.1.

Additionally, many of the current case studies in blended and online learning seem to be what Stake (1995) refers to as "intrinsic" case studies that are focused on understanding a particular case and are not particularly interested in understanding a particular theoretical concept better, like "instrumental" case studies are. The field could be strengthened if more researchers conducted instrumental case studies that create and/or elaborate on theoretical frameworks/models of blended learning (Graham, Henrie, & Gibbons, 2014).

Note

1 Note: This manuscript is a white paper published by the Innosight Institute (now the Clayton Christensen Institute for Disruptive Innovation). This is not a traditional research publication from an academic journal; however, it shows how cases of K–12 blended learning were used to develop models that are now widely referenced in the K–12 blended learning sector.

References

Bliuc, A.-M., Goodyear, P., & Ellis, R. A. (2007). Research focus and methodological choices in studies into students' experiences of blended learning in higher education. *The Internet and Higher Education, 10*(4), 231–244. doi:10.1016/j.iheduc.2007.08.001

Dron, J., Seidel, C., & Litten, G. (2004). Transactional distance in a blended learning environment. *Alt-J: Research in Learning Technology, 12*(2), 163–174. doi:10.1080/0968776042000216219

Gall, M. D., Borg, W. R., & Gall, J. P. (1996). *Educational research: An introduction* (6th ed.). White Plains, NY: Longman.

Graham, C. R. (2006). Blended learning systems: Definition, current trends, and future directions. In Bonk, C. J. & Graham, C. R. (eds) *Handbook of blended learning: Global perspectives, local designs* (pp. 3–21). San Francisco, CA: Pfeiffer Publishing.

Graham, C. R., Henrie, C. R., & Gibbons, A. S. (2014). Developing models and theory for blended learning research. In Picciano, A. G., Dziuban, C. D., & Graham, C. R. (eds) *Blended learning: Research perspectives, vol. 2* (pp. 13–33). New York: Routledge/Taylor Francis Group.

Graham, C. R., & Robison, R. (2007). Realizing the transformational potential of blended learning: Comparing cases of transforming blends and enhancing blends in higher education. In Picciano, A. G., & Dziuban, C. D. (eds) *Blended learning: Research perspectives* (pp. 83–110). Needham, MA: The Sloan Consortium.

Graham, C. R., Woodfield, W., & Harrison, J. B. (2013). A framework for institutional adoption and implementation of blended learning in higher education. *The Internet and Higher Education, 18*(3), 4–14. doi:10.1016/j.iheduc.2012.09.003

King, S. E., & Arnold, K. C. (2012). Blended learning environments in higher education: A case study of how professors make it happen. *Mid-Western Educational Researcher, 25*(1/2), 44–59.

Lincoln, Y. S., & Guba, E. G. (1985). *Naturalistic inquiry*. Beverly Hills, CA: Sage Publications, Inc.

Merriam, S. B. (1998). *Qualitative research and case study applications in education*. San Francisco, CA: Jossey-Bass.

Miles, M. B., & Huberman, M. (1994). *Qualitative data analysis: An expanded sourcebook* (2nd ed.). Thousand Oaks, CA: Sage Publications.

Moore, M. G. (2013). The theory of transactional distance. In Moore, M. G. (ed) *The handbook of distance education* (3rd ed.) (pp. 66–85). New York: Routledge.

Motteram, G. (2006). "Blended" education and the transformation of teachers: A long-term case study in postgraduate UK higher education. *British Journal of Educational Technology, 37*(1), 17–30. doi:10.1111/j.1467–8535.2005.00511.x

Osguthorpe, R. T., & Graham, C. R. (2003). Blended learning environments: Definitions and directions. *Quarterly Review of Distance Education, 4*(3), 227–234.

Patton, M. Q. (1990). *Qualitative evaluation and research methods* (2nd ed.). Newbury Park, CA: Sage Publications.

Porter, W. W., Graham, C. R., Spring, K. A., & Welch, K. R. (2014). Blended learning in higher education: Institutional adoption and implementation. *Computers & Education, 75*, 185–195. doi:10.1016/j.compedu.2014.02.011

Stake, R. E. (1995). *The art of case study research.* Thousand Oaks, CA: Sage Publications.

Stake, R. E. (2006). *Multiple case study analysis.* New York: Guilford Press.

Staker, H., Chan, E., Clayton, M., Hernandez, A., Horn, M. B., & Mackey, K. (2011). *The rise of K–12 blended learning: Profiles of emerging models. Learning* (p. 184). Retrieved from www.innosightinstitute.org/innosight/wp-content/uploads/2011/05/The-Rise-of-K-12-Blended-Learning.pdf [Accessed April 22, 2015].

Williams, D. D. (n.d.). Chapter 5—Standards and quality in qualitative inquiry. In *Qualitative inquiry in daily life: Exploring qualitative thought.* Retrieved from https://qualitativeinquirydailylife.wordpress.com/chapter-5/ [Accessed April 22, 2015].

Yin, R. K. (2003a). *Applications of case study research* (4th ed.). Thousand Oaks, CA: Sage Publications.

Yin, R. K. (2003b). *Case study research: Design and methods.* Thousand Oaks, CA: Sage Publications.

Chapter 9

Incorporating the Scholarship of Teaching and Learning (SoTL) into Instruction

Patsy D. Moskal

The scholarship of teaching and learning (SoTL) is not a new concept, having been defined by Ernest Boyer in 1990 in *Scholarship Reconsidered* (Boyer, 1990). Of course, teaching has always involved scholarship (to those true educators), as faculty are constantly involved with the art of trying new teaching practices, instructional methods, technologies, etc. in their classrooms in an effort to better reach students and effectively improve their instruction. However, the scholarship of teaching and learning involves more than the faculty member merely trying new things; instead he/she must systematically research the changes to instruction as a result of any modification he/she may have made to be able to determine and document what worked in detail. Faculty members often try new instructional techniques and new technologies as a way to augment or redesign what has been called the traditional classroom, perhaps by teaching in a blended or online format. So often, however, these changes occur with little or no research on their effectiveness, or, at best, only anecdotal evidence. SoTL provides a manner to formalize research on the impact of these instructional modifications. Grounding in evidence is key to SoTL. Sharing this information with others in the field helps impact evidence-based theory and practice, and ultimately provides for improvement in the educational enterprise—one class at a time.

SoTL research is perhaps most widely known among those in colleges of education, as much of their research areas may center on instructional-based techniques and methods; therefore, this research is valued by those faculty as part of their promotion and tenure process. While smaller, classroom-based pedagogical research projects may not be as widely recognized or valued in other disciplines, they nevertheless have the potential to inform, and ultimately revolutionize, instruction in classrooms, disciplines, colleges, and beyond. They can serve as a springboard to others' research, and through repetition and iteration, the lessons learned in similarly designed studies can determine what facets work well and what needs refining in a changing educational climate.

History of SoTL

Teaching is by its nature a scholarly activity. Ernest Boyer, in *Scholarship Reconsidered: Priorities of the Professoriate* (1990), delineated four overlapping forms of scholarship that scholar-educators embark on: discovery, integration, application, and teaching. The nature of the study promoted by scholarship of teaching and learning activities involves systematic reflection, research, and dissemination of the teaching process and its impact on student learning (Western Carolina University, 2015). Though dissemination opens the practitioner's research to the world, it also allows for others to critically review the instructional techniques and supporting research in a way that can foster a collaborative network of other like-minded faculty interested in similar topics designed to improve their teaching.

A number of organizations have been established to advance the mission of SoTL (Table 9.1). All of the organizations have extensive websites and can provide information on the origin and definition of SoTL, libraries and collections of SoTL examples, and resources to help promote this field of scholarly research. These web-sites can be helpful to those beginning with SoTL. They provide a guide for what is possible, as well as what others are doing in the field. The International Society for the Scholarship of Teaching and Learning (2014) also provides information on worldwide conferences devoted to SoTL. Learning from others is at the heart of SoTL, which is, in essence, the notion of "continuous quality improvement" incorporated into the teaching enterprise.

In addition to national organizations, there are many universities and colleges that have devoted significant support and resources to the enterprise of teaching and the scholarship of teaching and learning. For readers starting out with SoTL, Table 9.2 provides a list of several university sites containing resources that focus

Table 9.1 Organizations Devoted to SoTL

International Society for the Scholarship of Teaching and Learning
The Carnegie Foundation for the Advancement of Teaching
Carnegie Academy for the Scholarship of Teaching and Learning
American Association for Higher Education & Accreditation

Table 9.2 University Websites Focused on SoTL

Faculty Colloquium on Excellence in Teaching (FACET)—University of Indiana
University of Wisconsin Leadership Site for SoTL
Clark Atlanta University Center of Excellence in Teaching and Learning
University of Kansas Center for Teaching Excellence
State University of New York at Buffalo Teaching & Learning Center
George Mason University Center for Teaching Excellence
Illinois State Scholarship of Teaching and Learning
Abilene Christian University Scholarship of Teaching and Learning
Scholarship of Teaching and Learning at the University of Washington
University of Wisconsin-Madison Teaching and Learning Excellence
Vanderbilt University Center for Teaching
Western Carolina University Scholarship of Teaching and Learning
Western University Canada—Western Teaching Support Centre

on improving teaching and learning in an academic course or program. Many of these are sponsored by campus faculty development units and provide guidelines and classroom examples related to implementing educational innovation in varying disciplines in higher education.

Steps to SoTL

So, how does a faculty member begin a SoTL project? As with any research project, the most important first step is the research design. The researcher should have an idea of what it is he/she wants to examine. This is often influenced by the faculty member trying something new in his/her class—perhaps utilizing a new instructional technology (such as clickers), a new instructional approach (such as blended learning), or flipped classroom instruction. The teacher may have systematically changed something and wants to research the impact of the change, in terms of student learning or satisfaction. It may be sparked by faculty noticing something happening in their course—maybe women respond more to certain online discussion topics, or students tend to ignore online essay feedback. Once the idea is formed for research, then a plan is formulated to conduct a sound project to examine the questions that will guide the research. This step is critical, and it is best to spend more time in planning and design before beginning the research project. Because SoTL is incorporated into the classroom instruction, minimizing the disruption to students is critical. And, careful, up-front planning ensures that all pieces are in place for data collection. Uncollected data cannot be analyzed, and many researchers lament a missed opportunity to gather data.

Perhaps the most useful step to framing the SoTL project (not unlike any other research project) is to examine what other researchers have found. A thorough literature review is invaluable to determining both what others have done that is related to the topic and whether to replicate or extend that research, if any similarities exist. What data did others collect and what is available to the researcher? If student performance is being measured, the faculty has easy access to all grade book data—student scores for exams, quizzes, assignments, etc. What about institution level data? Data on students' transcripts—student demographics, prior achievement test scores (e.g., ACT, SAT, GRE), high school grade point average (GPA), transfer GPA, and overall GPA—are all available at the institution level, as well as any other data the university maintains in the student information system (SIS). This data can be obtained for each student in a given class.

What about student attitudes and opinions? If a survey is needed, the researcher will need to either find a suitable protocol that was used successfully by others, or construct a protocol from scratch. It is not unusual for at least some revision to an existing survey to be considered, as each research setting varies, and some questions that have been used in the past may not be relevant to the current sample. Permission must be obtained before a decision to use an existing survey is made. The faculty member can then assess what changes are relevant to his/her setting and whether additional questions may need to be added to capture the data he/she feels is necessary. Existing surveys often have data as to their reliability and validity, which is valuable. However, these analyses vary with each new administration and will need to be examined in any new research setting.

Careful planning must be made to determine the subjects to be recruited as participants, and the time frame for completion of the research. Time, support, and money all play into the design at this point. In the case of a researcher who is studying his or her class, this may be a simple task. However, in a class of twenty students it may be simple to collect data, but a class size of six hundred provides more challenges. If a survey is paper based, time and cost is involved and is directly proportional to the class size. While this is minimized by using an online survey, this method requires survey software, the knowledge to use it, and a means to keep the collected data secure.

Certainly, the research methods described in other chapters of this book are also relevant in this case. Survey design and implementation considerations are important, and the researcher will have to take into consideration his/her personal skill and knowledge in creation of paper or online surveys, and also in the ultimate analysis of data collected. At all times, the research questions should be used as a framework for the design of the research. Data do not equal information, and data gathered that does not address the questions the researcher sought to answer can result in wasted time and delays toward any meaningful interpretations.

Institutional Review Board (IRB)

Before we go further, it would be important to say a word or two about human subjects' rights. Most social science researchers and any who have sought grant funding are aware of the concept of human subject review and the effort involved with getting Institutional Review Board (IRB) approval prior to beginning any research that involves people. Grant agencies, such as the National Science Foundation, U.S. Department of Education, and National Institutes of Health, require proposals to have proof of IRB review and approval prior to submission. Each institution has an IRB committee—many have an IRB office that is devoted to reviewing all research involving human subjects and making a determination of whether the research meets the strict requirements of human subjects' rights. For faculty new to research, however, this may appear to be a strange and ominous hurdle.

Prior to submission of any research to the IRB for review, training is required that is specific to the nature of the area most commonly researched. For instance, the Collaborative Institutional Training Initiative (CITI) training (www.citiprogram. org/) involves researchers completing a number of online modules, all encompassing topics such as those found in Table 9.3. The intent of this training is the ethical treatment of people, such that the harm and risk to research participants is minimized, and assurance is provided that they are not in any way coerced to complete the research for fear of punitive measures or promise of rewards. Such training includes the historical need for human subject training and details on federal regulations that are critical for researchers to follow. Research can be high stakes, with promotion, tenure, grant funding, and reputations centered around the success and impact of completed projects. Ethics and high stakes have not always functioned harmoniously together, and so the current requirements have been influenced by prior missteps to help ensure that such blatant violations of human rights do not occur in the future. Any researcher who may see this as an annoying and unnecessary step would be wise to understand that the punitive measures against any university that does not abide by human subjects' rights can be severe. As an example, consider the well-publicized case against Johns Hopkins University. In 2001, the U.S. Department of Health and Human Services suspended all university medical

Table 9.3 A Sample of Human Subject Review Topics Covered in CITI Training

• IRB regulations and the review process	• Internet research
• Assessing risk to participants	• IRB member responsibilities
• Avoiding group harms	• IRB chair responsibilities
• Conflicts of interest	• Records-based research
• Cultural competence	• Research in schools
• FDA-regulated research	• Research with protected populations
• Genetic research	• Research with vulnerable subjects
• HIPAA-regulated research	• Unanticipated problems and reporting
• Informed consent	• Students in research
• International research	

research involving human subjects. The suspension impacted 2,400 human experiments, 15,000 patients and volunteers, and $300 million in federally funded clinical trials. The decision stemmed from the death of a twenty-four-year-old asthma study volunteer, Ellen Roche, who inhaled hexamethonium, an unapproved asthma drug, as part of a study into the causes of asthma. The Office for Human Research Protection found that Johns Hopkins had not researched the toxicity of the drug and had not adequately warned Roche about the potential risks involved with her participation (PBS News Hour, 2001).

While such serious consequences are more rare in social science research (as opposed to medical research), there are potential risks to study participants—impact on grades, for instance, or in the case of sensitive topics, possible emotional or mental impact on the subjects. Researchers can find the IRB process valuable to help assess and address any potential risks, and having other human subject experts examine the study provides further protection. As the point of our research involves helping students, this step is not a necessary evil, but rather a positive step toward improving our studies.

Once the researcher has obtained the required training qualifications, a university typically has protocols established for submitting a project description to the IRB. While many view this process as onerous and time consuming, it can help a researcher think more carefully of the research design and any unanticipated impact on participants. IRB staff are typically eager to provide help and guidance in this process. In fact, it's their job, and they are well versed in the details of human subject research, including what is ethical and not. They are experts in the area and can help maneuver smoothly around any potential snags in the process, as well as expedite the approval process. SoTL research is too important to not do well. Beginning with an ethical framework is critical.

Most research that is anonymous, or where participant information is kept confidential, is typically classified as exempt from review. Research review can also be expedited as determined by the IRB coordinator. However, research that involves more sensitive topics (e.g., sexual history, mental health history, sensitive medical details) or populations (children, prisoners, and pregnant women, for instance) may require review from the full IRB board before approval is obtained.

Once IRB approval is obtained, the researcher can continue with data collection and analysis. If researchers are unclear as to whether their projects fall under the umbrella of human subject review, a call to the institutional review board should be made to provide a quick determination of whether an IRB submission is warranted. It is important for the researcher to factor this time frame into the research design, however, as the time to complete any necessary training and produce, submit, and wait for IRB proposal review can delay the start of the research timetable. Classroom-based research may have a very strict timetable to complete during a quarter or semester, and so the IRB approval process must be completed prior to that time. In any case, the notion of IRB should not be considered a stumbling block to hinder research, but rather an important part of this process. And, researchers who find themselves unfamiliar and a bit intimidated by the process should not hesitate to ask for help from IRB personnel, or those familiar with the process on their campuses.

I Need Help!

It is certainly worth mentioning that many of those who may be interested in scholarship of teaching and learning research may find themselves unconfident in their skills at completing such a project. In reality, none of us are experienced in all areas of research and will often need help. Certainly, the authors of this book regularly seek advice and assistance from colleagues who may be more skilled in various facets of research and/or statistical methods. In addition, those whose primary responsibility is to teach rather than those required to conduct heavy research may consider SoTL even more intimidating, in spite of the benefit of its focus on teaching. For those of us on college campuses, there is a wealth of help available if we know where to look.

Faculty development offices or faculty centers for teaching and learning often have staff who are skilled in research or who can at least steer folks to those on campus who do have those skills. Institutional research staff are typically knowledgeable in data formatting and reporting. The office of research (responsible for any grant submissions) can also provide information on faculty who are experienced researchers. Some universities actually provide online resources and listings of research faculty who have prior grant submissions. This online listing can be used to help the researcher find others who have done work similar to his/her interests. Finally, faculty in statistics, psychology, sociology, and educational research departments are typically very familiar with social science research and are often willing and able to discuss ideas or collaborate with their fellow faculty from other disciplines. These faculty may be able to provide guidance not only in research design, but also in data collection and analysis.

The bottom line is that faculty who are interested in SoTL research should not let their fear of ignorance keep them from trying. We focus on telling our students where to go if they need help, and we should not be afraid to seek out help ourselves when needed.

A Word of Caution . . .

For those who are interested in SoTL research, there is a caveat to consider. If faculty are on a tenure track position that requires publishing and presenting research specific to their discipline, it is critical that they determine if SoTL research is valued in this process. While social science areas often see this research as extremely valuable, the hard sciences (e.g., physics, chemistry, engineering, biology, etc.) may not place as much value on research on education and teaching. That doesn't mean this research is less valuable toward improving teaching and learning, or that SoTL is less important toward improving teaching in those disciplines, but those who are interested should be aware of the specific requirements in their culture when it comes to promotion and tenure. Many fully tenured faculty work in SoTL, even if it isn't promoted in their discipline, since the faculty themselves understand the value of improving instruction in their field. Good teaching is good teaching, and this research can help improve any discipline in that regard. Check with your department or promotion and tenure committee to confirm the value of this type of research before you embark on a time-consuming research project that could have negative professional consequences.

Some Example SoTL Projects

To provide further clarification, this section provides some real-world examples that are relevant to blended learning from the author's experience supporting faculty with SoTL research. In many cases, these research ideas would certainly crossover to any course modality, and hopefully will spark some thought for readers regarding their own possibilities for SoTL. These are strategically organized by discipline to illustrate that SoTL is relevant to more than just colleges of education. However, the topics vary widely and could often fit any discipline and any modality of class.

Chemistry

Dimensional analysis is one of the early topics covered in general chemistry. But it is a topic that students have great difficulty mastering. Erin Saitta developed a collaborative, active learning activity that allowed students to manipulate chemical equations in a hands-on manner, rather than the static, paper-and-pencil method that is commonly used in textbooks. Students worked in pairs, which helped promote effective active learning and allowed them to learn from each other.

Results indicated that students who participated in the activity were more successful than those in the control group at solving problems using dimensional analysis. In addition, students' confidence in using dimensional analysis as a problem-solving tool improved as well (Saitta, Gittings, & Geiger, 2011).

Healthcare Management

Constructive engagement methodology (CEM) is a method of teaching that focuses on increasing student understanding as opposed to rote memorization of facts. Using a modified debate format, CEM requires active student participation in a five-step process (preparation, opening debate, intense interaction, closing, and evaluation), which helps promote in-depth understanding. Aaron Liberman incorporated this method into his healthcare risk management and healthcare organizational behavior classes and surveyed students to obtain their reactions.

This method is a stark departure from the multiple-choice question format that many students experience in their large classes, but students reported an increase in amount and quality of interaction with other students and an increase in amount of interaction with the instructor. Further, the process helped them confront and address fears with public speaking while creating an atmosphere of respect for others through the discourse required. While undergraduates were more positive than graduate students, both indicated high satisfaction with the experience. Students felt that it not only helped them better work in groups (an often lacking ability), but also helped them develop better communication skills (Liberman et al., 2005).

Communication and Anthropology

Tim Brown and Amanda Groff teach large classes in communications and anthropology, respectively. Their mutual curiosity about using social media in their classes led them to examine why students use various types of personal media and how appropriate certain types of communication are for relaying academic information.

They focused on the uses and gratifications approach as a framework to examine how students evaluated the appropriateness of certain academic information when communicated across various platforms, including email, social networking, and text messaging. The technology acceptance model (TAM) was used to evaluate how students' motivation for using social networking related to the evaluation of the appropriateness of transmitting academic information through various platforms for communication.

Results indicated that students preferred obtaining official "academic" information through what they perceived were official channels—email and the course management system. But, students were accepting of receiving certain types of information through more social channels (mobile devices and social networking) only if they did not have to share personal information (Brown & Groff, 2011).

Psychology and Communication

Alisha Janowsky and Kristin Davis noticed that students' online responses were often less civil than they believed students would be face-to-face. They examined students' perceptions of incivility in the online environment and in the face-to-face environment and compared them with faculty perceptions of student incivility, both online and face-to-face. Interestingly, cheating was seen as an indication of incivility by both students and faculty when considering online behavior (Table 9.4), but did not surface as incivility in the face-to-face setting—possibly an indication of the ongoing perception that students cheat more online. Students viewed disrespectful behavior as being uncivil in either online or face-to-face contexts, but mentioned inappropriate behavior and indifference only for the online setting. Faculty, in contrast, pinpointed indifference and class avoidance—behaviors not easily measured online—as being indicative of students' incivility in the face-to-face setting. Disrespect was mentioned only for the face-to-face setting, while inappropriate behavior was seen by faculty as student incivility in either setting (Davis & Janowsky, 2012).

Table 9.4 Student and Faculty Perceptions of Student Incivility

	Students	Faculty
Online	Disrespect	
	Cheating	Cheating
		Inappropriate behavior
		Disengagement
F2F	Disrespect	Disrespect
	Inappropriate behavior	Inappropriate behavior
	Indifference	Indifference
		Class avoidance

Anthropology

Online discussions are a popular tool in higher education, web-enhanced courses; however, there are mixed findings about their effectiveness in supporting critical thinking and engagement. A novel study by Beatriz Reyes-Foster and Aimee deNoyelles focused on the effectiveness of asking students to analyze word clouds (see Figure 9.1), which are graphical representations of word frequency in a given passage of text. They applied this pedagogical strategy to an anthropology course and rigorously measured engagement and critical thinking through content analysis of student discussion posts and a student survey. Results found that students

Figure 9.1 Word Cloud of John Lewis's Speech to the March on Washington

analyzing text in word clouds reported higher scores on engagement, critical thinking, and peer interaction than students analyzing text (such as a famous speech in history) in a linear fashion. Word clouds appeared to literally force students to articulate their thought processes and construct an understanding of the text, since they could not rely upon quotes or plot that were obvious in the actual speech. In addition, students were interested to see how their peers constructed different meanings from the same words. The results indicate that word clouds can be beneficial in improving learning when the focus is on the process rather than right-or-wrong answers (deNoyelles & Reyes-Foster, 2014).

Accounting

In teaching, Steven Hornik embraced new technologies and tried new approaches to reach his students. With the hype around virtual worlds, he wondered if using Second Life could better help him instruct and/or motivate students in his introductory accounting class. Working with an instructional designer (Aimee deNoyelles), he designed a survey to explore the dimensionality of college students' self-efficacy related to their academic activities in the open-ended virtual world of Second Life (SL). To do this, relevant dimensions of self-efficacy were theoretically derived, and items to measure these dimensions were developed and then assessed using a survey methodology. Using data from 486 students enrolled in an introductory accounting class that was supplemented by the use of SL, results confirmed the distinction of three dimensions of self-efficacy: virtual world-environment self-efficacy (VWE-SE), learning domain self-efficacy (LD-SE), and virtual world-learning domain self-efficacy (VWLD-SE). Additionally, this study found that both VWE-SE and VWLD-SE were correlated with course learning (deNoyelles, Hornik, & Johnson, 2014).

Sharing SoTL with Others

An important part of SoTL research is disseminating the results with others in the field. The publications and presentations that report the research circulate the study to others, both for critique and for learning. We can learn much from our peers, and allowing our research to be visible, used, and improved by others benefits scholarship for all. Teaching and learning is influenced by this process.

Tables 9.5, 9.6, and 9.7 include information on journals that publish a significant number of articles related to the teaching enterprise, including SoTL research. These are divided into general journals, discipline-specific journals, and those with a technology focus, which predominately examine research and topics within technology-enhanced education and online and/or blended instruction. It is wise to examine possible publication outlets *prior* to beginning to write, as each journal has its own guidelines and restrictions for article length, format, etc. In addition, it is helpful to find "similar" articles to what you are envisioning, as each journal has its own definition for the level of statistical rigor its audience expects. Looking at articles that have been published in a specific journal can give the researcher a good idea of whether his/her topic would be a good fit for the journal readership prior to starting the arduous task of writing. Furthermore,

Table 9.5 General Journals focused on SoTL

Journal of Scholarship of Teaching and Learning
Mountain Rise
International Journal for the Scholarship of Teaching & Learning
Achieving Learning in Higher Education
College Teaching
Teaching in Higher Education
Transformative Dialogues
Academic Exchange Quarterly
New Directions for Teaching and Learning
Journal on Excellence for Teaching and Learning
Journal of Cognitive Affective Learning
The National Teaching and Learning Forum
Higher Education Research and Development
Teaching and Teacher Education
Journal on Excellence in College Teaching
International Journal of Teaching and Learning in Higher Education
New Directions for Teaching and Learning

Table 9.6 Discipline-Specific Journals Focused on SoTL

Arts and Humanities in Higher Education
Studies in Art Education
American Biology Teacher
Journal of Education for Business
Teaching and Learning in Medicine
Journal of Nursing Information
Journal of Research in Science Teaching

the submit-review-revise-resubmit iterative nature of publishing can be daunting and time consuming for faculty. Careful selection of a publication outlet prior to writing can help minimize the potential struggle that a misfit can create when an article is submitted to a journal that may not quite be suitable for the journal's preferred clientele.

Conclusion

This purpose of this chapter is to provide those new to the scholarship of teaching and learning an overview of what this method of research entails, and also to provide some resources to help remove any obstacles that might discourage folks from

Table 9.7 Journals Devoted to Technology-Enhanced Education and Blended and Online Learning That Publish SoTL

Computers & Education

Contemporary Issues in Technology and Teacher Education

EDUCAUSE Quarterly

EDUCAUSE Review

Internet and Higher Education

Journal of Online Learning and Teaching

Online Learning (formerly Journal of Asynchronous Learning Networks)

Open Learning: The Journal of Open, Distance, and e-Learning

The International Journal for the Scholarship of Technology Enhanced Learning

embarking on SoTL research. It should be obvious that many of the remaining chapters of this book are also valuable to SoTL and would provide more detailed guidance on issues such as conducting a literature review or developing a survey. Those chapters span all forms of research, SoTL included.

The unique nature of SoTL is its emphasis on teaching and learning through a research lens. Scholarly teaching involves incorporating instructional techniques that have been tested and examined by others for their effectiveness. In SoTL research, the teacher opens the teaching and learning that occurs in his or her classroom to others, through his or her research on its effectiveness. Peer review of this research is an important part of SoTL, as disseminating results allows others to critically examine what has been done, and learn from colleagues to potentially duplicate and continue to improve those techniques.

SoTL research may not be as valued in all disciplines, and the researcher who is on a tenure track should confirm that this form of research is valued for that career step. However, for continually examining and improving our teaching and learning process, SoTL research is critical.

References

Boyer, E. L. (1990). *Scholarship reconsidered: Priorities of the professoriate.* Lawrenceville, NJ: Princeton University Press.

Brown, T., & Groff, A. (2011). But do they want us in "their" world? Evaluating the types of academic information students want through mobile and social media. In Kitchenham, A. (ed) *Models for interdisciplinary mobile learning: Delivering information to students* (pp. 49–65). Hershey, PA: Information Science Reference. doi:10.4018/978–1–60960–511–7.ch003

Collaborative Institutional Training Initiative at the University of Miami (CITI Program) (2014). Retrieved from www.citiprogram.org/ [Accessed April 20, 2015].

Davis, K., & Janowsky, A. (2012). *Perceived differences about incivility between faculty and students in higher education.* Presented at 18th Annual Sloan Consortium International Conference on Online Learning.

deNoyelles, A., Hornik, S., & Johnson, R. (2014). Exploring the dimensions of self-efficacy in virtual world learning: Environment, task, and content. *MERLOT Journal of Online Learning and Teaching, 10*(2), 255–271.

deNoyelles, A., & Reyes-Foster, B. (2014, October 29–31). *Using word clouds in online discussions to support critical thinking and engagement.* Presented at 20th Annual Online Learning Consortium International Conference.

International Society for the Scholarship of Teaching and Learning (ISSOTL) (2014). Retrieved from www.issotl.com/issotl15/ [Accessed April 20, 2015].

Liberman, A., Scharoun, K., Rotarious, T., Fottler, M., Dziuban, C., & Moskal, P. (2005). Teaching, learning, and the development of leadership skills through constructive engagement. *The Journal of Faculty Development, 20*(3), 177–186.

PBS News Hour (Producer) (2001). *Research halt.* Retrieved from www.pbs.org/newshour/bb/health-july-dec01-hopkins_7–20/.

Saitta, E.K.H., Gittings, M. J., & Geiger, C. (2011). Learning dimensional analysis through collaboratively working with manipulatives. *Journal of Chemical Education, 88*, 910–915.

Western Carolina University (2015). *The scholarship of teaching and learning.* Retrieved from www.wcu.edu/academics/faculty/coulter-faculty-commons/multiple-forms-of-scholarship/the-scholarship-of-teaching-and-learning/ [Accessed April 20, 2015].

Chapter 10

Longitudinal Evaluation in Online and Blended Learning

Patsy D. Moskal

In this book we have attempted to provide a variety of research methods that are commonly used to examine the impact of online, blended, and technology-enhanced instruction on faculty and students. So often we see these methods employed in a research study that captures what occurs at a single point in time—for instance, examining the change in student attitudes and performance when a course section is offered in a blended format instead of a "traditional" face-to-face modality, or examining whether students' use of clickers or practice quizzes resulted in gains in their performance.

These research studies are important and valuable for faculty to determine if changes to their instruction translate to intended outcomes and improvements. However, additional weight can be provided when studies are repeated in multiple instances over a longer time period. This chapter describes this type of *longitudinal* research conducted over time. The power of this method of evaluation is the ability to examine trends through repeated snapshots in time, or even following a cohort as they complete a module, course, or program in a given period of time. The repeated nature of longitudinal evaluation allows for potentially more precise findings, and the repeated nature of data collection helps provide an opportunity for iterative improvements to be made in instruction and data analysis, over the evolution of an initiative.

Perhaps the most familiar longitudinal evaluation in the United States is the U.S. Census. This survey, conducted every ten years as mandated by the U.S. Constitution, has the principal purpose of determining representation in the U.S. House of Representatives by population count. Data is aggregated for statistical purposes with identification of households and individuals being protected by law. Census general statistics are released for aggregate data as soon as they are available, but individual specific data is released seventy-two years after a given census (first proposed by the Census Bureau Director, Roy Peel, in 1952). Yet we are all familiar with the demographics of people across states, regions, and the country that we have seen over our lifetimes—demographics that were made possible by the repeated nature of this survey.

Similarly, we can have research designs that allow us to conduct, analyze, refine, and repeat experiments examining variables that can affect outcomes in online and blended learning over time. In fact, there are national organizations and studies that many may see often, and we provide some examples here.

Longitudinal Evaluation in Online and Blended Learning

There are a number of organizations that routinely conduct national longitudinal evaluations examining the impact of technology and/or online and blended courses in higher education. For instance, the Pew Research Center's Internet & American Life Project examines the "evolution of the Internet through surveys that examine how Americans use the Internet and how their activities affect their lives" (Pew Research Internet Project, 2014).

Figure 10.1 illustrates the 2013 survey data on the percentage of Americans, eighteen and older, who have access to dial-up versus broadband Internet at home. This longitudinal survey has allowed researchers to clearly document the growth of broadband and the demise of dial-up Internet throughout U.S. homes.

As educators involved with web-based learning, this information can be critical to determining the ability of potential and existing students to easily access any online information or course components. In fact, educators have monitored this data for years, and campuses have adjusted their on-campus labs and Wi-Fi access based on the proportion of students who might not have easy access to the Internet. Clearly, overall that is a very small minority at this point in time, but the value of this data is apparent—as is the value of continuing to monitor the trend through these many years. And, for those who may be in pockets of the U.S. that lag behind in Internet access, segmenting this data for those demographics continues to be critical.

Some organizations in higher education regularly survey faculty, students, staff, and/or administrators regarding issues that may be significant to other educators, institutions, and governments. For instance, the Online Learning Consortium (OLC) is "devoted to advancing quality online learning by providing professional development, instruction, best practice publications and guidance to educators, online learning professionals and organizations around the world" (Online Learning Consortium, 2014). Originally named the Sloan Consortium (Sloan-C), the OLC began with funding from the Alfred P. Sloan Foundation, through its interest

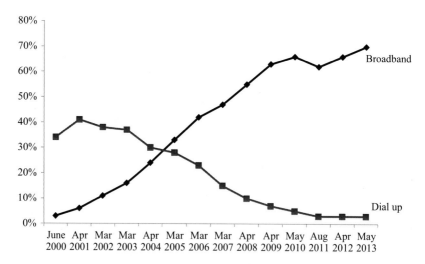

Figure 10.1 Home Broadband versus Dial-Up, 2000–2013

Adapted from Zickuhr, K., & Smith, A. (2013). *Home broadband 2013* (p. 2). Pew Research Center. Retrieved http://pewinternet.org/Reports/2013/Broadband.aspx [Accessed April 20, 2015].

in online learning in higher education with the Anytime, Anyplace Learning Initiative. The OLC has historically funded, supported, and provided outlets for disseminating research to help gauge the impact of web technologies on higher education teaching and learning.

Table 10.1 illustrates research conducted by the Babson Survey Research Group and supported by the Online Learning Consortium, that indicates the number of students learning online for the past decade. This research indicates that the growth rate for online learning appears to be slowing, but is still larger than the growth rate of higher education overall.

Table 10.2 provides an indication of the chief academic officers' (CAOs) perceptions of whether online education is critical to institutional strategy. The past decade has seen a steady increase in the number of leaders who agree with this premise, and in the latest 2013 survey, two-thirds of the respondents indicated that they felt that online education was critical to their institution's long-term strategy. These data indicate a growth in acceptance of online education and an indication that it is now in the mainstream of higher education.

Table 10.3 further indicates a positive trend by examining chief academic officers' perceptions as to whether online learning is inferior to face-to-face courses. Again, tracking this over time is valuable in illustrating the shift from the early, prevailing

Table 10.1 Total and Online Student Enrollment in Degree-Granting Postsecondary Institutions: Fall 2002 through Fall 2012

Fall	Total Enrollment	Annual Growth Rate Total Enrollment	Students Taking at Least One Online Course	Online Enrollment Increase Over Previous Year	Annual Growth Rate Online Enrollment	Online Enrollment as % of Total Enrollment
2002	16,611,710	N/A	1,602,970	N/A	N/A	6.9%
2003	16,911,481	1.8%	1,971,397	368,427	23.0%	11.7%
2004	17,272,043	2.1%	2,329,783	358,386	18.2%	13.5%
2005	17,487,481	1.2%	3,180,050	850,267	36.5%	18.2%
2006	17,758,872	1.6%	3,488,381	308,331	9.7%	19.6%
2007	18,248,133	2.8%	3,938,111	449,730	12.9%	21.6%
2008	19,102,811	4.7%	4,606,353	668,242	16.9%	24.1%
2009	20,427,711	6.9%	5,579,022	972,669	21.1%	27.3%
2010	21,016,126	2.9%	6,142,280	536,258	10.1%	29.2%
2011	20,994,113	−0.1%	6,715,792	572,512	9.3%	32.0%
2012	21,253,086	1.2%	7,126,549	411,757	6.1%	33.5%

Note: Adapted from "Grade change: Tracking online education in the United States," by I. E. Allen, and J. Seaman, 2014, *Babson Survey Research Group and Quahog Research Group, LLC.*, p. 33.

Reprinted with permission from Jeff Seaman

Table 10.2 Online Education Is Critical to the Long-Term Strategy of My Institution: 2002 to 2013

Fall	Agree	Neutral	Disagree
2002	48.8%	38.1%	13.1%
2003	53.5%	33.7%	12.9%
2004	56.0%	30.9%	13.1%
2005	58.4%	27.4%	14.2%
2006	59.1%	27.4%	13.5%
2007	58.0%	27.0%	15.0%
2009	59.2%	25.9%	14.9%
2010	63.1%	24.6%	12.3%
2011	65.5%	21.0%	13.5%
2012	69.1%	19.7%	11.2%
2013	65.9%	24.3%	9.7%

Note: Adapted from "Grade change: Tracking online education in the United States," by I.E. Allen, and J. Seaman, 2014, *Babson Survey Research Group and Quahog Research Group, LLC.,* p. 30.

Table 10.3 CAOs Reporting Learning Outcomes in Online Education as Inferior to Face-to-Face: 2003 to 2013

Year	Inferior	Somewhat Inferior
2003	10.7%	32.1%
2004	10.1%	28.4%
2006	7.8%	30.3%
2009	9.5%	23.0%
2010	9.8%	24.3%
2011	9.7%	22.7%
2012	5.3%	17.7%
2013	7.7%	18.2%

Note: Adapted from "Grade change: Tracking online education in the United States," by I.E. Allen, and J. Seaman, 2014, *Babson Survey Research Group and Quahog Research Group, LLC.,* p. 31.

concerns that online education was inferior to the more traditional face-to-face modality. Much research was completed in the past decade in an attempt to demonstrate the potential and promise of blended and online learning. These surveys, examining the views of CAOs, indicate a positive change of opinion toward the acceptance of online education.

EDUCAUSE is another national organization that "helps those who lead, manage, and use information technology to shape strategic decisions at every level" and "actively engages with colleges and universities, corporations, foundations, government, and other nonprofit organizations to further the mission of transforming higher education through the use of information technology" (EDUCAUSE, 2015). Understanding the value of ongoing research, EDUCAUSE formed the EDUCAUSE Center for Analysis & Research (ECAR) to help higher education professionals "predict, plan for, and act on IT trends in higher education." The EDUCAUSE Center for Analysis & Research conducts a yearly survey examining undergraduate students' experience with and preference for information technology (ECAR, 2015).

Historically, the *ECAR Study of Undergraduate Students and Information Technology* provides valuable information to higher education professionals on trends in student and faculty academic use of technology, preferences for blended and online learning resources, and perceptions regarding their institutional support for information technology. The 2014 survey incorporated data from 213 institutions and 75,306 students regarding their technology experiences (Dahlstrom & Bichsel, 2014).

The longitudinal nature of this survey allows ECAR to report trends through yearly reports, press releases, and presentations at annual conferences—a wide dissemination of data to professionals in the field, who may be in various stages of technology integration or adoption of online or blended learning. For instance, early surveys monitored participants' ownership of laptops versus desktop platforms (Figure 10.2), which clearly shows the rapid growth of laptops compared to desktops. Such information is critical to IT professionals in higher education, especially as the growth of web-based instruction has increased (Smith, Salaway, Caruso, & Katz, 2009). Issues such as wireless access, bring your own device, and lab or knowledge commons design have all seen growth in this time period. These initiatives have relied on ongoing research providing information on technology and laptop growth over time to leaders anticipating campus infrastructure, lab, and technology needs.

Administered yearly, these surveys change slightly as researchers tweak, add, and omit questions due to the fast-paced growth of new technologies and changes in technology use. It is critical to monitor the appropriateness of questions and adjust those that may be ambiguous or fail to provide the feedback that is needed to inform the audience. Unlike surveys that are administered only once, the ongoing nature of longitudinal surveys—create, administer, review, edit, revise, and repeat—requires yearly review and allows for continual improvement to ensure that the content is appropriate and informative for today's "market."

The most recent *ECAR Study of Undergraduate Students and Information Technology* (Dahlstrom & Bichsel, 2014) shows the change in technologies now studied (Figure 10.3). No longer is IT measured in the difference between laptops and desktops. Now, mobile technologies such as e-readers, tablets, and smartphones are included. Figure 10.3 illustrates the growth in these new technologies, as well as students' perceptions of their value toward their educational success. Once again, the value in examining these trends over time becomes obvious when looking at the change that has occurred. Being aware that students now have mobile devices and that they perceive these as valuable to their academic success can inform higher education professionals who may be responsible for both information technology

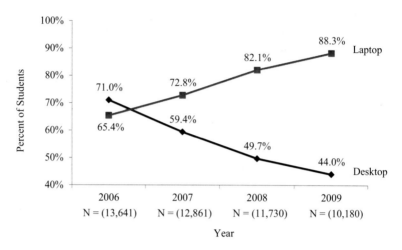

Figure 10.2 Students' Desktop versus Laptop Use, 2006–2009

Adapted from Smith, S. D., Salaway, G., Caruso, J. B., & Katz, R. N. (2009). *The ECAR Study of Undergraduate Students and Information Technology, 2009* (p. 43). Boulder, CO: ECAR.

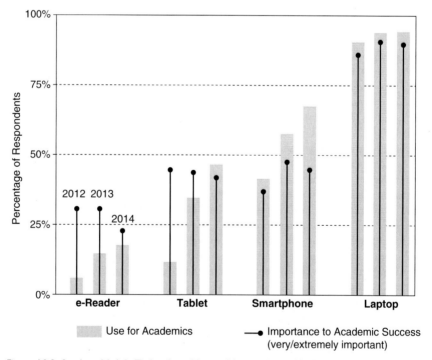

Figure 10.3 Student Mobile Technology Use and Importance, 2012–2014

Adapted from Dahlstrom, E., & Bichsel, J. (2014). *ECAR study of students and information technology, 2014.* Research report, Louisville, CO: ECAR.

and instructional technology. These data are critical to decisions regarding the use of various web technologies and applications, including examining their accessibility and usability on various mobile platforms. Continuing to examine this trend helps universities to maintain quality instruction and know what platforms to support and what issues may arise as students attempt to access their course and campus online components in the way most convenient to them.

Longitudinal Evaluation at an Institutional Level

While we often see long-term studies conducted by national organizations such as the Online Learning Consortium, Pew Research Center's Internet and American Life Project, or the EDUCAUSE Center for Analysis & Research, such research does occur on a smaller scale at an institutional, program, or even class level, and can provide valuable information to those stakeholders over time.

New initiatives, such as the implementation of blended learning, often take time to get established, and they morph and evolve over time. While a quick and early study can be valuable, a long-term evaluation can provide more detailed information on the progression of the initiative in terms of enrollment, faculty and student satisfaction, technology acceptance, and student and faculty perception of institutional support. All of these factors are critical to ensuring a program, department, or campus-wide initiative is successful and that it provides quality instruction to the students we serve. Such longitudinal evaluations require a supported and sustained level of buy-in and funding by administrators to ensure that staff and support are available to conduct a quality, objective evaluation for a longer period of time. We present several campus initiatives here to illustrate the value of longitudinal research to them.

A Long-Term Study on Engagement

Dringus and Seagull (2013) reported on their four-year evaluation of the effectiveness of blended learning initiatives on Nova Southeastern University (NSU). As part of their Southern Association of Colleges and Schools (SACS) accreditation process, schools are required to complete a Quality Enhancement Plan (QEP). NSU's QEP centered around enhancing student engagement, and Dringus and Seagull's department faculty utilized online delivery systems in campus courses—using discussion boards for facilitating group project discussion, lecture recaps, student resource sharing, and online question and answer sessions in their classes to increase engagement.

Accreditation or other mandated requirements can be a strong motivator for completing longitudinal research. As part of their QEP, Dringus and Seagull allowed faculty to define the manner in which they enhanced student engagement using online activities. Then they gathered data yearly from students and faculty regarding the success of the implementation. Data were collected examining student satisfaction, student assessment of learning, and instructor satisfaction in an effort to gain student and faculty perspectives on engagement in each course and gather a perspective of the activities undertaken in the Graduate School of Computer and Information Sciences at Nova Southeastern University. Blended learning had been adopted to extend support for masters' students who were known to be

Table 10.4 Students' Satisfaction and Perceived Enhanced Learning by Interaction Strategy

Interaction Strategy	n	Satisfaction in %	Enhances Learning in %
Discussion Boards	60	87	77
Distributed Articles	53	97	83
Synchronous Lectures	21	81	62
Discussion Forms	77	84	67
Online Discussions	81	75	58
Lecture Recaps	44	73	59
Share Resources	12	83	75
Create Online Q & A	14	71	71

campus based. Given that engagement is related to student learning and having the awareness that learning exists beyond the physical classroom, they wanted to explore various technologies for access and exchange outside of class time. Blended learning afforded the opportunity to incorporate these technologies into existing courses while maintaining a face-to-face presence.

Evaluating blended learning in their program from 2008–2011 allowed Dringus and Seagull (2013) to collect data from 1,032 students (duplicated headcounts) and fifteen faculty and adjuncts. End-of-term surveys were conducted with students, incorporating items that measured the impact and utility of the faculty-implemented online-interactivity methods. Faculty were then surveyed for their perceptions and comments regarding the implementation of the online interaction method in their courses, with regard to its ability to increase student engagement during nonclass time. Finally, analytics data collected by the learning management system were collected as a proxy for student engagement and interaction with a course (e.g., discussion posts). Table 10.4 illustrates the aggregation of student data across the various interaction strategies that faculty chose to use. Overall, student satisfaction was slightly higher than student perception of enhanced learning due to the interaction, but students were satisfied with the approaches.

The nature of this project required time to implement and collect data. So, a longitudinal approach was required to effectively gather data across courses, semesters, and years. Aggregating the data across the four years of the project provided an overall look at students' perceptions of the incorporated engagement strategies (Table 10.5). In addition, Dringus and Seagull gathered individual comments from faculty on how the strategies worked in their courses. These provide valuable context to support and provide more detail to the Likert-style survey responses. Faculty commented that on-campus students still preferred face-to-face interaction, pointing out constraints that impact the significance of the outcomes, even though students appear to be satisfied. They also indicated the difficulty in overcoming the "course and a half" perception (Kaleta, Skibba, & Joosten, 2007) when adding new course strategies. Students often feel stress with the amount of classwork required. Faculty teaching course sections with online components need to be careful not to add more work than is necessary and focus on those components directly related to the course content instruction.

Table 10.5 Students' Overall Satisfaction and Perceived Higher Learning by Year

Year	n	Satisfaction in %	Perceived Higher Learning in %
2008	183	89	85
2009	142	74	69
2010	158	83	65
2011	131	83	69

Dringus and Seagull (2013) point out that while we often see that once the need (in this case, the SACS QEP requirement) is over, evaluation stops, this is not the best course of action. In fact, they comment that "one should not discount that to sustain positive efforts there is a need for ongoing evaluation of the effectiveness of this modality to refine effective practices" (p.137).

A Long-Term Evaluation of Blended Learning

The University of Central Florida (UCF) began offering blended courses in 1997. A mandatory faculty development program was established from the beginning for any faculty member teaching either fully online or blended courses (UCF's blended courses by definition have reduced face-to-face seat time). In addition, the administration was forward thinking and established an evaluation unit that has conducted an ongoing evaluation of the initiative since that time.

The Research Initiative for Teaching Effectiveness (RITE) developed a research design that has provided the fundamental direction for the evaluation, while evolving slightly as time and technology have progressed (Moskal, 2009). Data focuses on examining the impact the web modalities have on faculty and students, and data collection involves surveys, institutionally collected data from the student information system, and university-mandated student evaluations of instructors. As an illustration of this longitudinal evaluation, data from students is presented here.

It seems that when any institution begins incorporating a new technology or new modality into its courses, the prevailing question is always: "Is it as good as face-to-face?" Grades are used as a surrogate for student learning, collected and maintained in the student information system (SIS) along with other course and student demographic information. As such, course grades are the one common indicator of student learning available across all colleges. Success rates (A, B, or C grade) are then calculated, along with percentage of those who withdraw each semester for each course. The aggregate data is monitored for trends across courses, departments, colleges, and the university to determine any changes that may occur for given modalities. Table 10.6 presents the success and withdrawal rates from spring 2009 through spring 2014.

These data have been collected each semester since blended learning has been offered, and a common trend is that blended course sections typically have higher success rates than face-to-face courses and comparable withdrawal rates. While a lack of every modality for every course prevents exact comparison in most cases, the overall trend still continues for courses across departments and colleges. RITE

Table 10.6 Student Success and Withdrawal in Face-to-Face and Blended Courses

	Success				Withdrawal			
	Blended		Face-to-Face		Blended		Face-to-Face	
Semester	n	%	n	%	n	%	n	%
2009								
Spring	9,177	88	133,561	87	9,228	4	146,714	4
Summer	3,943	95	40,258	91	3,943	2	43,712	2
Fall	9,386	91	148,990	87	9,464	3	164,438	3
2010								
Spring	10,336	91	140,981	88	10,416	3	157,288	3
Summer	5,314	94	41,598	91	5,351	1	46,821	2
Fall	12,325	90	150,640	87	12,439	3	169,717	3
2011								
Spring	12,969	90	140,941	87	13,202	3	158,840	3
Summer	5,986	94	42,059	91	6,002	2	46,316	2
Fall	13,379	90	153,299	87	13,548	4	170,674	4
2012								
Spring	12,495	90	143,624	87	12,793	4	159,607	4
Summer	5,757	94	41,263	90	5,757	3	45,822	3
Fall	15,538	90	148,452	87	15,888	4	166,967	5
2013								
Spring	14,852	92	138,994	88	15,112	3	155,795	3
Summer	6,021	94	38,636	91	6,022	2	43,248	3
Fall	15,684	91	145,970	87	15,940	3	164,726	5
2014								
Spring	15,777	90	134,075	88	16,385	4	151,195	4

uses these data to help faculty, programs, and colleges conduct similar research based on their needs.

In addition to monitoring student performance, student attitudes toward blended learning have been collected through the student perception of instruction (SPI) administered electronically each semester for each course, as mandated by the university. These metrics use five-point Likert items to give an indication of student satisfaction with a given course, and changes in students' ratings can indicate a problem, especially when the course has been altered, such as being redesigned as blended learning. Because the course demographics are also maintained, comparisons are made across various modalities for a given course. Table 10.7 presents the percentage of student overall excellent ratings for blended and face-to-face courses for spring 2009 through spring 2014. While there are differences across semesters, in general students rate blended instruction more positively than face-to-face. Again, these data are collected for each course, each semester and are collected anonymously.

Figure 10.4 shows the data for the average (mean) ratings for the same time period. Again, the trend clearly indicates that blended course ratings are, on average, higher than face-to-face sections; but it also illustrates that the ratings for face-to-face are relatively high as well. However, these data are also limited in the lack of comparison data for each course. Each course does not have a comparable section

Table 10.7 Student Perceptions of Overall Excellent Ratings

Semester	Blended		Face-to-Face	
	N	%	N	%
2009				
Spring	6,003	50.5	86,228	49.7
Summer	2,794	60.5	28,166	54.1
Fall	6,783	50.1	109,288	45.1
2010				
Spring	6,287	50.5	85,104	46.8
Summer	3,056	58.6	25,426	53.4
Fall	5,275	50.9	70,346	48.1
2011				
Spring	6,998	49.9	76,091	48.4
Summer	3,617	57.8	25,660	54.1
Fall	3,865	56.3	48,079	54.6
2012				
Spring	6,588	53.7	77,334	51.0
Summer	3,316	58.7	25,915	55.1
Fall	7,399	55.6	74,485	52.0
2013				
Spring	8,287	55.1	79,550	53.1
Summer	4,481	59.3	28,496	55.6
Fall	9,027	56.4	90,876	51.8
2014				
Spring	10,269	53.9	87,460	54.0

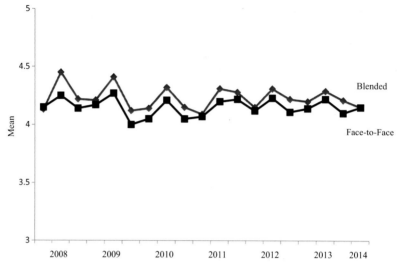

Figure 10.4 Student Perception of Overall Excellence by Semester

for both blended and face-to-face modalities. RITE does support program and faculty-initiated research, which can compare the two in a more controlled manner over time.

Critical to the success of this evaluation has been that the data are routinely shared and used to inform and improve the ongoing initiative. Each semester, the CIO, Associate Vice President for Distributed Learning, and those who head faculty development and evaluation meet with college deans and their representatives to discuss any issues and concerns that arise with regard to web courses, and also to plan for any future needs with regard to faculty or student support, new programs, or faculty development. Having years of data has helped provide information for any questions that may occur regarding any specific demographic. For instance, if there is a concern regarding minority success or freshmen withdrawal rates, these can be historically examined for any anomalies.

In addition, the big data sets that such a long-term evaluation provide allow for researchers to examine profiles across the numerous variables. For instance, in examining what makes an "excellent" teacher in the eye of the student, a classification and regression tree approach was used to examine all items on the student evaluation of instruction form, along with the course level (lower undergraduate, upper undergraduate, or graduate) and modality, to determine what factors students interpret as being critical to "excellent" instruction. As illustrated in Table 10.8 and discussed in Chapter 11, this produces a rule indicating that a faculty member has a 98% probability of receiving an overall rating of excellent if they receive an excellent rating on facilitating learning and an excellent rating on communicating ideas effectively.

As an illustration of how powerful a longitudinal evaluation can be, these results were found for a new student evaluation form, created and sanctioned by the university's faculty senate and implemented since spring 2013. But, the results mirror prior similar results found for the past SPI version, in effect for decades (Wang,

Table 10.8 A Decision Rule for the Probability of a Faculty Member Receiving an Overall Rating of Excellent (n = 126,672)

If...					
SPI Survey Items	Excellent	Very Good	Good	Fair	Poor
Facilitating learning	✓				
Communicating ideas	✓				
Then ...					
The probability of an *overall* rating of *Excellent* = .98					
The probability of an *overall* rating of *Fair* or *Poor* = .00					

Dziuban, Cook, & Moskal, 2009). Repeating the study adds further credibility to the power of these items toward what students deem is excellent instruction. These results have also been used to inform the campus Faculty Center for Teaching and Learning, which works with faculty on methods to improve their instruction, including how they facilitate learning and communicate ideas to students. As the SPI is high stakes at UCF—incorporated into faculty awards and tenure and promotion—this is valuable information that can be used to help support faculty success not only in blended learning, but across the university as well.

Guidelines for Longitudinal Evaluation

This chapter has focused on the merits of longitudinal evaluation, namely by providing examples of where it has been used to inform stakeholders through national and university higher education institutions. But, this method of research is not limited to such a large scope. In fact, an individual faculty member can conduct a long-term evaluation of an instructional change implemented in his/her course over time, incorporating these results into adding improvements and tweaks to provide the best instruction possible to his or her students. Programs of study can also find this valuable to study cohorts as they begin and progress through the program to find issues that may cause students to stumble or pinpoint courses or changes that may impede student success or retention. Faculty, departments, colleges, or universities can use this to study interventions aimed at improving student success. The following are guidelines to consider in this process.

Collect All the Data

One of a researcher's nightmares is a missed opportunity. A key principle to keep in mind is that uncollected data cannot be analyzed. It is easy to ignore data that have been collected, but it is impossible to analyze data not collected. If you think there might be value in collecting data and you have the ability to do so, gather it while you can. There are issues that impact data—such as ongoing student information system (SIS) updates—that can change data and require more work or make it impossible to collect data in the future. For instance, pulling two-year-old data may mean that a student two years ago has today's academic standing if he/she is currently enrolled.

Continually Improve

The very nature of research is to learn from the experiments conducted, and use these lessons to improve for the future. Repeating surveys and/or data collection adds strength to the findings and an indication that they are not an anomaly. Evaluations also evolve and change. With each new administration of a survey, evaluate the questions for their appropriateness. While keeping a core group of questions helps validate your study with repeated use, technology changes rapidly and, depending on the length of time of your evaluation, it is worth examining the appropriateness of questions with each administration. Has anything changed that might make some questions irrelevant or ambiguous? Look at the data collected and examine whether the answers provided the information you intended with regard to the input you sought. If it is clear that a question was interpreted differently by respondents than you expected, then determine if you can change the wording to make it more explicit in the future. Weigh the advantages of changing the item with not changing the item.

The very nature of longitudinal evaluation implies changes will occur across time. And, the fact that our work with blended learning involves technology means this will be multiplied even further by changes in future technologies. The notion of "big data" was foreign to all but a very few with supercomputers a decade ago. Yet today, it is possible for a faculty member to collect large amounts of data and store and analyze it on a desktop or laptop computer, given the appropriate resources.

The examples provided in this chapter involve surveys that center around student and faculty use and perception of instructional technology. And it is obvious that the technologies available, as well as their use and availability, affect students, faculty, and the academy. This needs to be considered and regularly examined in any longitudinal evaluation.

Be Prepared for Cleaning

The nature of data means it can be messy. This can be magnified with longitudinal evaluation as things change over time, including data. With data you are in control of, this may be less so, but even small changes to a student database or learning management system can affect surveys that are sent through that system.

Data captured through the student information system (SIS) is subject to changes mandated by the university, such as a move to plus or minus grading, additions or deletions to student or course demographics, and added questions or variables that you may find important to include in your research. In addition, changes to the system—a move to PeopleSoft, for instance—can impact how you obtain the data. In the UCF example provided above, there have been many changes in the eighteen years of evaluation—adoption of PeopleSoft and move to Instructure Canvas campus wide; reorganization of colleges, including a merger of two colleges and renaming of others; the addition or deletion of departments; the move to plus or minus grades; and changes to designations for ethnicity, to name a few. The student perception of instruction has had three redesigns in that time period as well. All of these changes were incorporated into the ongoing research and impacted merging any datasets that existed, as well as changing any reporting in the future. So, be prepared for change!

Ask for Help When Needed

The point has been made in other chapters as well, but if you need help with research, there are typically people who are able and willing to help you with anything from research design to data analysis—so seek them out. Faculty in sociology, psychology, statistics, math, and educational research may all have some experience in research, so collaboration can help you deal with limited time and limited experience in order to accomplish a strong evaluation. And, those people, along with experts in institutional research and others who maintain data on campus, can be critical to conducting longitudinal evaluation.

Disseminate the Results to Others

Certainly, one of the most valuable aspects of research is disseminating the results of your efforts. Whether you intend to orally present for your campus faculty, administration, or professional colleagues, or produce a white paper for your department or a manuscript for others in the field, how you present your research is critical to the message you are distributing to others. Data do not equal information. You must be the conduit that tells the story so that others can find value and information in the research you conduct. This is a critical piece of research in blended learning and one that allows the efforts of your hard work to inform the field and help others. In essence, it is the main reason why we do research.

Conclusion

There is a strong need for longitudinal evaluation on online and blended learning. Examining the variety of online and blended models, approaches, and integration of instructional methods repeatedly over time can help inform and provide critical insights to policymakers, researchers, and faculty. Any of the research methods discussed in this book can provide valuable information to help educators ensure that their approach to online and blended learning provides quality instruction to students, as well as identify any potential challenges that can be addressed early to minimize their negative impact on student and faculty. Hopefully, this chapter has illustrated the advantages of longitudinal evaluation and provided those considering this method with the motivation to examine it as a possibility for their research in the future.

References

Allen, I. E., & Seaman, J. (2014). *Grade change: Tracking online education in the United States*. Babson Park, MA: Babson Survey Research Group and Quahog Research Group, LLC. Retrieved from www.onlinelearningsurvey.com/reports/gradechange.pdf [Accessed April 20, 2015].

Dahlstrom, E., & Bichsel, J. (2014). *ECAR study of students and information technology, 2014*. Research report, Louisville, CO: ECAR. Retrieved from www.educause.edu/library/resources/study-students-and-information-technology-2014 [Accessed April 20, 2015].

Dringus, L. P., & Seagull, A. B. (2013). A five-year study of sustaining blended learning initiatives to enhance academic engagement in computer and information sciences campus courses. In

Picciano, A. G., & Dziuban, C. D. (eds) *Blended learning: Research perspectives, vol. 2* (pp. 122–140). New York: Routledge/Taylor Francis Group.

ECAR (2015). *ECAR: EDUCAUSE Center for Analysis and Research.* Retrieved from www .educause.edu/ecar [Accessed April 20, 2015].

EDUCAUSE (2015). *About EDUCAUSE.* Retrieved from www.educause.edu/about [Accessed April 20, 2015].

Kaleta, R., Skibba, K., & Joosten, T. (2007) Discovering, designing, and delivering hybrid courses. In Picciano, A. G. & Dziuban, C. D. (eds) *Blended learning: Research perspectives* (pp. 111–144). Needham, MA: Sloan-C.

Moskal, P. (2009). Dancing with a bear: One university's experience with evaluating blended learning. *Journal of Asynchronous Learning Networks, 13*(1), 65–74.

Online Learning Consortium (2014). *What we're all about.* Retrieved from http:// onlinelearningconsortium.org/about/ [April 20, 2015].

Pew Research Internet Project (2014). *About the project.* Retrieved from www.pewinternet.org/ about/# [April 20, 2015].

Smith, S. D., Salaway, G., Caruso, J. B., & Katz, R. N. (2009). *The ECAR study of undergraduate students and information technology, 2009.* Research report, Boulder, CO: ECAR. Retrieved from www.educause.edu/ecar [Accessed April 20, 2015].

Wang, M. C., Dziuban, C. D., Cook, I. J., & Moskal, P. D. (2009). Dr. Fox rocks: Using data-mining techniques to examine student ratings of instruction. In Shelley, M. C., Yore, L. D., Hand, B. (eds) *Quality research in literacy and science education: International perspectives and gold standards* (pp. 383–398). Dordrecht, NL: Springer.

Zickuhr, K., & Smith, A. (2013). *Home broadband 2013.* Pew Research Center. Retrieved from http://pewinternet.org/Reports/2013/Broadband.aspx [Accessed April 20, 2015].

Chapter 11

Big Data in Online and Blended Learning Research

Charles D. Dziuban

In this chapter we consider a phenomenon that has created considerable interest in the areas of online and blended learning research: the concept of big data (Kolb & Kolb, 2013; Mayer-Schönberger & Cukier, 2013; Needham, 2013; Sathi, 2012; Siegel, 2013; Silver, 2012). Picciano (2012) attributes this development to the evolution of data-driven research and decision making that took place in the 1980s and 1990s. Just as statistical computation power has increased over recent decades, so has our ability to handle, with relative ease, data sets of a size that would have previously been unimaginable to evaluators. At its core big data has given us the ability to find important patterns and relationships that simply are not possible with smaller sample sizes.

However, just as Picciano (2012, 2014) cites the enthusiasm and adoption of big data principles in research and evaluation in online and blended learning, he points to the rapid formation of advocates and cynics of the concept. There is no difficulty in finding those who believe that big data will open up new vistas of decision making (McAfee & Brynjolfsson, 2012; Hidalgo, 2014; Brown, Chui, & Manyika, 2011; Lohr, 2012; Siegel, 2013). Conversely, there are many critics who feel that the big data concept is fraught with serious problems that need to be overcome before reaching its full potential (Boyd & Crawford, 2012; Waterman & Hendler, 2013; Mayer-Schönberger & Cukier, 2013; *The Economist Technology Quarterly*, 2014a; Craig & Ludloff, 2011). This seems particularly true in online and blended learning. In this chapter we discuss big data from three specific perspectives:

1. Big data in industry and marketing
2. The application of big data principles to predictive analytics
3. Analysis of very large, same-instance data sets in online and blended learning research

There is a fundamental dichotomy between thinking "statistically" and thinking "big data" that frames differences in analysis and interpretation strategies. As statisticians, we are primarily concerned with sampling, estimation, and hypothesis testing. As big data analysts, we are more concerned with modeling, prediction, and machine learning. This is an important distinction, and one that forces us to rethink how we approach converting data into useful information, because data sets, no matter how large and comprehensive, do not lessen our responsibilities as researchers to interpret findings so that they are informative and useful. Table 11.1 presents some potential big data analyses.

Table 11.1 Big Data Analysis Potential

- Thoroughly explore and describe your data
- Construct similarity and distance models
- Develop look-up models for retrieving information
- Identify strong and weak relationships
- Construct prediction models, including regression, multiple regression, logistic and multinomial regression, fixed and hierarchical effects
- Develop useful if-then decision rules
- Conduct network analysis
- Identify affiliated classification groups of individuals or variables
- Conduct time sequence analysis
- Discover patterns
- Detect underlying clusters, such as nearest neighbors
- Develop association rules
- Construct new variables by combining the variables at hand
- Reduce your variables to a small set of underrating dimensions
- Work with several variables simultaneously
- Perform extensive graphical analysis

Big Data Thinking

We noted that big data is characterized by three elements: modeling, prediction, and machine learning. From these elements, it seems clear that the approach is much more about effective and accurate decision making than it is about the actual data. If you accept the proposition that big data analysis is much better considered as a process rather than a research method, then there are many different ways to go about predicating, modeling, and letting the algorithms run on their own. Therefore, if there are many ways to approach big data, we should not be surprised that they can, and often do, compete with each other. There is an evaluation irony in this. The term "big data" appears to convey a message stressing the importance of the number of observations that we have, but in most cases this number is so large that the question is moot. In our judgment, the important questions for big data appear in Table 11.2:

The movie *Close Encounters of the Third Kind* foreshadows machine learning when the computer systems engineers said, "we are taking over this conversation now"—the machine learned while the scientists coped with the language of the extraterrestrial visitors.

Some Definitions in Industry and Marketing

The big data process is replete with many terms that seem to be of fairly recent origin: data science, data intelligence, data visualization, data shaping, brain science, high performance computing, optimization, the cloud, scalability, Hadoop, real time, operationalization, segmentation, adaptive analytics, and risk management, to name a few. Given this new and rapidly emerging vocabulary and language that comes with the big data enterprise, we offer a small sample of definitions found in the literature in Table 11.3:

Few of the definitions on the topic relate to online and blended learning. From these examples it should be clear that, because definitions range from data sets that depend on the interactions of technology, analysis, and mythology to

Table 11.2 The Important Questions for Big Data

- Can you build an accurate model of what happened or is happening?
- Will that model prove useful for predicting future outcomes or behaviors?
- Will you be able to build a system that will take input and make accurate decisions in a pseudo-intelligent and autocatalytic way?
- What do you want to do about it?

Table 11.3 Current Big Data Definitions

Boyd & Crawford (2012)	"Big Data as a cultural, technological, and scholarly phenomenon that rest on the interplay of: technology. . ., analysis . . ., and mythology" (p.663).
Dumbill (2013)	"Big data is data that exceeds the processing capacity of conventional database systems. The data is too big, moves too fast, or doesn't fit the structures of your database architectures. To gain value from this data, you must choose an alternative way to process it" (p.1).
Provost & Fawcett (2013)	"Datasets that are too large for traditional data-processing systems and that therefore require new technologies are used for many task, including data engineering" (p.54).
Sathi (2012)	"There are two common sources of data grouped under the banner Big Data . . . within the corporation . . . (and) more data outside the organization" (p.2).
Kolb & Kolb (2013)	"It's the buzzword they use to say they are using 'bleeding edge' technology . . . there is no uniformly accepted definition because people use the term to mean a wide variety of things to suit their purposes. It has been used to describe data tools, data sets, questions, problems and answers" (p.69).
Needham (2013)	"Big Data is the commercial equivalent of HPC, which could also be called high-performance commercial computing or commercial supercomputing . . . it is less about equations and more about discovering patterns" (p.3).
Lohr (2013)	"Big Data is a vague term, used loosely, if often, these days. But put simply, the catchall phrase means three things. First, it is a bundle of technologies. Second, it is a potential revolution in measurement. And third, it is a point of view, or philosophy, about how decisions will be—and perhaps should be—made in the future."

high-performance computing, we will have difficulties developing a generally accepted version for research. This relates to Chapter 12 on assessing outcomes, in which we discuss the boundary object phenomenon. Big data seem to be well defined within individual constituencies, but not so universally understood in the general research community in which we work—i.e., online and blended learning. Perhaps then, instead of relying on hypothesis tests, big data should be understood in the context of how very large data sets force us to develop explanatory models and useful decision rules.

An Example of Big Data in Industry and Marketing

Big data has made possible the development of processes and models that in business, industry, and marketing have created predictive analytics—something that each of us encounters on a daily basis. Usually, this is accomplished with a program called a recommendation engine or a system that uses linear algebra to determine your preferences (O'Neil & Schutt, 2013). Conceptually, two domains are formulated—potential users (customers) and items or products that might be recommended to those users, each having a unique designation. Therefore, when a user expresses an opinion about an item or product (good, bad, or indifferent), the system processes that information to train itself so that it is able to make additional recommendations to the customer. Those recommendations constitute the output form engine. In addition, many of these systems incorporate metadata (gender, age, zip code, etc.) to increase the accuracy of their predictions. As the engines are fed more and more data they begin to incorporate procedures such as nearest neighbor analysis where they can predict one individual's preferences from another individual's because of the fact that they are very close to each other in the variable space.

Every time an online shopping or search site makes a purchasing suggestion to you, it happens because a recommendation engine has analyzed your shopping and search preferences and has developed a profile for you (Anderson, Jolly, & Fairhurst, 2007; Sen, Dacin, & Pattichis, 2006; Siegel, 2013; *The Economist Technology Quarterly*, 2014a, 2014b). A browser who spends most of his search time with classic literature, statistics, data-mining books, fountain pens, running shoes, and fishing equipment will find that his search preferences will surface relatively quickly. Each time he logs on, the system will show him a new pen, a new translation of *Anna Karenina*, a new data-mining book, a new tarpon rod, and a pair of running shoes that claim to make old men run like young men. If he buys two of those items, when he initially had no intention of purchasing anything, the suggestions worked by motivating sales. The organization has collected this information on millions of people, and the system gets more sophisticated using any number of predictive modeling techniques, selecting the best-performing one or simply averaging them to develop predictive models that do an even better job—models that can be updated very quickly. As a result, profits begin to rise much more rapidly because big data analytics identified patterns that never could have been recognized any other way. The most powerful thing about this process is that it happens in real time and changes with your search patterns.

Let's run some numbers. Suppose a browser goes to the dominant online search engine, and finds the gross and net profits to date of the leading Internet sales company. Let's say that is a gross profit of $25.35 billion, with a net of $300 million. Hypothetically, assuming that the marketing strategy based on big data resulted in

Table 11.4 Big Data Applications

Amazon.com generates 35% of all sales by product recommendations.

Netflix influences 70% of their customers' movie choices with their recommendation engine.

Clinical researchers predict impending divorce with a high degree of accuracy.

Investigators use machine learning to accurately predict which movies at the box office will be hits.

Banks model mortgages to predict which of their customers will refinance their home loans and thus take their business to another bank.

Credit card companies use customer relations management to accurately determine who will pay off their bill each month, who will pay the minimum, and who will default.

Health organizations, such as the Centers for Disease Control and Prevention, develop models of disease progression.

Many companies and organizations use big data approaches to determine billing errors that have cost them millions of dollars.

The criminal justice system uses big data analytics to anticipate crime recidivism and probable repeat incarceration of prison inmates.

---

a modest 5% increase in sales, the gross profits climb by about $1.26 billion, with a net increase of $15 million, if the 5% applies equally to net and gross.

This kind of power demonstrates why big data mining has taken such a prominent position in sales and marketing (Shaw, Subramaniam, Tan, & Welge, 2001; Ling & Li, 1998; Olson & Delen, 2008). Siegel (2013) provides some real-world examples about the potential impact of data analytics (listed above in Table 11.4).

These few examples present a powerful picture of the influence that data and analytics play in our daily lives. As researchers, we must be aware that these approaches capitalize on the information contained in data. We should give serious consideration to further developing our ability and skills in processes such as data mining to increase the possibility of obtaining information that will benefit our students, faculty members, and institutions—something we all need to do, including the authors of this book. There is new potential in big data—potential that enables us to reconsider just how we have been going about the business of conducting research.

Big Data Thinking in Online and Blended Learning Research

In conducting research on the impact of online and blended learning, one can easily see the potential for big data, predictive analytics, and large data sets. Many learning management systems, such as Blackboard, Brightspace, and Canvas by Instructure, collect and provide the means for analyzing student behavior, engagement measures, and performance. With the proper institutional review board (IRB) approval, investigators can obtain access to large data sets that their institutions collect on a regular basis. If that is possible, then we have the ability to potentially identify students who are most at risk of not succeeding. Table 11.5 provides some example identifiers for at-risk students.

Table 11.5 Identifiers for At-Risk Students

- Lack of engagement
- Lower academic ability levels
- Inability or unwillingness to use institutional resources, such as the writing center or student academic services
- Socioeconomic disadvantages
- Poor program planning
- Unaware that they are at risk in a course
- Poorly developed academic skills; i.e., poor study habits
- Inability to align with the proper student cohort
- Toxic schedule

A reasonable and important follow-up to identifying students, as they align to one or more of these categories, is to select or design interventions that will help them avoid the problems they are likely to encounter. The research component plays a vital role in student intervention. By using big data procedures, investigators may determine which of these are likely to impact various student cohorts or individuals. Picciano (2012) references an IBM white paper, entitled *Analytics for Achievement* (2001), that identifies several components of education intervention: monitoring learning behavior, data disaggregation, identifying candidates for intervention, predicting potential, preventing attrition, developing effective instructional techniques, developing effective assessment practices, and curriculum assessment. Predictive analytics play an important role in this process.

Some Approaches to Predictive Analytics in Online and Blended Learning that Provide Usable Data

Over recent years several organizations and institutions have applied predictive analytic techniques and processes that have proved effective for predicting students' success, or lack thereof, while at the same time creating data for further analysis. Some of them are included in Table 11.6.

For investigators, each platform for conducting predictive analytics produces data that can be useful for further analysis and reporting. For instance, the Predictive Analytics Reporting (PAR) Framework and CIVITAS Learning work with terabytes of data from across many institutions at virtually all measurement levels. Course Signals produces information that is both nominal and ordinal. Starfish incorporates faculty judgment in addition to student outcome measurement. Degree Compass aligns students with the most likely demographic and achievement profiles that maximize potential for success. SoLAR (Society for Learning Analytics Research) is an organization dedicated to improving all approaches to learning analytics and legacy analytics and to developing strategies within the context of a particular organization by capitalizing on existing data resources (Dziuban, Moskal, Cavanagh & Watts, 2012).

In addition, institutions across the country (for example, University of Maryland, Baltimore Campus; Carnegie Mellon University; Capella University; Sinclair Community College; South Orange Community College; University of Texas, El

Table 11.6 Examples of Predictive Analytic Approaches

- PAR Framework
- CIVITAS Learning & The CIVITAS Learning Space
- Course Signals
- RioPace
- Starfish
- Open Learning Initiative (OLI)
- Map-Works
- Degree Compass
- SoLAR
- Legacy Analytics

Paso; and the University of Central Florida) have translated big data thinking into predictive analytics approaches to help students succeed. Research in the area has the potential to identify at-risk students and cohorts, allowing timely interventions.

Very Large Data Sets

Mayer-Schönberger and Cukier (2013) present three positive impacts of working with large data sets. First, we can analyze far larger numbers of observations than ever before, and in some cases we can simply work with all the data at hand. Historically, we have had to resort to sampling, which, according to Mayer-Schönberger and Cukier, is an artifact of scarcity in an analog information society. In our judgment, this tacitly raises the question—"when does a sample stop being a sample?"—an important question, but with no simple answer. Second, with less concern about sampling error we can accept more measurement error, were it simply not as important that we collect data on the exact variables in the domains under investigation. Finally, we can be much less concerned with causality models, because complex patterns are more readily identifiable in their nuanced form (Wang, Dziuban, Cook, & Moskal, 2009).

In Chapter 6 we emphasized the importance of prior planning and decision making before analyzing data. In the previous section of this chapter, we also indicated that educators have a tendency to approach big data as a very large snapshot of observations that can yield important information for possible future modeling, prediction, and machine learning. In many cases we typically collect data in a single instance, run a statistical analysis, and report the results. Very large data sets pose substantial challenges for our statistical approaches. Also, we noted that, because sample sizes increase with big data sets, the power of statistical hypothesis tests rises dramatically. Therefore, we increase the risk of making a type one error—that is, citing a finding as significant when in reality it makes little or no practical difference.

Statistical Thinking with Large Data Sets

Next, we demonstrate this phenomenon with data collected by the Research Initiative for Teaching Effectiveness (RITE) at the University of Central Florida (UCF) in connection with UCF's distributed learning program, an organization that has specialized in large data set analysis for the past twenty years.

Table 11.7 Correlations of Success with SAT and ACT Aptitude Tests and High School Grade Point Average (GPA)

Correlation and Probability	SAT (n = 174,414)	ACT (n = 108,432)	HS GPA (n = 149,766)
r	.006	.021	.124
p	.010	.000	.000
r²	.00036	.00044	.0029

The first example of this phenomenon pertains to correlations and significant correlations where the hypothesis testing population value is zero. Table 11.7 presents the point-biserial correlations among success rates (a C grade or better) in courses of all modes and SAT and ACT total scores, in addition to high school grade point average (GPA).

From Table 11.7 you can see that the derived correlations are very small (.006, .021, and .124). When you convert them to r^2 values in terms of a shared variance, they all approach zero. However, the computed probabilities lead to a rejection of the null hypotheses. These correlations are statistically significant, but the actual relationship is virtually zero. A better research pursuit in this case would be a post hoc analysis to determine why the actual values are so small. These findings can lead you to an erroneous conclusion that suggests that GPAs may not relate to success, when most likely you have encountered the artifact of attenuation. The vast majority of students at UCF succeed, and to some degree the intuition uses cut scores for ability and high school performance; therefore, the range of each one of those variables is considerably restricted, producing what might well be artificially low correlations that very large sample sizes identify as "significant." Working statistically with large samples can be challenging.

A second example originates from data for students' end-of-course evaluations, on a Likert rating scale for overall rating of the course, with items ranging from a low of 1 to a high of 5. Table 11.8 presents the results of an analysis of variance on the means of that item for blended, face-to-face, and online courses. Again, the readers can see that the data sets (if samples) are very large.

To even the most casual observer who is familiar with rating scales, the mean differences across course modalities appear to be trivial at best (.01, .08, .09). However, the analysis of variance procedure would lead the investigator to reject the null hypothesis. Further, the Bonferonni post hoc (Hochberg, 1988) procedure would also lead one to reject the null hypothesis for all pairwise comparisons. Making decisions about instructor effectiveness for promotion, raises, and teaching awards based on these differences would be misleading and inappropriate. One last point is that the American Psychological Association (APA) (Fidler, 2010) recommends an effect size calculation, in this case Hedges's g (Hedges, 1981), which indicates that the impact of course mode is essentially zero.

These two examples show important impacts that the number of observations has on outcomes and investigators' decisions about them. A large number of observations and the big data process require investigators to think carefully beforehand about what kind of difference will be important to them. In the electronic culture, obtaining observations and data is accomplished with much less difficulty. How we

Table 11.8 Mean Overall Course Rating by Modality with Post Hoc Test and Effect Sizes

Course Modality	M	SD	F*	p
Blended (n = 53,476)	4.19	1.029	166.99	.00
Face-to-Face (n = 726,342)	4.11	1.066		
Online (n = 121,257)	4.10	1.800		

* MS between = 159.21; df = 2
MS within = 1.136; df = 901,072

Bonferroni Probabilities	p	Hedges's g
Blended—Face-to-Face	.000	.075
Blended—Online	.006	.093
Online—Face-to-Face	.013	.009

analyze them and what we report requires much more careful and thorough planning. We can no longer let the machine decide what is important and what should be discounted.

The Other Too Many

We are all familiar with the phrase "too much of a good thing." In the previous section we hope that we have convinced you that when dealing with large data sets the number of observations can have important implications for the results you obtain and how you interpret them. However, the number of variables that you include in your data set has consequences of its own. Certainly, more variables carry a larger amount of information that increases the ability to provide descriptive information, but there is a downside to adding all possible variables to your analysis. Several authors (Dziuban, Shirkey, & Peoples, 1979; Wheelan, 2013; Taleb, 2010, 2012) have documented that many classification, prediction, and modeling procedures used in big data analysis are highly sensitive to the number of variables included in the analysis. The variables that you choose for input and how many of them you use have a dramatic effect on the results.

Linoff and Berry (2011) give examples of a number of things that can happen with an overabundance of variables, two of which are most relevant to research in online and blended learning. The first problem—multicollinearity—results from input variables being highly correlated with each other. This problem results in big data solutions that become highly erratic. This problem is best solved by examining the scatterplots or the correlation matrix among the input variables and removing the redundancies at the beginning of the analysis. Linoff and Berry (2011) provide an excellent discussion of other techniques for dealing with this problem.

A second and more serious problem that can occur with a large number of input variables is the problem of overfitting your model. The solution works well on the data used for development, but when the result is applied to other situations it becomes ineffective. That happens because the solution was too dependent on the special case of your development data and cannot work very well in other situations (Linoff & Berry, 2011; Silver, 2012; Siegel, 2013; Tabachnick & Fidell, 2012; O'Neil & Schuut, 2013). Silver (2012) describes this as developing an overly specific answer to a much more general problem. The optimal situation is to develop a model that is acceptable, but not too tightly wound around your data. The best way for you to gain a better understanding of these two problems is to run an analysis that involves relationships among multiple variables. Remove a few or add a few more and watch what happens. Once you do this you will understand the meaning of "if the shoe fits."

Information from Large Data Sets

Large data sets provide useful information for making decisions about the impact of online and blended learning programs. We provide a few examples of how data can be helpful in the tables that follow, taken from work completed by RITE at UCF. Table 11.9 displays percentages of student cohorts enrolled in online, blended, and face-to-face courses at UCF in a group of approximately half a million student registrations. Collectively, the data show that the largest registration occurs in face-to-face courses, but that noteworthy trends do emerge. The results show increased student involvement in technology-enhanced learning as students progress from the lower undergraduate to graduate levels; approximately 86% of freshmen and sophomores are involved in face-to-face learning, with about 14% of their learning taking place in online or blended learning courses. Graduate students have technology components in their work about 36% of the time, with upper undergraduates not far behind at approximately 28%. In presenting these data to colleges and departments, the feedback from these groups indicates an awareness of the fact that lower undergraduate students are most subject to withdrawing early in their educational careers. These data have proved very useful in various units of the university, as it focuses on the philosophy that students need extended time on campus in order to acclimate to academic life and have access to on-campus resources that will help them remain in college. Therefore, this large data set has served as a discussion point to help the university develop its policies and procedures, and provide support for online and blended learning. The fact that the data set was so large and comprehensive helped departments understand how their particular policies and procedures coincided with what was trending across the university.

Table 11.10 presents the results of a logistic regression analysis determining which variables are most effective for predicting whether or not a student is likely to succeed in a particular class (success measured by a binary variable: C or better = 1, less than a C = 0). A number of variables were entered one at a time, and the pseudo r^2 computed giving the incremental gain by adding each variable. The findings show that adding variables starting with course modality through high school grade point average accounted for only 7.4% of the variance in course success. However, adding college grade point average increased that number to over 40%. Note that those results presented in graphical form (Figure 11.1) demonstrate the impact of previous academic accomplishment in predicting future success. Table 11.10 and Figure 11.1, both based on a large data set, have proved instrumental in fostering conversation and debate about the best way to intervene in order to help students who are at risk.

Table 11.9 Percentage of Students Enrolling in Online, Blended, and Face-to-Face (F2F) Courses by Level

Course Level	n	Online	Blended	F2F
Lower undergraduate	175,712	10.1	4.1	85.8
Upper undergraduate	279,185	21.3	7.1	71.6
Graduate	42,873	23.4	12.3	64.2

Table 11.10 Add One Logistic Regression Analysis for Predicting Success (n = 258,212)

Predictor Variables	r^2
Modality	.003
Course level	.022
Class size	.024
Gender	.029
Ethnicity	.035
Age	.035
SAT	.034
College	.047
High school GPA	.074
Cumulative college GPA	.405

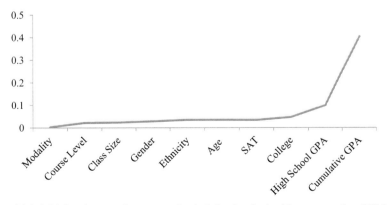

Figure 11.1 Add One Logistic Regression Analysis for Predicting Nonsuccess (n = 258,212)

Table 11.11 contains a large data set approach using classification and regression trees to determine what variables will predict whether or not a student will assign an overall rating of excellent to an instructor. Once again, the predicted variable is whether or not an instructor received an excellent rating (yes = 1, no = 0). The predictor variables were course level (lower undergraduate, upper undergraduate, graduate), as indicated in Table 11.9, the college in which the student was enrolled, and the other items on the end-of-course survey (course organization, facilitating learning, explaining requirements, communicating ideas, respect and concern for students, stimulating interesting in the course, creating a helping, learning environment, providing useful feedback, and helping students achieve course objectives). The results of the predictive modeling are presented in Table 11.11 and show that two items on the final evaluation form (facilitating learning and communicating ideas) accounted in the vast majority of variance in achieving excellent ratings. The results present themselves in an easily understood, if-then decision rule that states: If a student assigns an instructor a rating of excellent on "facilitating learning" and "ability to communicate," then the chance of his/her receiving an overall rating of excellent is .98 and the probability of receiving a rating of poor is 0. This rule holds true irrespective of student course level and college status and his/her responses to the other remaining rating scale items.

Table 11.12 demonstrates the application of the rule to students' status on a question that asked about their desire to enroll in a course. The left-hand column of the table shows the overall percentage of excellent ratings, ignoring the rule. The students who showed the lowest desire to take the course assigned an overall excellent score at a rate of 26%, while 78% of the students who exhibited a strong desire to take the course assigned an overall excellent score. However, if the investigator used the rule and aggregated all the students who conformed to it, then redistributed students into their original motivation categories, virtually all of them assigned an excellent rating to their instructor. Furthermore, the researchers at RITE have been unable to break that rule with virtually every classification variable (see Table 11.10) to be found at the university. The rule works and is robust.

This large data set analysis has proved informative at a number of levels. First, it appears to identify the two characteristics of instructors that students value most highly. Second, it provides an excellent base for discussion of effective pedagogy.

Table 11.11 A Decision Rule for the Probability of a Faculty Member Receiving an Overall Rating of Excellent (n = 126,672)

If...					
Rating Scale Question	*Excellent*	*Very Good*	*Good*	*Fair*	*Poor*
Facilitating learning	✓				
Communicating ideas	✓				
Then ...					
The probability of an *overall* rating of Excellent = .98					
The probability of an *overall* rating of Fair or Poor = .00					

Table 11.12 Percentage of Excellent Under Rule 1 for Question "I had a Strong Desire to Take This Course" (n = 126,672)

Likert Rating	Overall Excellent	If Rule 1 Excellent
Strongly disagree	26	96
Disagree	34	95
No opinion	38	95
Agree	48	96
Strongly agree	78	98

Third, it helps faculty members consider what they might do to improve their high stakes end of course evaluations. Finally, these results provide a good indication about where faculty development centers might concentrate their development efforts.

These examples give a demonstration of how large data sets can provide comprehensive information about the teaching and learning culture across many constituencies of a college or university. Each analysis was relatively straightforward and not particularity complicated. Taken as a whole, however, this work with large data sets can provide information that is simply not possible in a more traditional analysis approach. Big is not in itself effective, but it can provide excellent discovery opportunities.

Some Final Thoughts

Of course, this newfound power comes at a cost. Silver (2012) cautions about the ease with which we identify false positives that don't really make any appreciable difference, and Taleb (2012) warns about big data's propensity to make spurious relationships appear important. Those of us who work in this area are well aware that, as data sets get larger, the chance of erroneous information (otherwise known as mistakes) increases very quickly. For instance, Wang, Dziuban, Cook, and Moskal (2009), who have analyzed institution-wide data sets for years, spend a good deal of their time cleaning data that, allegedly, were in good shape. Additionally, there are major societal concerns with big data that revolve around security and individual privacy. Certainly, these questions have been raised about Google (Levick, 2012) and Amazon (*The Economist Technology Quarterly*, 2014b) collecting data about customers' search and buying habits. More recently, Edward Snowden's (*The Economist Technology Quarterly*, 2014a) divulging the data-harvesting practices of the National Security Agency on American citizens, foreign leaders, and political figures without their knowledge has raised major concerns about big data at the governmental level. Recent information about supposed free apps that harvest all the information on our cell phones (McAfee & Brynjolfsson, 2012) has raised consumer stress levels, in addition to the hacking of customer databases. In many respects, big data seems to be the best of times and the worst of times because we find information that we never thought possible, but we can also find ourselves analyzing trivial noise. Silver summarizes the issue this way:

We have to view technology for what it has always been-a tool for the better-ment of the human condition. We should neither worship at the altar of tech-nology nor be frightened by it. Nobody has ever designed, and probably no one ever will, a computer that thinks like a human being. But computers are a reflection of human progress and human ingenuity: it is not really "artificial" intelligence if a human designed the artifice.

(2012, p.293)

As Picciano (2014) points out, there are opportunities for using big data in the areas on online and blended learning research. From a positive perspective we now have the potential for developing real-time analysis procedures that index students' progress as they move through their educational programs. Second, we have the ability to identify critical incidences and markers that will alert us to the possibil-ity that students have a higher risk of not succeeding. Hopefully, with that prior knowledge researchers might be able to help identify strategies that will prove effective in helping students overcome those risks—a worthy research problem. Finally, big data sets now allow us to find important patterns and relationships that can assist with decision making and assessing learning outcomes. Big data work will require continual retraining for those of us who have been working in online and blended learning. Finally, there is a need for a meeting of the minds among experts in big data analysis, data mining, and education on the potential and proper strategic use of these procedures in online and blended learning.

References

Anderson, J. L., Jolly, L. D., & Fairhurst, A. E. (2007). Customer relationship management in retailing: A content analysis of retail trade journals. *Journal of Retailing and Consumer Services, 14*(6), 394–399. doi:10.1016/j.jretconser.2007.02.009

Boyd, D., & Crawford, K. (2012). Critical questions for big data. *Information, Communication & Society, 15*(5), 662–679.

Brown, B., Chui, M., & Manyika, J. (2011). Are you ready for the era of "big data?". *McKinsey Quarterly, 4*, 24–35.

Craig, T., & Ludloff, M. E. (2011). *Privacy and big data.* Sebastopol, CA: O'Reilly Media, Inc.

Dumbill, E. (2013). Making sense of big data. *Mary Ann Liebert Inc., 1*(1), 1–2.

Dziuban, C. D., Moskal, P., Cavanagh, T., & Watts, A. (2012). Analytics that inform the university: Using data you already have. *Journal of Asynchronous Learning Networks, 16*(3), 21–38.

Dziuban, C. D., Shirkey, E. C., & Peeples, T. O. (1979). An investigation of some distributional character-istics of the measure of sampling adequacy. *Educational and Psychological Measurement, 39*(3), 543–549.

Fidler, F. (2010, July). The American Psychological Association publication manual sixth edition: Implications for statistics education. In *Data and context in statistics education: Towards an evidence based society* (Proceedings of the 8th International Conference on Teaching Statistics).

Hedges, L. (1981). Distribution theory for Glass's estimator of effect size and related estimators. *Journal of Educational and Behavior Statistics, 6*(107), 107–128. doi:10.3102/10769986006002107

Hidalgo, C. A. (2014). Saving big data from big mouths. *Scientific American.* Retrieved from www.scientificamerican.com/article/saving-big-data-from-big-mouths/ [Accessed April 20, 2015].

Hiding from big data. (2014a, June). *The Economist Technology Quarterly,* 23–24.

Hochberg, Y. (1988). A sharper Bonferroni procedure for multiple tests of significance. *Biometrika, 75*(4), 800–802. doi:10.1093/biomet/75.4.800

How far can Amazon go? (2014b, June). *The Economist Technology Quarterly,* 11.

Kolb, J., & Kolb, J. (2013). *The big data revolution: The world is changing are you ready?*. Chicago, IL: Applied Data Labs.

Levick, R. (2012, May 3). *Big Google is watching you* [web blog]. Retrieved from www.forbes.com/sites/richardlevick/2012/05/03/big-google-is-watching-you/ [Accessed April 20, 2015].

Ling, C. X., & Li, C. (1998). Data mining for direct marketing: Problems and solutions. *KDD, 98*, 73–79.

Linoff, G. S., & Berry, M. J. (2011). *Data mining techniques: For marketing, sales, and customer relationship management.* Indianapolis, IN: Wiley Publishing, Inc.

Lohr, S. (2012). The age of big data. *The New York Times.* Retrieved from www.nytimes.com/2012/02/12/sunday-review/big-datas-impact-in-the-world.html?pagewanted=all&_r=0 [Accessed April 20, 2015].

Lohr, S. (2013). Sizing up big data, broadening beyond the Internet. *The New York Times.* Retrieved from http://bits.blogs.nytimes.com/2013/06/19/sizing-up-big-data-broadening-beyond-the-internet/?_php=true&_type=blogs&_r=0 [Accessed April 20, 2015].

Mayer-Schönberger, V., & Cukier, K. (2013). *Big data: A revolution that will transform how we live, work, and think.* New York: Houghton Mifflin Harcourt Publishing Company.

McAfee, A., & Brynjolfsson, E. (2012). Big data: The management revolution. *Harvard Business Review*, 2–9.

Needham, J. (2013). *Disruptive possibilities: How big data changes everything.* Sebastopol, CA: O'Reilly Media, Inc.

Olson, D. L., & Delen, D. (2008). *Data mining techniques* (1st ed.). New York: Springer Publishing Company.

O'Neil, C., & Schutt, R. (2013). *Doing data science: Straight talk from the front line.* Sebastopol, CA: O'Reilly Media, Inc.

Picciano, A. G. (2012). The evolution of big data and learning analytics in American higher education. *Journal of Asynchronous Learning Networks, 16*(3), 9–20.

Picciano, A. G. (2014). Big data and learning analytics in blended learning environments: Benefits and concerns. *International Journal of Artificial Intelligence and Interactive Multimedia, 2*(7), 35–43.

Provost, F., & Fawcett, T. (2013). Data science and its relationship to big data and data-driven decision making. *Mary Ann Liebert Inc., 1*(1), 51–59.

Sathi, A. (2012). *Big data analytics.* Boise, ID: MC Press Online, LLC.

Sen, A., Dacin, P. A., & Pattichis, C. (2006). Current trends in web analysis. *Communications of the ACM, 49*(11), 85–91. doi:10.1145/1167838.1167842s

Shaw, M. J., Subramaniam, C., Tan, G. W., & Welge, M. E. (2001). Knowledge management and data mining for marketing. *Decision Support Systems, 31*(1), 127–137. doi:10.1016/S0167-9236(00)00123-8

Siegel, E. (2013). *Predictive analytics: The power to predict who will click, buy, lie, or die.* Hoboken, NJ: John Wiley & Sons, Inc.

Silver, N. (2012). *The signal and the noise: Why so many predictions fail-but some don't.* New York: The Penguin Press.

Tabachnick, B. G., & Fidell, L. S. (2012). *Using multivariate statistics.* Upper Saddle River, NJ: Pearson, Inc.

Taleb, N. N. (2010). *The black swan: The impact of the highly improbable fragility.* New York: Random House LLC.

Taleb, N. N. (2012) *Antifragile: Things that gain from disorder.* New York: Random House.

Wang, M. C., Dziuban, C. D., Cook, I. J., & Moskal, P. D. (2009). Dr. Fox rocks: Using data-mining techniques to examine student ratings of instruction. In Shelley II, M. C., Yore, L. D., & Hand, B. (eds) *Quality research in literacy and science education: International perspectives and gold standards* (pp. 383–398). Dordrecht, NL: Springer.

Waterman, K. K., & Hendler, J. (2013) Getting the dirt on big data. *Mary Ann Liebert Inc., 1*(3), 137–140.

Wheelan, C. (2013). *Naked statistics: Stripping the dread from the data.* New York: W.W. Norton & Company.

Chapter 12

Assessing Outcomes in Online and Blended Learning Research

Charles D. Dziuban

Today, students in the online and blended learning environments understand the importance of regular and meaningful feedback about their academic performance. Openly, they express their view that effective teaching must be embedded in benchmarks describing how they progress through their courses and programs (Wang, Dziuban, Cook, & Moskal, 2009). One side effect of the heightened interactivity in distributed learning has been a shift away from the assessment methods of the past and a movement toward processes that are more contextual and relevant to what will be expected of students once they complete their studies. Interviews with potential employers demonstrate that they are much less interested in test scores, transcripts, grade point averages, and student class ranks. They are more concerned with issues such as a student's understanding of the organization's business value proposition, problem-solving skills, and the ability to work effectively in teams. Although objective testing is still highly prevalent and useful in our society, students have become more involved in the assessment process through online and blended learning; therefore, educators are developing procedures that require instructors to be much more reflective (Bennett & Lockyer, 2004).

These developments suggest that outcomes in online and blended learning convey information about students (and faculty) in three general areas. The first domain, and the one that receives the most attention, is the cognitive area: What do they know, what can they produce, and what can they create (Bloom, 1956) (usually framed in the context of student learning outcomes)? The second area relates to student (and faculty) attitudes toward their online and blended learning experiences. This assessment method can take on many formats, but in recent years attitudes have been measured with Likert scales. However, assessment options that produce excellent information include paired comparisons, equal appearing intervals, Guttman scales, and latent structure analysis (Schuessler, 1971; David, 1963; Edwards & Kenney, 1946; Van Schuur, 2003; Bradley & Lang, 1994). In addition, contemporary measurement techniques that use item response theory (Baker, 2001; Hambleton, Swaminathan, & Rogers, 1991; Linacre, 2006; Lord, 1980; Lord & Novick, 1968) produce measurement scales—both achievement and attitude—that possess more elegant measurement properties and permit extended data analysis options. Third, because of online and blended learning experiences, a great deal of interest is directed toward student (and faculty) behavior, involving problem-solving exercises, presentations, speeches, and projects (e.g., the evidence-based practice initiative in nursing and other areas) (Pravikoff, Tanner, & Pierce, 2005; Duong, 2010).

However, this chapter concentrates on the first area—assessment of the knowledge domain in the online and blended learning environments.

This change in emphases has impacted the conversation about outcome measurement with the multiple-choice question and its assessment analogs—true/ false, fill in the blank, etc. Researchers have criticized these forms, asserting that they enable unethical online academic behavior, assess lower cognitive levels, and are based on memorization (Rovai, 2000; FairTest, 2014). Therefore, we will consider the assessment issues in online and blended learning, followed by a demonstration of how taxonomies have shaped our thinking about learning. Then we will consider three approaches to assessment by concentrating on the multiple-choice question as a representative of an objective approach, authentic assessment using rubrics, and criterion-referenced assessment. These methods parallel the scaling levels discussed in Chapter 6 on data analysis: interval, ordinal, and nominal. The three examples here are simply prototypes for many approaches that can be incorporated in each category. As an evaluator, the reader will have to decide which measurement level is most appropriate for assessing learning impact within context.

Constructs, Boundary Objects, and Surrogates in the Assessment Process

Through the years of online and blended learning, educators have found themselves pressured by the questions about student learning effectiveness (Hwang & Chang, 2011; Herron & Wright, 2006). These viability concerns are framed around constructs such as quality, engagement, motivation, learning, critical thinking, learning style, disruption, transformation, and ambivalence, among others. Most professionals believe that each concept is a key element for effective teaching and learning and that each derives from theoretical foundations in learning theory. The assessment problem comes from the fact that these constructs are abstractions that we incorporate into the educational narrative and subsequently believe are objective and concrete (Postman, 2011). The process for measurement seems straightforward; but this is not necessarily true. Each element typifies a boundary object, a concept described by Susan Leigh Star and James R. Griesemer:

> Boundary objects are objects which are both plastic enough to adapt to local needs and constraints of the several parties employing them, yet robust enough to maintain a common identity across sites. They are weakly structured in common use, and become strongly structured in individual-site use. They may be abstract or concrete. They have different meanings in different social worlds but their structure is common enough to more than one world to make them recognizable, a means of translation. The creation and management of boundary objects is key in developing and maintaining coherence across intersecting social worlds.
>
> (1989, p.393)

Critical thinking conforms precisely to this specification. In the broader education community, there is virtually unanimous support for the importance of critical thinking in the learning process, and we profess to integrate it into our courses and programs so that students attain high levels of this characteristic. However, trying to develop a universally accepted definition and measurement scale for critical thinking is problematic. To experience this phenomenon, we encourage readers to interview faculty members in several departments across campus. We believe that the determination of what elements compromise critical thinking in departments such as mathematics, rhetoric, chemistry, philosophy, biology, psychology, foreign language, women's studies, and statistics will be well articulated, but differ greatly. Neil Postman has suggested that this has reified many abstract and complex constructs:

> The first problem is called reification, which means converting an abstract idea (mostly a word) into a thing. In this context reification works this way. We use the word "intelligence" to refer to a variety of human capabilities of which we approve. There is no such thing as "intelligence." It is a word not a thing and a word of a very high order of abstraction. But if we believe it to be a thing like the pancreas or liver, then we believe scientific procedures can locate and measure it.
>
> (2011, p.130)

Many of the important ideas and issues in online and blended learning (motivation, engagement, disruption, and transformation) exhibit Postman's characterization. Therefore, as researchers, we must be cognizant that we are forced to select surrogates to assess the characteristics in which we are interested. For instance, student engagement is measured by participation in discussion groups, critical thinking by contrived scenarios, satisfaction by rating scales, and problem-solving ability by unstructured response exercises. As researchers, our responsibility is to understand that at best these surrogates only approximate the construct with which we are interested. They are fallible measures, where adequate assessment may require the collection of several measures for a single construct.

Taxonomies as a Guide to Learning Outcomes

At the instructional level, online and blended learning have rekindled interest in learning taxonomies as blueprints for assessing student learning outcomes. These classification schemes serve to guide our thinking about structuring effective learning experiences for students, and creating a foundation for assessment at several levels. A relatively brief Internet search will identify a large number of resources for learning taxonomies.

Table 12.1 presents a small sample of taxonomies that have been proposed over the years—most long before the emergence of the distributed learning environment. Many other human domains can be described through a taxonomic approach—e.g., affective and psychomotor (Krathwohl, Bloom, & Masia, 1964; Harrow, 1972). However, a number of scholars have considered learning taxonomies in the context of instructional technology, and these are illustrated in Table 12.2 (Anderson, 2008; Ally, 2004; Koszalka & Ganesan, 2004; Blignaut & Trollip, 2003; Cicognani, 2000).

Table 12.1 Examples of Learning Taxonomies

Taxonomy	Categories
Cognitive domain Bloom (1956)	• Knowledge • Comprehension • Application • Analysis • Synthesis
A revision of Bloom's taxonomy Anderson et al. (2001)	• Remembering • Understanding • Applying • Analyzing • Evaluating • Creating
Levels of geometric thinking Van Hiele (1986)	• Visualization • Analysis • Informal deduction • Formal deduction • Rigor
SOLO taxonomy Biggs & Collis (1982)	• Prestructural • Unistructural • Multistructural • Relational • Extended abstract
Learned capabilities Gagne & Briggs (1979)	• Motor skills • Attitude • Verbal information • Cognitive strategy • Intellectual skills
How people learn Bransford, Brown, & Cocking (1999)	• Learner centered • Knowledge centered • Community centered • Assessment centered

Table 12.2 Examples of Taxonomies for Online and Blended Learning

Taxonomy	Categories
Foundational theory for online learning Ally (2004)	• Preparation • Activities • Interaction • Transfer
Instructor postings Blignaut & Trollip (2003)	• Administrative • Affective • Corrective • Informative • Socratic

(Continued)

Table 12.2 (Continued)

Strategic course management systems Koszalka & Ganesan (2004)	• Email • Discussion • Shared whiteboards • Chat rooms • Audio/video conferencing
Concept mapping online and blended learning Cicognani (2000)	• Generalization • Focusing • Application • Consolidation

Learning taxonomies have certain characteristics in common. They tend to be monotone to higher levels of thinking; that is, they provide rank ordering of skills or behaviors that progress from lower to higher levels. With this kind of organization they can serve as guides for constructing assessment protocols, with the caveat that the higher you progress in the taxonomy, the more difficult and time consuming it becomes to construct effective measurement devices. Taxonomies arrange themselves as hierarchies, meaning that accomplishment at the higher levels requires satisfaction of the lower-level knowledge and skills. In the original Bloom (1956) taxonomy of the cognitive domain, comprehension requires satisfaction of the knowledge level first; in the revised version (Anderson et al., 2001), application is preceded by remembering and understanding. According to Van Hiele's (1986) model of thought, rigor requires visualization through formal deduction. Others, such as the structure of observed learning outcomes (SOLO) taxonomy, propose that student functioning at the highest level must deal with a lack of closure so that students are required to construct new knowledge in order to accomplish the task (Biggs & Collis, 1982). In the Gagne and Briggs (1979) formulation, motor skills become the foundation for progression through the learning hierarchy. Learning taxonomies can also be formulated in a nonhierarchical format (Fink, 2003; Dodge, 1995). Theories such as these bring structure to the learning experience, but do not impose progressive levels for achieving learning outcomes. Examination of most learning taxonomies will prove them to be essentially content agnostic, so that they have application to almost any discipline.

Because of their inherent interactive and collaborative nature, online and blended learning environments present excellent opportunities for collecting student assessment data at the higher level of understanding. The general principle is that these higher levels involve production and creation, along with substantial evaluative reflection, both by students and their instructors, making the assessment process much more participatory.

The Multiple-Choice Questions as a Source of Outcome Data

Multiple-choice questions have been a mainstay for assessing student learning outcomes (Bacon, 2003; Brady, 2005; Simkin & Kuechler, 2005). Virtually every educator has had some training in constructing these items, and knows how difficult it is to formulate effective questions. One never knows how an item will perform until it has been administered a number of times. A critical component of multiple-choice assessment is control of the environment in which the items are administered, and maintenance of the test's security. Obviously, the loss of these two environmental elements—especially in online learning—has led to difficulties with multiple-choice tests (Miners, 2009; Howell, Sorensen, & Tippets, 2009). This problem is exacerbated when test item banks are produced by publishers as supplements to their textbooks and can be found online. Some universities have developed solutions by establishing testing facilities, such as the Thomas L. Keon Testing Center in the College of Business Administration at the University of Central Florida (Moskal, Caldwell, & Ellis, 2009). Despite difficulties, multiple-choice questions can be effective in the online and blended learning environments and can provide useful data for outcomes research. Careful planning and innovative work can still render them effective for outcomes assessment and, therefore, a good source of research data.

One can find information in textbooks and on the Internet about how to construct effective questions that can be assigned to various levels of learning taxonomies (Case & Donahue, 2008; Daggert, 2007; Fisher, 2008). The items can be constructed in a number of formats: correct answer, best answer, multiple response, incomplete statement, negation, passages to be read, incomplete alternatives, and combined response. They have potential for assessing knowledge, comprehension, rule allocation, generalization, sequencing, misconceptions, vocabulary, key words, analogies, sources, data recognition, operations, computation, information use, argument adequacy, inferences, logical conclusions, classification, explication, examples, prediction, and unnecessary information. They permit a much more comprehensive content sampling than do other assessment formats, and may be objectively scored. They are appropriate for statistical analyses that are useful in diagnosing why a particular student missed the question and how the class as a cohort is progressing. Multiple-choice tests will produce a large number of meaningful statistics and data that can help the investigator make informed decisions about the impact of online and blended learning. Table 12.3 presents a partial summary of information that may be gathered for many statistical platforms.

Table 12.3 Example Statistics That May Be Obtained from Multiple-Choice Tests

Total mean, variance, standard deviation

Item mean, variance, standard deviation

Test reliability—alpha, split half, and others

Inter-item correlation matrix

Inter-item covariance matrix

Scale mean with each item deleted one at a time

Scale variance

Item discrimination index—item total score correlation

Squared multiple correlation of each item with the remaining items on the test

The reliability of the test if the item is deleted

The proportion of individuals who selected each option for each question

The disadvantages of using multiple-choice questions when assessing learning outcomes in online and blended learning include that they often test recall of knowledge, are a poor vehicle for testing written and oral expression, often require one correct answer for complex situations, and usually have a substantial amount of student test-taking ability comingled with their responses. Another challenge with using the multiple-choice test formats is the predesign needed by content experts. In most cases investigators are not qualified to construct items in subjects such as chemistry, mathematics, health care administration, social work, rhetoric, etc.—a subject matter expert is necessary. This alone has caused instructors, departments, and even colleges to rely on prepublished item banks that may cause difficulties with academic integrity and group test–taking behavior.

Authentic Assessment in Online and Blended Learning

An enduring criticism of objective testing for assessment in online and blended learning is the lack of authenticity of the results yielded by the instruments—the nontransferability of the data obtained from multiple-choice tests to performance in the workplace (FairTest, 2014). For example, the written portion of the driver's license examination may or may not predict how well a candidate will perform on the driving exercise. These objective measures certify minimum knowledge competency. If an applicant wants to obtain a driver's license, an understanding of the law regarding driving safety is a reasonable requirement. Basic knowledge assessment, while indicating minimum competency, is not necessarily predictive of future performance. As a result, a community of scholars argued for more authentic assessment procedures (Wiggins, 1991; Shepard, 1989; Stiggins, 1991; Resnick & Resnick, 1992). The issue has resurfaced with the advent of technologies in the online and blended learning environments (Ashford-Rowe, Herrington, & Brown, 2013). Table 12.4 provides examples of authentic assessment devices.

While Table 12.4 provides several possibilities for developing authentic assessment exercises, Ashford-Rowe, Herrington, and Brown (2013) suggest the following criteria for authentic assessment; we present them with our modifications:

- Be challenging.
- Involve a performance or product—one with an added process.
- Transfer skills and abilities to relevant context.
- Involve metacognition.
- Ensure accuracy of assessment.
- Ensure that assessment is part of the learning process.
- Involve continual and meaningful feedback.
- Involve some form of collaboration.

Generally, authentic exercises evaluate a student's ability to operate effectively in his/her future roles. In this assessment context, students are asked to apply their acquired knowledge and skills to tasks, projects, problem solving, leadership, and other areas requiring a higher level of integration. Authentic assessment deemphasizes rote learning, memorization, and test-taking ability. In the learning taxonomies

Table 12.4 Examples of Authentic Assessment Processes

Traditional	Online and blended
Experiments in the sciences	Virtual-world exercises (i.e., Second Life)
Service learning	Discussion boards
Interpretation of literature and scientific research	Peer-created questions for virtual discussion
Assembly of e-portfolios	Chat rooms
Open responses	Videos
Problem solving in group situations	Gaming
Self-assessment (metacognition)	Simulations
Peer evaluation	PowerPoint presentations
Simulations	Observation log
Debates	Reflection posts
Case studies	Videos
Observations reports	Contribution to a wiki
Physical performance exercises	Construction of a website
Recorded logs	Use of mobile device for course
Oral presentations	

that we have examined, authentic assessment requires students to function at the higher level of those classification schemes.

Using authentic assessment devices for evaluating the impact of online and blended learning provides several advantages, the most important of which is that it closely parallels future performance expectation. This method of assessment also becomes part of the instructional process; it is much more active than objective tests by requiring reflective thought, having a large formative component, and being a drastic departure from the teach-then-test model. The process includes more careful monitoring, continual feedback to students, and a much less–structured environment. The question for evaluators then becomes, "what kind of evaluative data can be obtained for these devices?" The answer has several components. The data coming from authentic assessment are less precise than data coming from objective tests, because the categories will be limited to a brief rank ordering over four or five categories with explanations and interpretations in narrative form that reflect the judgment of the instructor, a group of experts, peer evaluators, or comparison to some predetermined prototypes, and subsequently that of the evaluator. Given these requirements, almost all processes and products that come from authentic assessment are scored with a predetermined rubric that informs students about their status (from novice to proficient). An important aspect of outcomes assessment using rubrics is the flexibility for providing usable data in multiple contexts. Often this more than compensates for the lack of preciseness of the device.

Probably the best-known program that bases itself on a rubric assessment is Quality Matters (Kreie & Bussmann, 2014). The devices in this program are primarily intended for indexing online and blended courses, using the concept of alignment. The construct hinges on critical course components: learning objectives, assessment and measurement, instructional materials, course activities and learner interaction, and course technology that provides an effective learning environment. The annotation component of the rubric is documented by fitting alignment to eight general standards:

1. Course overview and introduction
2. Learning objectives (outcomes)
3. Assessment and measurement
4. Instructional materials
5. Course activities and learner interaction
6. Course technology
7. Learner support
8. Accessibility and usability

To demonstrate this flexibility, the authors have developed a rubric (Table 12.5) to determine the level of research and data analysis skills of students and others. We

Table 12.5 A Research Skill Rubric Based on Question Narratives

	Data Analysis Platforms	Hypothesis Testing	Variables and Scales	Data Interpretation
Stage I Minimal understanding, wants context-free rules	What should I use to analyze my data?	What hypothesis should I test?	What kind of measurement device can I use?	What does this mean?
Stage II Some experience, develops strategic knowledge	I think I can do this with statistical package for the social sciences (SPSS)	I'll look for a significant difference.	I was considering a Likert scale.	I understand some of this.
Stage III Makes conscious choices about alternatives, sets priorities	I think I will have more options with R.	I'll look for a two–standard deviation difference.	I plan to develop and validate my own instrument.	I can get what I need from the output.
Stage IV Uses know-how and intuition	I'll use the best of SPSS, statistical analysis systems (SAS), and R.	I plan to do a sample size and power analysis.	I'm going to get the variance component for my scale.	I find the results from platform "X" more useful than those from platform "Z."

have found this important in understanding how to provide meaningful advice to researchers about data analysis platforms, hypothesis testing, variables, scales, and data interpretation. The rubric is not designed as a third-person description of individual research skills, but rather a narrative guide based on the kind of language used in the questions posed. The use of a rubric prevents providing information that offers little or no assistance to the investigator: novice information to the proficient or proficient information to the novice.

Criterion-Referenced Assessment and Adaptive Learning

Writing in the *American Psychologist*, Glaser (1963) described the need for an assessment system that was the basis for evaluating human performance based on predetermined standards rather than comparing individuals to each other. That foreshadowed the concept of criterion-referenced measurement (also known as criterion reference testing, CRT), which gained traction in education. Instead of distinct comparison processes, CRT refers to a predetermined standard approach to interpreting and reporting an individual's test or rubric score (Popham, 1971). Therefore, any assessment device can reflect a criterion score. Whether you passed the written portion of the driver's license examination or not is the criterion-referenced interpretation. Your actual score may be important to you, but the Department of Motor Vehicles (DMV) is only concerned about whether or not you passed the test—a prototype criterion-referenced interpretation. The University of Central Florida assigns a student to the success category if he/she achieves at least a "C" grade in a course. Students receiving an "A" or "B" are also placed in the pass category. The fundamental point for criterion performance assessment using more traditional instruments is that there must be a standard (test score, minimum percentage, etc.) that can be used to determine whether or not a student has achieved a particular criterion (Bond, 1996; Haertel, 1985). Criterion-referenced testing is summarized and contrasted with norm-referenced testing in Table 12.6.

Table 12.7 presents some examples of activity in online and blended learning that can have a criterion-referenced interpretation.

Newer adaptive learning procedures bear a direct relationship to criterion-referenced assessment (Meskauskas, 1976; Hambleton, Swaminathan, Algina, & Coulson, 1978; Berk, 1984) and use the decision-making power of algorithms to determine which course objectives students have attained and which objectives comprise the best learning path for each individual. Several platforms are currently on the education market. The ultimate strength of these platforms is that they form an evaluative perspective that may help students determine whether or not they have achieved each course objective as a criterion reference. Some examples of possible adaptive, criterion-referenced assessment resources in online and blended learning are listed in Table 12.8; however, many more programs are being developed and regularly made available to investigators.

A Blended Approach to Outcomes Assessment

Sampling in outcomes assessment includes two issues: a statistical approach and a psychometric concern. The statistical approach concentrates on obtaining an

Table 12.6 Criterion-Referenced versus Norm-Referenced Tests (Finch, 2000)

	Criterion-Referenced Tests	*Norm-Referenced Tests*
Test characteristics		
Underlying purposes	Foster learning	Classify/group students
Types of decisions	Diagnosis, progress, achievement	Aptitude, proficiency, placement
Levels of generality	Classroom specific	Overall, global
Students' expectations	Know content to expect	Do not know content
Score interpretations	Percent	Percentile
Score report strategies	Scores and answers go to students	Only scores go to students
Logistical dimensions		
Group size	Relatively small group	Large group
Range of abilities	Relatively homogeneous	Wide range of abilities
Test length	Relatively few questions	Large number of questions
Time allocated	Relatively short time	Long (two to four hours) administration

Table 12.7 Examples of Possible Criterion-Referenced Assessment in Online and Blended Learning

Log onto the course during the first week

Attend the first face-to-face section of blended course

Log onto the course once a week following the first week

Attend multiple face-to-face sections of a blended course

Opt out of certain class activities by passing a pretest

Post discussion questions

Respond in discussion threads

Post required videos

Post PowerPoint slides for virtual presentations

Submit weekly assignments

Complete weekly quizzes/tests

Watch posted videos/presentations/lectures

Attend all face-to-face sections of a blended course

Complete all quizzes/tests

Submit all of the required assignments

Achieve a certain grade—A, B, C, etc.

Pass or fail the course

Table 12.8 Adaptive Learning Programs

Acrobatiq—Carnegie Mellon	Adapt Courseware
ALEKS	aNewSpring
ASSISTments—Worcester Polytechnic Institute	Cengage Learning—Aplia
Cognitive Tutor—Carnegie Learning	CogBooks
DreamBox	eSpindle Learning—LearnThat
Grockit	Knewton
OLI—Carnegie Mellon	Pearson Adaptive—SuccessMaker
PrepMe	Sherston Software—Planet Sherton
MindEdge	Smart Sparrow
RealizeIt	

adequate sample of individuals for a specified population—the classic sampling issue that dominates data analysis and outcomes assessment problems. The second sampling issue, however, asks the question that must be considered if outcomes assessments for online and blended learning are to have any real meaning: "Did you develop a good sample of items or activities for a domain of interest?"

The taxonomies we examined tend to progress from concrete to increasingly abstract. At the concrete level, objective measures such as multiple choice and other forms appear to be most useful for assessing basic cognitive achievement of students. However, when progressing up the taxonomic domains, authentic assessment and criterion-referenced testing would produce additionally informative information. Multiple devices, though possibly costly and more time consuming, will provide more meaningful results, because the investigators will be able to comprehensively assess the cognitive (what do they know), affective (what are their attitudes), and behavioral (what do they do) in technology-mediated learning environments. Our job as evaluators is to provide useful information, not simply report data. By combining many methods, techniques, and domains, blended assessment, like blended learning, can bring the best of many approaches to the impact evaluation process.

References

Ally, M. (2004). Foundations of educational theory for online learning. In Anderson, T., & Elloumi, F. (eds) *Theory and practice of online learning* (pp. 15–44). Athabasca, AB: Athabasca University.

Anderson, L. W., Krathwohl, D. R. (eds), Airasian, P. W., Cruikshank, K. A., Mayer, R. E., Pintrich, P. R., . . . & Wittrock, M. C. (2001). *A taxonomy for learning, teaching, and assessing: A revision of Bloom's taxonomy of educational objectives.* Boston, MA: Pearson Education Group.

Anderson, T. (2008). Towards a theory of online learning. In Anderson, T., & Elloumi, F. (eds) *Theory and practice of online learning* (pp. 45–74). Athabasca, AB: Athabasca University.

Ashford-Rowe, K., Herrington, J., & Brown, C. (2013). Establishing the critical elements that determine authentic assessment. *Assessment & Evaluation in Higher Education, 39*(5), 205–222.

Bacon, D. R. (2003). Assessing learning outcomes: A comparison of multiple-choice and short-answer questions in a marketing context. *Journal of Marketing Education, 25*(1), 31–36.

Baker, F. B. (2001). *The basics of item response theory* (2nd ed.). College Park, MD: University of Maryland, ERIC Clearinghouse on Assessment and Evaluation.

Bennett, S., & Lockyer, L. (2004). Becoming an online teacher: Adapting to a changed environment for teaching and learning in higher education. *Educational Media International, 41*(3), 231–248.

Berk, R. A. (1984). *A guide to criterion-referenced test construction.* Baltimore, MD: Johns Hopkins University Press.

Biggs, J., & Collis, K. (1982) *Evaluating the quality of learning: The SOLO taxonomy.* New York: Academic Press.

Blignaut, S., & Trollip, S. R. (2003). Developing a taxonomy of faculty participation in asynchronous learning environments—An exploratory investigation. *Computers & Education, 41*(2), 149–172.

Bloom, B. S. (1956). *Taxonomy of educational objectives, handbook I: The cognitive domain.* New York: David McKay Co Inc.

Bond, L. A. (1996). *Norm- and Criterion-Referenced Testing. ERIC/AE Digest.* Retrieved from http://files.eric.ed.gov/fulltext/ED410316.pdf [Accessed May 20, 2015].

Bradley, M. M., & Lang, P. J. (1994). Measuring emotion: The self-assessment manikin and the semantic differential. *Journal of behavior therapy and experimental psychiatry, 25*(1), 49–59.

Brady, A. M. (2005). Assessment of learning with multiple-choice questions. *Nurse Education in Practice, 5*(4), 238–242.

Bransford, J. D., Brown, A., & Cocking, R. (eds) (1999). *How people learn: Brain, mind, experience, and school* (pp. 285–348). Washington, DC: National Academy Press.

Case, S. M., & Donahue, B. E. (2008). Developing high-quality multiple-choice questions for assessment in legal education. *Journal of Legal Education, 58*, 372.

Cicognani, A. (2000). Concept mapping as a collaborative tool for enhanced online learning. *Educational Technology & Society, 3*(3), 150–158.

Daggert, L. M. (2007). All of the above: Computerized exam scoring of multiple choice items helps to: (a) Show how exam items worked technically, (b) maximize exam fairness, (c) justly assign letter grades, and (d) provide feedback on student learning. *Journal of Legal Education, 57*, 391.

David, H. A. (1963). *The method of paired comparisons* (vol. 12). London: Charles Griffin.

Dodge, B. (1995). Some thoughts about WebQuests. *The Distance Educator, 1*(3), 12–15.

Duong, D. N. (2010). The evidence-based practice concept: Engaging interest and participation. *Nursing research, 59*(1), S7–S10.

Edwards, A. L., & Kenney, K. C. (1946). A comparison of the Thurstone and Likert techniques of attitude scale construction. *Journal of Applied Psychology, 30*(1), 72.

FairTest: The National Center for Fair and Open Testing (2014). Retrieved from www.fairtest.org/ [Accessed April 20, 2015].

Finch, A. E. (2000). *A formative evaluation of a task-based EFL programme for Korean university students.* Manchester, UK: Manchester University. Retrieved from www.finchpark.com [Accessed April 20, 2015].

Fink, L. D. (2003). *Creating significant learning experiences: An integrated approach to designing college courses.* San Francisco: Jossey-Bass.

Fisher, J. W. (2008). Multiple choice: Choosing the best options for more effective and less frustrating law school testing. *Capital University Law Review, 37*, 119–136.

Gagne, R. M., & Briggs, L. (1979). *Principles of instructional design.* New York: Holt, Rinehart and Winston.

Glaser, R. (1963). Instructional technology and the measurement of learning outcomes. *American Psychologist, 18*(8), 519–521.

Haertel, E. (1985). Construct validity and criterion-referenced testing. *Review of Educational Research, 55*(1), 23–46.

Hambleton, R. K., Swaminathan, H., Algina, J., & Coulson, D. B. (1978). Criterion-referenced testing and measurement: A review of technical issues and developments. *Review of Educational Research, 48*(1), 1–47.

Hambleton, R. K., Swaminathan, H., & Rogers, H. J. (1991). *Fundamentals of item response theory*. Newbury Park, CA: Sage Press.

Harrow, A. J. (1972). *A taxonomy of the psychomotor domain: A guide for developing behavioral objectives*. New York: David McKay.

Herron, J. F., & Wright, V. H. (2006). Assessment in online learning: Are students really learning. In Wright, V. H., Sunal, C. S., & Wilson, E. K. (eds) *Research on enhancing the interactivity of online learning* (pp. 45–64). Scottsdale, AZ: Information Age Publishing, Inc.

Howell, S. L., Sorensen, D., & Tippets, H. R. (2009). The new (and old) news about cheating for distance educators. *Online Journal of Distance Learning Administration, 12*(3). Retrieved from www.westga.edu/~distance/ojdla/fall123/howell123.html [Accessed April 20, 2015].

Hwang, G. J., & Chang, H. F. (2011). A formative assessment-based mobile learning approach to improving the learning attitudes and achievements of students. *Computers & Education, 56*(4), 1023–1031.

Koszalka, T., & Ganesan, R. (2004). Designing online courses: A taxonomy to guide strategic use of features available in course management systems (CMS) in distance education. *Distance Education, 25*(2), 243–256.

Krathwohl, D. R., Bloom, B. S., & Masia, B. B. (1964). *Taxonomy of educational objectives, handbook II: Affective domain*. New York: David McKay Company Inc.

Kreie, J., & Bussmann, S. (2014). Course redesign based on the Quality Matters program: Examples of before and after. *Proceedings of the Information Systems Educators Conference, USA, 2167*(31), 1–16.

Linacre, J. M. (2006). Data variance explained by Rasch measures. *Rasch Measurement Transactions, 20*(1), 1045–1054.

Lord, F. M. (1980). *Applications of item response theory to practical testing problems*. Mahwah, NJ: Lawrence Erlbaum Associates.

Lord, F. M., & Novick, M. R. (1968). *Statistical theories of mental test scores*. Reading, MA: Addison-Wesley.

Meskauskas, J. A. (1976). Evaluation models for criterion-referenced testing: Views regarding mastery and standard-setting. *Review of Educational Research, 46*(1), 133–158.

Miners, Z. (2009, June 23). One third of teens use cellphones to cheat in school. *U.S. News and World Report*. Retrieved from www.usnews.com/blogs/on-education/2009/06/23/one-third-of-teens-use-cellphones-to-cheat-in-school.html [Accessed April 20, 2015].

Moskal, P., Caldwell, R., & Ellis, T. (2009). Evolution of a computer-based testing laboratory. *Innovate: Journal of Online Education, 5*(6), 1–7.

Popham, W. J. (ed) (1971). *Criterion-referenced measurement: An introduction*. Englewood Cliffs, NJ: Prentice-Hall.

Postman, N. (2011). *Technopoly: The surrender of culture to technology*. New York: Random House Digital, Inc.

Pravikoff, D. S., Tanner, A. B., & Pierce, S. T. (2005). Readiness of US nurses for evidence-based practice: Many don't understand or value research and have had little or no training to help them find evidence on which to base their practice. *The American Journal of Nursing, 105*(9), 40–51.

Resnick, L. B., & Resnick, D. P. (1992). Assessing the thinking curriculum: New tools for educational reform. In Gifford, B. R., & O'Connor, M. C. (eds) *Future assessments: Changing views of aptitude achievement and instruction* (pp. 37–75). Boston, MA: Kluwer.

Rovai, A. P. (2000). Online and traditional assessments: What is the difference? *The Internet and Higher Education, 3*(3), 141–151.

Schuessler, K. (1971). *Analyzing social data: A statistical orientation*. Boston: Houghton Mifflin Company.

Shepard, L. A. (1989). Why we need better assessments. *Educational Leadership, 46*(7), 4–9.

Simkin, M. G., & Kuechler, W. L. (2005). Multiple-choice tests and student understanding: What is the connection? *Decision Sciences Journal of Innovative Education, 3*(1), 73–98.

Star, S. L., & Griesemer, J. R. (1989). Institutional ecology, translations and boundary objects: Amateurs and professionals in Berkeley's Museum of Vertebrate Zoology, 1907–39. *Social Studies of Science, 19*(3), 387–420.

Stiggins, R. J. (1991). Facing the challenges of a new era of educational assessment. *Applied Measurement in Education, 4*(4), 263–273.

Van Hiele, P. M. (1986). *Structure and insight: A theory of mathematics education.* New York: Academic Press.

Van Schuur, W. H. (2003). Mokken scale analysis: Between the Guttman scale and parametric item response theory. *Political Analysis, 11*(2), 139–163.

Wang, M. C., Dziuban, C. D., Cook, I. J., & Moskal, P. D. (2009). Dr. Fox rocks: Using data-mining techniques to examine student ratings of instruction. In Shelley, M. C., Yore, L. D., & Hand, B. (eds) *Quality research in literacy and science education: International perspectives and gold standards* (pp. 383–398). Dordrecht, NL: Springer.

Wiggins, G. (1991). Standards, not standardization: Evoking quality student work. *Educational Leadership, 48*(5), 18–25.

Chapter 13

What the Future Might Hold for Online and Blended Learning Research

Charles D. Dziuban and Anthony G. Picciano

The point was made in Chapter 1 of this book, when discussing today's research efforts in online and blended learning, that "it would have been unheard of to consider any of these scenarios as little as twenty years ago." The Internet was just beginning and no one predicted the rapidity with which it would permeate all aspects of society, including education. In this final chapter, an attempt will be made to predict where research in online and blended learning is going and some of the issues it will be facing. This is a risky undertaking at best, since predicting the future, and in this case the evolution and growth of technology, new products, and services, is difficult. While many try to predict *what* will happen and sometimes get it right, predicting *when* something will happen is far more challenging. Before discussing the future of research in online and blended learning, it might be prudent to discuss the future of online and blended learning. And before doing that, a review of the history of online and blended learning is in order.

Online learning as conceived today started in the 1990s, with the Internet and World Wide Web. Online learning applications using local and wide area networks existed before the Internet, but the model that evolved over the past twenty or more years relies on ubiquitous data communications that are owned and operated routinely by all segments of the population. Today, people use laptops, cell phones, and other portable devices daily to stay connected with family, friends, and their studies.

The First Wave (The Beginning)—1990s

The technology of the first wave of online learning was based on slow-speed, dial-up modem lines. As a result, many of the earliest online learning courses were text based and relied heavily on asynchronous learning. Digital multimedia was difficult and time consuming to develop and was incredibly slow in download-ing to student computers. The main pedagogical model was a highly interactive, asynchronous learning network made popular by the Alfred P. Sloan Foundation's grant program, entitled *Anytime/Anyplace Learning*. The first major award in the program was made in 1993. The Sloan Foundation also funded the *Journal of Asynchronous Learning Networks* (*JALN*), which started publishing in 1997 and was the first refereed journal devoted entirely to online learning (recently renamed *Online Learning*). At that time, software such as learning/course management systems was rudimentary, and a number of schools resorted to developing their own platforms.

The colleges and universities most interested in online learning during this decade were those that had established distance education programs using other modalities such as television, radio, and course packs. Public institutions such as the Penn State World Campus and the University of Maryland University College were early leaders in the development of the online learning initiative. Also, for-profit colleges such as the University of Phoenix invested heavily in developing online learning programs. The phenomenon in K–12 schools was slow to develop until the latter part of the decade, when statewide virtual schools such as the Florida Virtual School were first established.

Online learning during the first wave was not without its critics. Social commentators such as Neil Postman (1992) and David Noble (1998) cautioned against the new online technology and its incursion into teaching and learning. Neil Postman (1992) saw virtual learning as a poor substitute for face-to-face instruction and said so in *The End of Education*. David Noble (1998) went further in his criticism and warned that online learning was ushering in the era of "digital diploma mills." Regardless, online learning development pushed on. By the end of the 1990s, hundreds of thousands of college students were enrolling in online courses every year. Allen & Seaman (2014) estimated that 1.6 million students were enrolling yearly in fully online courses by 2002. Regarding K–12, data are not available, and the sense is that no more than 100,000 or so students were enrolled in online courses during this period.

The Second Wave (Into the Mainstream)—Early 2000s

By the early 2000s, Internet technology had advanced to the point where most people were able to afford high-speed cable modems or DSL. This enhanced connectivity opened up the possibility of incorporating multimedia (pictures, sound, video) into online learning development. Social media such as blogs, wikis, and YouTube also came on the scene, allowing for greater interaction. Faculty from around the country began sharing learning tools and objects in digital depositories such as Merlot. Perhaps the most important development of this second wave was that online learning was no longer seen solely as a vehicle for distance education, but could be used in mainstream education in almost any class and any subject matter. The predominant pedagogical model of this wave was blended learning, as faculty and teachers from most sectors of education began to use online facilities to enhance their courses and replace seat time in regular face-to-face courses.

In 2004, the Alfred P. Sloan Foundation funded an invitation-only workshop focusing on blended learning and hosted by the University of Illinois-Chicago (Picciano, 2009). One of the major purposes of this workshop was to develop a definition of blended learning. The workshop participants were unable to agree until almost a year later, and even then the definition was imperfect. The issue of a definition or lack thereof continues to dominate any discussion of blended learning today, as educators continue to define blended learning to suit their own institutions and academic departments.

Also during the second wave, many colleges and universities scaled up their online and blended learning activities. Learning/course management systems such as Blackboard, Desire2Learn, and Moodle were acquired throughout education, including K–12. For-profit colleges expanded their programs significantly as venture capital flooded into the sector. The fully online model continued to be the mainstay of the for-profit colleges, mainly because it was cost effective for those institutions that did not have brick and mortar campuses.

Perhaps the most serious concerns of the second wave were in response to the remarkable growth of the for-profit sector, which came under scrutiny for recruitment and questionable financial aid practices. The Education Trust estimated that the for-profit sector grew 236% from 1998 to 2008, while the public and nonprofit sectors grew 21% and 17%, respectively (Lynch, Engle, & Cruz, 2010). The University of Phoenix, one of the top recipients of federal student financial aid, was the focus of highly publicized federal government investigations on its recruitment practices in 2003 and 2004. The university subsequently settled these investigations by making significant payments to the federal government without admitting wrongdoing.

It was estimated that by 2008, 4.6 million students enrolled yearly in fully online courses in public and nonprofit colleges and universities (Allen & Seaman, 2014). Data for the for-profit colleges and universities are sketchy, but it is likely that over one million additional students were enrolled in fully online courses in this sector. In higher education, data on enrollments in blended courses are practically nonexistent due to the problem of definition discussed earlier in this chapter. In K–12 schools, over one million students were enrolled in online and blended courses, mostly in rural districts where student populations are small and funding is limited (Picciano & Seaman, 2008). Data on blended courses in K–12 are more reliable, mainly because school districts need to maintain careful records for funding purposes based on class attendance. Also, with so many fewer course offerings, high school administrators maintain a much tighter rein on the teaching modalities utilized by staffs. Lastly, estimates are that hundreds of thousands of K–12 students are being homeschooled using online learning, but accurate data on this population are not available.

The Third Wave (The MOOC Phenomenon)—2008 to 2013

The term "MOOC" (massive open online course) was coined in 2008 by Dave Cormier and Bryan Alexander to describe an online course led by George Siemens of Athabasca University and Stephen Downes of the National Research Council. The course enrolled more than 2,000 students. With this course, the third wave of online learning development began. In 2011, Stanford University offered several MOOCs—one of which, led by Sebastian Thrun and Peter Norvig, enrolled more than 160,000 students. Thrun shortly thereafter started his MOOC company, Udacity. A few months later, Andrew Ng and Daphne Koller, both from Stanford University, launched Coursera, another MOOC provider. The MOOC model was grounded in improving student access to higher education and cost effectiveness. The emphasis was surely on "massive" enrollments. Venture capital flowed into MOOC development, especially as for-profit colleges lost some of their appeal due to ongoing federal investigations of recruitment and financial irregularities.

The major interest in MOOC technology was not its pedagogical benefits. Nevertheless, courses that were enrolling hundreds of thousands of students attracted deserved attention. Faculty from big-name institutions such as Stanford University, Harvard, and the Massachusetts Institute of Technology became associated with the MOOC phenomenon. MOOCs were glamorized by their founders at Udacity,

Coursera, and edX as the technological revolution that would indeed change higher education. Significant investments of capital into MOOC companies were made by private investors and venture philanthropies. As a result, the media went into a frenzy. *The New York Times* declared 2012 as "the year of the MOOC" (Pappano, 2012). Education policymakers and university trustees took notice and thought they had found a solution to their education-funding woes. Some, such as those at the California State University system and the University of Virginia, pushed for major new MOOC initiatives.

As the MOOC phenomenon took off, a closer examination of the pedagogical basis of the course design was made by faculty and instructional designers, many of whom were experienced online learning developers. The computer-assisted instruction (CAI) style of many early MOOCs, based on "read, watch, listen, and repeat" course materials, was questioned by experienced online learning developers who preferred more socially constructed, pedagogical approaches that emphasize extensive interaction between students and faculty. In addition, the high student dropout rates of 90% in some MOOC courses could not be easily explained away. Lastly, but perhaps most significantly, was the failure by educational leaders and faculty to jump at the chance to use course materials developed by the faculty at Ivy League and other highly selective universities. To the contrary, faculty and administrators saw this as elitism and arrogance on the part of the MOOC providers.

By the end of 2012, more than seven million students were enrolling every year in for-credit online courses in public and private, nonprofit universities (Allen & Seaman, 2014). Many more were enrolled in for-profit colleges and universities. MOOC courses added hundreds of thousands of additional students in mostly non–credit bearing courses. In K–12, enrollments continued to grow, but accurate data are lacking. It is known, for instance, that in addition to rural school districts, urban and suburban schools significantly expanded the use of online, credit recovery programs during this period (Picciano & Seaman, 2010).

At the end of 2013, the media's infatuation with MOOCs receded. The story of new technologies overhyped by the media only to be followed by a backlash has been a recurring theme in American culture. Products such as the Apple Liza, Windows Vista operating system, Microsoft Zune, and Linden Lab's Second Life are examples of technologies that never lived up to their promotion. To a degree, MOOCs followed the same pattern. One major development that occurred in 2013 spurred the backlash. California's San Jose State University was the focus of a well-publicized experiment in which several basic courses in mathematics and statistics were developed by Udacity and offered in the spring of 2013. In comparing completion rates and grades, students taking the MOOC courses did not fare as well as students in previous years' face-to-face courses (Collins, 2013). In December 2013, Sebastian Thrun, the founder of Udacity, opened the flood gates for criticism in an interview with *Fast Company*, where he was quoted as saying that he was throwing in the towel and that "we [Udacity] have a lousy product" (Chafkin, 2013). Actually, Thrun may have been too harsh on his company, but the quote was out there, and doubts about the efficacy of MOOCs grew. Daphne Koller, founder of Coursera, was more moderate in her comments about her own company's MOOC products. In November 2013, she commented at the Sloan Consortium International Conference on Online Learning that students who have remediation and other learning needs, and who lack the basic skills of reading, writing, and arithmetic, would probably better be served by face-to-face instruction (Koller, 2013). Koller went on to say that MOOC companies should consider the development of more pedagogically sound course materials that can be used in blended online formats rather than fully online formats. In a sense, Coursera and other MOOC providers might rebrand themselves as producers of high-quality content that gives faculty the option as to how best to use their materials, rather than as course providers and developers.

The Fourth Wave (Reconciliation of the Blended Learning and MOOC Models)—2014 and onward

In 2014, the fourth wave arrived, wherein blended learning technologies that allow for more extensive and personal faculty interaction began to be integrated with well-financed course content developed by MOOC providers and others for instructors to use as they see fit. The fourth wave model extends and combines the development of the second wave (blended learning) and the third wave (well-designed MOOC content) and will incorporate a variety of pedagogical approaches using multiple content forms and instructional tools. Social and multimedia use will expand, in that students will rely on portable devices (laptops, tablets, PDAs) for accessing and participating in course activities. In addition, a number of new facilities and approaches that were in their nascent stages in previous waves will expand. These include:

1. Learning analytics
2. Adaptive or differentiated learning
3. Competency-based instruction
4. Open resources, including material meant to replace traditional textbooks
5. Gaming and multi-user virtual environments (MUVE)

All of the above, as well as traditional lectures, class discussions, laboratory work, internships, etc., that are typical in face-to-face classes will be at the disposal of faculty. Pedagogy will drive technology in a comprehensive and sophisticated blended learning environment.

The evolution of the fourth wave blended/MOOC model will require careful nurturing. The potential for friction over whether content and course materials are developed within or outside of individual colleges and universities is great. In a survey of college presidents, conducted by *The Chronicle of Higher Education* on change and innovation, important insights were provided as to where campus leaders think online and blended learning are going. The following is an excerpt from the executive summary:

Direction:	Two-thirds of presidents of public institutions think that higher education is headed in the right direction, as do well over half of their private campus peers.
Modality:	An overwhelming majority of presidents—three quarters at private institutions and even more at public campuses—think that blended courses that contain both face-to-face and online components will have a positive impact on higher education.

Focus: Presidents say that when it comes to innovation in higher educa-
                      tion, reformers pay too much attention to cutting costs and not
                      enough to changing the model of teaching and learning.

Change Drivers: Two-thirds of public-institution presidents think that politicians
                      are the most influential drivers of change in higher education and
                      half of private-campus presidents agree with that assessment. The
                      presidents on both types of campuses believe strongly that faculty
                      should be the number one drivers of change.

                                                                        (Selingo, 2014)

The last item on *Change Drivers* is most telling. Faculty should indeed be the
number one drivers of change, and to a degree many have been at the forefront
of the twenty-year period of evolution of online and blended learning. They will
have to continue to be at the forefront, understanding full well that forces outside
of the university will be moving to exert great influence on teaching and learning.

In sum, the fourth wave of online and blended learning provides fertile ground
for research now and in the future.

Research in Online and Blended: What is Driving the Agenda?

Creative Destruction

The June 28–July 4, 2014 edition of *The Economist* was titled "Creative Destruction:
Reinventing the University." That issue featured three articles that foreshadowed
developments facing higher education: rising cost, changing demand, and disruptive technology. The editors argued that American higher education constitutes one
of the great success stories of the welfare state by shifting educational opportunities from a privileged few to the middle-class masses, largely because of governmental support. At the same time, however, they provided evidence of decreasing
public support for education, with colleges and universities passing the financial
responsibility onto students. The journal characterized the first issue as Baumol's
disease—rapidly rising costs in a labor-intensive market faced with stagnant pro-
ductivity. They noted that, although prices of many commodities, especially in the
technology sector, have fallen dramatically, the cost of education has exceeded
inflationary trends by 1.6% every year. This is disruptive, because from a research
perspective, spiraling cost impacts access, quality, value added, outreach, long-term
debt, and educational opportunity costs, with the resulting uncertainty about directions for future inquiry.

A second issue, the changing labor market, is causing an almost equal impact
on education and, compounded with rising costs, presents a complicated problem
that requires attention in the new research agenda. Historically, students went to
college, obtained a degree, and worked in their chosen field for the remainder of
their careers. Education was a good investment with an excellent net return. However, two things have changed. In this present climate no one is surprised that the
staggering educational debt facing students diminishes the financial advantage of a
college education—equally impacting both blue- and white-collar workers. Compounding the problem, *The Economist* (2014, p.11) cites data from an Oxford study
predicting that 47% of today's jobs face a high probability of being automated in

the foreseeable future. Should this prediction prove accurate then the phrase "life-long learning" will take on added meaning in the face of changing labor markets, because education, the ultimate human capital, will require constant revision and retooling. From a research perspective we need a clearer understanding of how online and blended learning, as well as other instructional technologies, can address this problem. Unfortunately, research about this issue is not as straightforward as *The Economist* would have us believe. For instance, Charette (2013) argues that the shortage of labor in the areas of science, technology, engineering, and mathematics is a myth because we have miscalculated the size of the available workforce.

The first two issues, rising cost and changing labor markets, will force a reinvention of higher education, but the third phenomenon, technology, makes it inevitable. Underlying this assertion, *The Economist* cites the unbundling effect that technology has had on established traditions in American culture (newspapers, book stores, music, retail sales, etc.), and the writers argue that higher education is squarely in the crosshairs. They use the massive open online courses (MOOCs) as the principal impact factor for the reinvention of higher education, by arguing that they will dramatically reduce cost and greatly expand access. However, the data are unclear about the potential impact of MOOCs for their quality of knowledge acquisition and how they will interface with colleges and universities, both private and public. Nonetheless, MOOCs are causing us to reevaluate our educational value propositions. *The Economist* argues that instead of propping up the old models of learning, we should reengineer new ones that work more effectively. Certainly, this should be part of the next generation research agenda.

Changing Base Lines and the Long View

The four waves of online and blended learning constitute rapid change in the extreme. Aligned with this has been a long array of research questions that have been explored over the years, ranging from the "no significant difference phenomenon" and metadata to the impact of MOOCs and predictive analytics. The upshot of these trends coincides with Roberts (2007), where he documents constantly changing baselines. He argues that a kind of collective amnesia surrounds changes that happened over a more distant time frame. We tend to trust what we have seen for ourselves and dismiss events that occurred in the more distant past. He stresses that incremental changes inch up on us (noise pollution, diminishing green space, and longer commutes to work), and we fail to notice them. In education, for instance, we can overlook the impact caused by changes in learning space (Norberg, Dziuban, & Moskal, 2011), instantaneous communication (Seife, 2014), information overload (Wurman, 1989; Wurman et al., 2001), and the remarkably altered role expectations for students and instructors in online and blended learning (Wang, Dziuban, Cook, & Moskal, 2009). Diamond (1999) defines this as landscape amnesia, where we forget anything but what we are experiencing at the moment and assume that the present is the way it has always been. Many of us are subject to this phenomenon. We have been working in online and blended learning research for so long that the structure of earlier education is slipping away. Johnson (2014) develops this idea further when he explores the notion of the long view. He documents the impact of six developments in the world: glass, cold, sound, clean, time, and light. For example,

Johannes Gutenberg's printing press created a surge in the demand for spectacles, as the new practice of reading made Europeans across the continent suddenly realize that they were farsighted; the market demand for spectacles encouraged a growing number of people to produce and experiment with lenses, which led to the invention of the microscope, which shortly thereafter enabled us to perceive that our bodies were made up of microscopic cells. You wouldn't think that printing technology would have anything to do with expansion of our vision down to the cellular scale . . .

(2014, pp.4–5)

As we enter the next phase of online and blended learning, researchers may develop more productive studies by turning their attention to longer-term outcomes and issues in education. These become evolutionary questions revolving around changes in our institutions, our instructors and students, learning outcomes, educational cost, policy, diversity, opportunity, access, and the broader issues about how our society plans to educate a growing population of students that express increasing ambivalence about the value of a formal education. One example might be how online and blended learning have impacted the tragedy of the commons, where disciplines continue to believe that they are distinct from each other (Diamond, 2005). These are big problems composed of a complicated network of smaller problems that we need to address one at a time. These bigger issues are solved by operating at the boundaries—for instance, determining more meaningful ways to evaluate whether or not students have acquired knowledge and information that will enable them to function effectively upon leaving institutions in which they have learned through online and blended learning. This is a problem that might be resolved by developing and evaluating a number of smaller assessment practices that change the paradigm for indexing learning outcomes. In spite of the enthusiasm for initiatives such as learning analytics, adaptive learning, competency-based instruction, open resources, and multi-user environments, their enduring impact on education, for the most part, remains undocumented.

"The Speed of Light"

An additional factor impacting the next generation of research is the viral nature of digital information. Seife (2014) characterizes this as a disconnect from all that we have known before. Information moves around the world instantaneously and can be stored with perfect reliability. In an epidemiological sense, he compares digital information to a super virus that invades all aspects of society and education, changing the way we understand how students acquire knowledge. Powers describes this digital environment:

We're all busier. Much, much busier. It's a lot of work managing all that connectedness. The e-mail, texts, and voicemails; the pokes, prods, and tweets; the alerts, and comments; the links, tags, and posts; the photos and videos; the blogs and vlogs; the searches; downloads, uploads, files and folders; feeds and filters; walls and widgets; tags and clouds; the usernames, passcodes, and access keys; pop-ups and banners; ringtones and vibrations. That's just a small sample of what we navigate each day in the room. By the time you read this there will be completely new modes of connecting that are all the rage. Our tools are fertile, constantly multiplying.

(2010, p.2)

In many respects, impact data behave this way. The future research agenda will call for us to manage these very large data sets that are in constant motion. The historical research paradigm may not be nearly as informative when we assess short-term changes (as in pretest-posttest differences), but more effective by examining the trends and trajectories of our data the way Rosling, Rönnlund, and Rosling accomplished it with their Gapminder approach (Gapminder World, 2014). Even in this day of online journals, delay can make some of our research obsolete by the time it becomes available. We are convinced that research results need to move faster to keep up with digital information and data in contemporary education settings—especially online and blended learning.

Complexity

Another important consideration for next generation research will be the development of methods for dealing with and extracting information from complex systems such as classes, departments, colleges, and universities consortia, as well as state and national educational organizations. Complex systems constitute substantial challenges to cause and effect thinking. Jay Forrester (1971, 1993) showed us that complexity exhibits certain characteristics:

1. Generally, it is impossible to predict how an intervention will ripple through a complex system.
2. Very often outcomes will be counterintuitive.
3. There will be both positive and negative side effects.

There are examples of this phenomenon from virtually all areas. Levitt and Dubner (2014) cite the bounty effect, where offering financial incentives intended to eliminate pests actually increases the infestation because certain segments of the population resort to pest farming as a cottage industry. Another example of counterintuitive side effects comes with the United Nations Carbon Credit program to reduce greenhouse gases, which motivated certain countries to produce more of the most harmful substances to obtain higher credits for the increased financial incentives (Levitt & Dubner, 2014). Grosz (2013) described an unanticipated outcome that involves praising children for their excellent work. The natural assumption is that such praise would be motivating, but he cites a body of research that presents evidence showing the opposite effect. The praise proves to be a disincentive to the work ethic of children, interfering with their perseverance with more difficult tasks.

In the online and blended learning environments, we find ourselves conducting research where the results run counter to our expectations. Seife (2014) describes the increase of sock puppetry on the Internet, where individuals manufacture completely fraudulent environments, creating a subculture that believes what is being portrayed is genuine. Further, he documents side effects such as politicians hiring companies to artificially inflate their Twitter following to make them appear much more popular than they really are (Seife, 2014). Of greater concern is the process of search engine optimization (SEO), where organizations specialize in gaming search engines with vocabulary and syntax to elevate websites, articles, journals, products, and other items to the front pages in order to create more business. This can be particularly troublesome in the search for valid and reliable information when one assumes that he/she has found the most often referenced resources, but their popularity is the result of manipulation.

Taleb (2007) describes the issue this way: Complex systems (we add blended and online learning) are fraught with interdependences that are extremely difficult to deconstruct and hardly ever exhibit linearity in their relationships. This means that if you double the online time in a blended course it does not follow that learning gains will double. They may triple or quadruple, or conversely diminish by half. The relationships we identify in complex systems can increase or decrease in an exponential function (Silver, 2012). Additionally, the relations are not necessarily reciprocal. For instance, finding a high positive correlation between students' attending the wellness center regularly and their remaining in school does not mean that requiring all students to visit the center will result in higher retention rates. Most likely there are many complicated interactions that result in good students attending the wellness center—their motivation, work ethic, educational engagement, compulsivity, and an embraced connection between healthy bodies and healthy minds. Therefore, using the wellness center is an outcome and not a cause.

Uncertain Mediation, Ambiguity, and Ambivalence

Setényi (1995), when discussing the evolution of Hungary from communism to democracy after the fall of the Soviet Union, coined the term "uncertain mediation." By that he meant that there are never enough data to allow individuals, organizations, or governments to make clear-cut decisions. Actions must be taken, legislation passed, policies developed, and curriculum designed in the face of incomplete evidence. This theory relates closely to the notion of open systems that have continual input from external sources—as opposed to closed systems where inputs are finite (Magee, 2009). This thinking pattern has implications for research in online and blended learning in the future. Contemporary educational environments are continually bombarded with external inputs. Questions about quality, learning outcomes, student engagement, faculty rolls, return on investment, policy, learning environments, value added, regulation, assessment, and more find their way onto the agendas of researchers and evaluators, who are expected to provide compelling evidence where no such evidence exists. This development will impact future research agendas and is likely to expand in the coming years.

Compounding uncertain mediation difficulties in research is the notion of ambiguity, which is a cognitive phenomenon characterized by a confusion of ideas or facts (Dequech, 2000). If I see something coiled up in the corner of the barn and can't tell whether it is a rope or a snake, I suffer from ambiguity and don't know how to act until I determine which it is (Weigert, 1991). Many times we have encountered students that indicate they did not know what the instructor expected of them in their online or blended course. A study completed for the Sloan Consortium (now the Online Learning Consortium) by Dziuban, Moskal, Brophy-Ellison, and Shea (2007) identified several elements that must be resolved about a course if ambiguity is to be diminished: reduced ambivalence, enriched learning environments, clear rules of engagement, instructor shows commitment to learning, instructor shows respect and concern, and instructor shows engagement. Levine (1985) and Weigert (1991) contend that a flight from ambiguity characterizes modern society and education, both of which are committed to the need for clarity. As researchers, we are continually asked whether something is this or that—is online learning effective or not, will analytics increase retention or not, are MOOCs effective learning devices or not, are students satisfied with online courses or not? Often, these kinds of questions are generated from external sources in an open system and suffer from the binary fallacy. In almost all cases they cannot be answered by a yes or a no response. They will continue to impact future research in online and blended learning and require uncertain mediation.

The third construct that has research implications is that of ambivalence, described by Long (2011), Weigert (1991), and Craig and Martinez (2005). Ambivalence is an emotional response characterized by simultaneous positive and negative feelings. Weigert (1991) cites several issues that foster ambivalence in contemporary society and education: pluralism, value relativity, increasing technological control of everyday life, a bewildering array of choices, instant communication, and exponential growth of available information. Craig and Martinez (2005) raise this question: Have we not experienced mixed feelings about virtually everything we have encountered in life at one time or another—loved ones, children, government, charities, the economy, bosses, friends, and, in education, our classes, instructors, universities, classmates, the education we received, and our prospects for the future? Long (2011) used the ambivalence concept to explain the behavior of adolescents as they make the journey from childhood to adulthood, perplexed by positive and negative feelings toward authority figures (parents, teachers, and adults), and argued that ambivalence is an important catalyst for change in society. Ambivalence underlies a fundamental uncertainty about culture, society, and education. Mixed emotions in culture are characterized in any number of contradictory proverbs: Look before you leap; he who hesitates is lost; if at first you don't succeed, try again; don't beat your head against a wall; many hands make light work; too many cooks spoil the broth. Some contradictions relate to education: You can't teach an old dog new tricks, you are never too old to learn, a word to the wise is sufficient, talk is cheap. Ambivalence can also be found in online and blended learning: I love the convenience of online learning but miss the face-to-face time, I love working at my own pace but dislike having to log on every day, I love the technology but hate it when it breaks. The irony seems to be that ambivalence can be both a bad and good thing. How is that for an ambivalent statement? In the online and blended learning environment, ambivalence about those modalities leads to student confusion about satisfaction. However, at the same time, Dziuban, Moskal, Kramer, and Thompson (2012) have shown that ambivalent students are the most reflective and thoughtful about the quality of their education. Their ambivalence about online learning helped them identify the positive and negative aspects of what they experienced. Although on course evaluations their overall ratings appeared neutral, the underlying reasons were considerably diverse.

Uncertain mediation, ambiguity, and ambivalence will impact future research. As the issues become more complex and develop with cumulative rapidity, evaluation procedures will have to accommodate unstructured situations. Direct interpretation will become more difficult, much like complex interactions in analysis of variance or suppressor variables in regression. Investigators will have to be more subtle and nuanced in their interpretations. Levitt and Dubner state, "these are multidimensional cause-and-effect questions, which means their outcomes are both distant and nuanced. With complex issues, it can be ridiculously hard to pin a particular cause on a particular effect" (2014, p.23).

While this may disappoint those who want direct and unequivocal answers, future research will be addressing authentic questions in the educational environment, instead of procedures like the "no significant difference phenomenon" that, in our opinion, was an answer looking for a question.

Not Knowing and Being Wrong

Schultz cites a quote by Leonard Susskind, professor of physics at Stanford, member of the National Academy of Sciences, and pioneer in the development of string theory:

> If I were to flip a coin a million times, I'd be damn sure that I wasn't going to get all heads ... I'm not a betting man, but I'd be so sure that I'd bet my life and my soul on it ... I'm absolutely certain that the laws of large numbers—probability theory—will work and protect me. All of science is based on it ... I can't prove it, and I don't really know why it works.
>
> (2011, p.141)

As we progress to next generation research, it is going to become increasingly important to recognize that we simply don't know why certain things happen and that often our assumptions and conclusions prove to be wrong. Historically, we have avoided the three words "I don't know" in favor of conjectures that proved wrong over the long term. Many examples come to mind: speculation that many universities will close their doors, there will be a markedly decreased need for faculty members, universities will become diploma mills, the quality of learning will decrease because of the absence of face-to-face time, and on-the-job performance of online graduates will decrease. Each of these predictions has impacted higher education, but not in the way so-called experts originally predicted. Levitt and Dubner cite Niels Bohr as saying, "prediction ... is very difficult, especially if it's about the future" (2014, p.23). They go on with this anecdote:

| Moderator: | Tonight, our guest: Thomas Sargent, Nobel laureate in economics and one of the most-cited economist in the world. Professor Sargent, can you tell us what CD rates will be in two years? |
| Sargent: | No. |

(2014, p.27)

What are some of the reasons that so many of our assumed outcomes in online and blended learning have been something less than correct? Taleb (2007) points out that we are simply not very good at calculating the probability of the extremely small likelihood of events. He shows that these black swans have had an impact on culture, society, or education. Once they happen we tend to reconstruct a set of causal connections that explain why the event took place. There are many examples of black swans: 9/11, the Harry Potter novels, Google, the severe recession of 2008, MOOCs, and Facebook. Lazarsfeld (1949) provides an example of how we tend to backfill incorrect explanations. In describing the study of the American soldier, he presented several findings about the characteristics of American military personnel in World War II. The results he reported were the opposite of what the study concluded. He documented that most everyone produced an explanation for why those erroneous results were true. However, when the results were corrected, people built alternate narratives about the correct results without hesitation.

As researchers in the coming years of online and blended learning, we will have to be cognizant of our tendencies toward confirmation bias (Kahneman, 2011; Watts, 2011), which is a strongly held belief that education will be benefitted by all aspects of instructional technologies. This can happen quite easily, since we tend to frequent groups and individuals who embrace our own beliefs. Additionally, we have to be careful of distorted memory, such as the lecture teaching and learning method, that is inherently flawed. There are problems with lecturing in the digital world, but to assume that it should be completely abandoned is erroneous thinking. Further, the idea of sunk cost can lead us astray. That is, so much has been invested that we can't afford to abandon or discard the initiative. Avoiding the conclusion that the optimal decision that this intervention should not be implemented aligns with sunk cost. This corresponds to the Bayesian theory (Barber, 2012), where the best decision is not to implement the study. Finally, as researchers in the next generation, we will have be wary of common sense thinking, because, as Kahneman (2011) and Watts (2011) point out, rarely does it lead us to the correct finding or conclusion—especially in a research context.

Things to Consider as We Advance

The increasing impact of instructional technologies in online and blended learning will intensify the demand for information about their effectiveness. This places added responsibility on investigators to design and implement studies that respond to the needs of decision makers while simultaneously extending the boundaries of research into new areas. We live in a time of the perceived unbundling of higher education, increased complexity, uncertain mediation, ambiguity, ambivalence, and uncertainty. These challenges come from a changing educational landscape, in which information grows exponentially—much of which is valid, but unfortunately, some of which is inaccurate. Therefore, filtering and monitoring the digital world will require a coalition of educational professionals: administrators, faculty members, instructional designers, faculty center staffs, students, and educational researchers, among others. These are not new role expectations, but rather ones that have become much more important in recent years. Therefore, as we move into the next generation research agenda, a number of concepts might serve as useful benchmarks.

Beware of False Positives

Silver (2012) cites the frequency with which we report false positives in our research. False positives come from studies that cite a significant difference, a strong relationship, an interaction pattern, a compelling narrative, an important demographic trend, or a reflective insight that may have been the result of a particular study but in practice has no lasting impact. In statistical terms this is a type one error. This phenomenon can occur with research methods of virtually any method. These errors are costly and difficult to correct because they can lead to premature policy decisions and substantial resource allocation. As responsible researchers in online and blended learning, we have to be aware of the relative (and absolute) costs of specifying a false positive against its opposite—a false negative; i.e., concluding from your study that an intervention was ineffective when it would have created an impact.

Research Context is Increasingly Important

In the changing educational environment we cannot approach inquiry into online and blended learning as if it were free from situational circumstances. We have entered a period of context-driven research. For instance, the answer to the question—" are predictive analytics effective for increasing student retention?"—has to be: *it depends on the context.* As we evaluate analytic procedures we find that many are tied to specific institutions with cultures that dictate what will be effective (Dziuban & Moskal, 2013). This is also true for online and blended learning. Therefore, as next generation researchers, we will have to spend time and resources defining the context in which we conduct our studies. Certainly, this has been a requirement of research over the past decades, but it will be more important for the new educational environments in which we conduct research.

Research context closely relates to the framing of your study—the way you establish the mental picture of what you hope to accomplish. Lakoff argues that reframing a particular situation or context is the catalyst for change. He describes the process this way: "Frames are mental structures that shape the way we see the world. As a result they shape the goals we seek, the plans we make, the way we act and what counts as a good or bad outcome of our actions" (2004, p.xv).

Others (Gould, 1996; Goffman, 1974) show that the manner in which you frame a situation or research study constitutes the primary determinant of how people will interpret what you report. Often this is accomplished through the use of metaphors: "If we are right in suggesting that our conceptual system is largely metaphorical, then the way we think, what we experience, and what we do every day is very much a matter of metaphors" (Lakoff & Johnson, 1980, p.3).

Meyer (2005) makes a strong case that metaphors have been essential for enhancing our understanding of distance education (we substitute online and blended learning): the World Wide Web, information highway, virtual, surfing, file, hard drive, mouse, and many others. These frames transform things from a terminology that we may not fully understand to terms of something with which we have more familiarity. However, Meyer (2005) and Lanier (2010, 2013) point out that these frames define the situation. For instance, *first do no harm with online learning* causes people to think in terms of possible damage caused by it. Alternatively, *searching for possible benefits of online learning* creates a distinctly different context. Outcomes that you find may not be all that you hoped for, but the second frame doesn't immediately direct people to look for harmful effects. Carefully choosing a frame for your study is an important first step in creating proactive and clearer understanding of what you wish to accomplish in your work.

The Best of All Worlds

The future research agenda will force us to devise an effective way to combine the old and the new research methodologies. Jenkins (2006) argues that in some cases new technologies replace old ones immediately, but the most common occurrence is an evolutionary convergence, incorporating the best aspects of both by building a kind of eutectic structure. Diamond (2013) makes the same point, answering the question from an anthropological perspective: What can we learn and take from traditional societies? The increasing demand for information places the responsibility on the research community to combine the best aspects of more established research methods and the emerging models being generated by online and blended learning. This convergence, however, places an important expectation on the research culture. No longer can we afford to collect data—be they quantitative, qualitative, artifacts, or observations—without some prior consideration of outcomes that will make a difference and will result in the implementation of a program, initiative, or policy. The argument may be made that prespecifying the outcomes is subjective and would invalidate the study. However, we contend that some aspect of all studies, even the most tightly controlled experiments, have a number of subjective elements to them (Walster & Cleary, 1970). Gibbons and Bunderson (2005) emphasize this point when they classify research into explore, explain, and design, where the final category places the responsibility on the researcher for some predetermined outcome that will lead to action.

This notion parallels the area of design-based research (DBR), also referred to as educational design research (McKenney & Reeves, 2012, 2014; Wang & Hannafin, 2005; Reeves, Herrington, & Oliver, 2005; Barab & Squire, 2004). DBR is best conceived of as a process, rather than a set of procedures. Proponents of this approach acknowledge that the methods of implementing it can vary widely, but the purpose remains constant. Solve practical problems through an iterative feedback approach while simultaneously discovering new knowledge.

In speculating about the future of research in online and blended learning, it seems clear that although many of the methods considered in this book appear disparate, there is a constant that pervades. All of the approaches to research become much more effective if the investigators can answer the question: "What will make a difference?"

The Need for Collaboration and Flexibility

David Straus (1988) and his colleagues created their facilitative leadership model based on a series of new directions and assumptions that effective leaders continually interact with their constituencies in an ongoing process. In another initiative, but aligned with facilitative leadership, Washington State University (WSU), the National Learning Infrastructure Initiative (NLII), the Coalition for Networked Information (CNI), and the TLT Group developed their transformative assessment paradigm. We quote from their rubric:

> The assessment results are designed for multiple constituencies; the assessment plan includes feedback and corresponding resources and protocols for improving student learning, faculty teaching, administrative support, or some combination of these features. Assessment is open and fosters reflection.
>
> (2003, p.1)

The transformative assessment initiative reflects the facilitative leadership model and gives us some insight about effective research in online and blended learning. We take Straus's work, together with transformative assessment and some of our own thoughts, and recast it into a facilitative research context:

1. Contemporary research is always formative and involves a series of continuous feedback loops that generate new questions as the previous ones have been addressed. Effective research is a series of iterative approximations.
2. Research in online and blended learning will, by the nature of change, have to be opportunistic, because innovations happen rapidly in this new environment.
3. Collaboration among many constituencies in the research process will increase the potential for: creating a motivating vision for research; focusing on relationships, processes, and outcomes; being good role models; and making research much more celebratory. Working in isolation produces less than optimal results.
4. Aligning oneself with a particular research method is not a particularly functional idea because of the number of research approaches that are available. This becomes a problem in conducting online and blended learning research. The briefest of searches for types of research methods can be overwhelming. We present the results of that search in Table 13.1, in no particular order (Vogt, Vogt, Gardner, & Haeffele, 2014):

The list of research methods in Table 13.1 is by no means exhaustive and can be extended almost indefinitely. However, the common thread in all of these seemingly disparate approaches is that they respond to different contexts in order to produce useful information. In addition, there has been a long-standing initiative in the research community to blend research into more comprehensive, underlying constructs. A predominant example is the extensive work that has been done to unify the classic divide between quantitative and qualitative research into mixed methods (Creswell, 2013, 2015; Creswell and Clark, 2010; Hesse-Biber, 2010; *Journal of Mixed Method Research*). Other investigators, through careful analytic work, argue that the differences between quantitative and qualitative methods are much more perceived than actual; i.e., the difference in theory and practice is minimal (Crowe & Sheppard, 2010). This mutually exclusive distinction has never been productive; qualitative and quantitative studies can enhance each other in many and varied contexts. For instance, a complicated path diagram developed by a structural equation modeler is virtually incomprehensible to most people without a compelling explanatory narrative. However, an interesting narrative gains much more clarity if there are some data to verify its conclusions.

And Finally ...

Online and blended learning have forced contemporary researchers to reconsider many of their approaches to inquiry—approaches that have remained stable and valid for a number of decades. New learning environments force educational institutions to change and adapt. Therefore, the way we create and use information has become more complex. With this change, we have gained research knowledge and insight into effective pedagogy, how students engage and learn, how educational institutions are impacted, what will be required of effective teachers in the future, how students value education, and what might be reasonable learning outcomes for

Table 13.1 A Sample of Research Methodologies for Online and Blended Learning

Comparison	Descriptive	Meta-analysis	Participant observation
Survey methods	Phenomenographic	Retrospective analysis	Experimental research
Quasi-experimental	Cohort studies	Case studies	Predictive
Action research	Data mining	Literature reviews	Grounded theory
Focus groups	Longitudinal studies	Secondary data analysis	Historical research
Exploratory	Case control design	Reflective practice	Model building
Mixed methods	Theory-based research	Cross-cultural comparison	Cross-institutional studies
Interaction analysis	Demographic analysis	Inductive reasoning	Personal experience
Archival research	Deductive reasoning	Quantitative research	Qualitative studies
Empiricism	Observational studies	Phenomenology	Pre-experimental research
Correlational	Ethnography	Developmental research	Trend prediction
Ex post facto	Randomized trials	Decision-oriented studies	Design-based research
Diagnostic studies	Content analysis	Graphic analysis	Correlational research
Modeling	Interviews	Graphic analysis	Artifact analysis

higher education. However, very few of these results have been entirely conclusive. That we talk about the new learning *environment* is probably a misnomer. We should be speaking about the new learning *environments*, because there are many. The considerable years of research experienced by the authors of the book convince us that understanding online and blended learning will be an incremental, upward spiral. For every one issue addressed, several more will be created. The new research agenda will involve a continuing conversation among many constituencies, where each one of them can make contributions to the research agenda.

We have considered many approaches to research in this book—some of them quite traditional, while others have been tailored to the new teaching and learning environments. We hope that we have made a case that important results and useful information can come from every approach to research. Our questions are extensive, and we need to use every resource at hand. This calls for much more collaboration among historical competitors if we are to understand the emerging learning environments that are dissolving the boundaries among disciplines, institutions, and national initiatives. In the new world, no one appears to own anything exclusively. In the future we will need serious reconsideration of established research cultures that have evolved over the years and have devoted considerable effort to finding fault with approaches other than their own. The time is long overdue for us to vacate research comfort zones where, for example, psychometric researchers should take a serious look at how grounded theory might help them and grounded theorists explore the research possibilities modeling procedure. Such seemingly diverse approaches must have some things in common that would be mutually beneficial. Ideas are much better shared than protected.

We end with Johnson's (2010) thinking about where good ideas and research emerge. The first is the notion of the adjacent possible that he attributed to the complexity theorist Stuart Kaufman (Johnson, 2014). The idea is that we ratchet progress through a series of small-step progressions of what is reasonably possible. We didn't jump from the magnifying glass to the electron microscope. That took many years. Initially, we didn't understand that student satisfaction with online learning was not one dimensional but much more complex (Dziuban, Moskal, Kramer, & Thompson, 2012). That took two decades.

The second idea that facilitates research is the liquid network. Throughout this book we have stressed the need for collaborative work. This means that an idea is not a single thing but resides in many places. An idea intersects with multiple groups and is considered developed, reframed, and improved by each of them. The close proximity of individuals, either physically or virtually, working on an idea has the potential for making progress by an order of magnitude. Liquid networks increase the likelihood of discovering the next adjacent possible, because the problem is exposed to diverse perspectives of people who make progress by tinkering. An example of this liquid network in action is the Sloan Consortium (Bourne, 2004)—now rebranded the Online Learning Consortium—working on the concept of asynchronous learning networks and localness. That took a long time and a number of people to design working blueprints.

The third notion is the slow hunch. This means that we have to take an idea and stay with it for a long time and allow it to develop. We like to think about eureka moments, but they are rare occurrences. Darwin and Edison worked on their ideas for years before they came to fruition. This proves to be true for most important discoveries and inventions. Arguably, we are in a slow hunch period with online and blended learning. We have learned much about them, but we have to stay on board for the long term to see their full impact. Unfortunately, answers don't come easily. In the final analysis, however, our research future in online and blended learning is full of promise. Thank you for reading our book, and welcome to the new old frontier.

References

Allen, E., & Seaman, J. (2014). *Grade change: Tracking online education in the United States*. Needham, MA: Babson College Survey Research Group.

Barab, S., & Squire, K. (2004). Design-based research: Putting a stake in the ground. *The Journal of the Learning Sciences, 13*(1), 1–14.

Barber, D. (2012). *Bayesian reasoning and machine learning*. Cambridge: Cambridge University Press.

Bourne, J. R. (2004). *Elements of quality online education: Into the mainstream*. Needham, MA: Sloan-C.

Chafkin, M. (2013, December). *Udacity's Sebastian Thrun, godfather of free online education, changes course*. Fast Company. Retrieved from www.fastcompany.com/3021473/udacity-sebastian-thrun-uphill-climb [Accessed April 20, 2015].

Charette, R. N. (2013, August). *The STEM crisis is a myth*. IEEE Spectrum. Retrieved from http://spectrum.ieee.org/at-work/education/the-stem-crisis-is-a-myth [Accessed April 20, 2015].

Collins, E. D. (2013, September). *Preliminary summary: SJSU and augmented online learning environment pilot project*. The Research and Planning Group for California Community Colleges (RP Group). Retrieved from www.sjsu.edu/chemistry/People/Faculty/Collins_Research_Page/AOLE%20Report%20Final%20Version_Jan%201_2014.pdf [Accessed April 20, 2015].

Craig, S. C., & Martinez, M.D. (2005). *Ambivalence and the structure of political opinion*. New York: Palgrave Macmillan.

Creative destruction: Reinventing the university. (2014, June). *The Economist*, 11.

Creswell, J.W. (2013). *Research design: Qualitative, quantitative, and mixed methods approaches* (4th ed.). Thousand Oaks, CA: SAGE Publications.

Creswell, J. W. (2015). *A concise introduction to mixed methods research*. Thousand Oaks, CA: SAGE Publications.

Creswell, J. W., & Clark, V.L.P. (2010). *Designing and conducting mixed methods research*. Thousand Oaks, CA: SAGE Publications.

Crowe, M., & Sheppard, L. (2010). Qualitative and quantitative research designs are more similar than different. *The Internet Journal of Allied Health Sciences and Practice, 8*(4), 1–7.

Dequech, D. (2000). Fundamental uncertainty and ambiguity. *Eastern Economic Journal, 26*(1), 41–60.

Diamond, J. (1999). *Germs, guns, and steel: The fates of human societies*. New York: W.W. Norton & Company, Inc.

Diamond, J. (2005). *Collapse: How societies choose to fail or succeed*. New York: Penguin.

Diamond, J. (2013). *The world until yesterday: What can we learn from traditional societies?*. New York: Penguin.

Dziuban, C., & Moskal, P. (2013, June 3). *Analytics and metaphors: Grounding our understanding in a conceptual framework* [webinar]. ELI Webinars. Retrieved from www.educause.edu/library/resources/analytics-and-metaphors-grounding-our-understanding-conceptual-framework [Accessed April 20, 2015].

Dziuban, C., Moskal, P., Brophy-Ellison, J., & Shea, P. (2007). Technology-enhanced education and millennial students in higher education. *Metropolitan Universities, 18*(3), 75–90.

Dziuban, C., Moskal, P., Kramer, L., & Thompson, J. (2012). Student satisfaction with online learning in the presence of ambivalence: Looking for the will-o'-the-wisp. *The Internet and Higher Education, 17*, 1–8.

Forrester, J.W. (1971). Counterintuitive behavior of social systems. *Technology Review, 73*, 52–68.

Forrester, J. W. (1993). System dynamics and the lessons of 35 years. In Greene, K. B. (ed) *A systems-based approach to policymaking* (pp. 199–240). New York: Springer Science and Business Media.

Gapminder. (2014, December). *Data in Gapminder World* Retrieved from www.gapminder.org/data/ [Accessed May 27, 2015].

Gibbons, A. S., & Bunderson, C. V. (2005). Explore, explain, design. *Encyclopedia of Social Measurement, 1*, 927–938.

Goffman, E. (1974). *Frame analysis: An essay on the organization of experience*. Lebanon, NW: Northeastern University Press.

Gould, S. J. (1996). *The mismeasure of man*. New York: W. W. Norton & Company.

Grosz, S. (2013). *The examined life: How we lose and find ourselves*. New York: W. W. Norton & Company.

Hesse-Biber, S. N. (2010). *Mixed method research: Merging theory with practice*. New York: The Guilford Press.

Jenkins, H. (2006). *Convergence culture: Where old and new media collide*. New York: New York University Press.

Johnson, S. (2010). *Where good ideas come from*. New York: Penguin Group.

Johnson, S. (2014). *How we got to now: Six innovations that made the modern world*. New York: Penguin Group.

Kahneman, D. (2011). *Thinking, fast and slow*. New York: Farrar, Strauss, Giroux.

Koller, D. (2013, November). *Online learning: Learning without limits*. Keynote presentation at the 19th Annual Sloan Consortium Conference on Online Learning, Orlando, FL.

Lakoff, G. (2004). *Don't think of an elephant! Know your values and frame the debate*. White River Junction, VT: Chelsea Green Publishing Company.

Lakoff, G., & Johnson, M. (1980). *Metaphors we live by*. Chicago, IL: The University of Chicago Press.

Lanier, J. (2010). *You are not a gadget*. New York: Vintage Books.

Lanier, J. (2013). *Who owns the future*. New York: Simon & Schuster.

Lazarsfeld, A. F. (1949). An American soldier: An expository review. *The Public Opinion Quarterly, 13*(3), 377–404.

Levine, D. N. (1985). Trust as a social reality. *Social Forces, 63*, 967–985.

Levitt, S. D., & Dubner, S. J. (2014). *Think like a freak*. New York: HarperCollins Publishers.

Long, W. A. (2011). *Your predictable adolescent*. Charleston, SC: BookSurge Publishing.

Lynch, M., Engle, J., & Cruz, J. L. (2010). *Subprime opportunity: The unfulfilled promise of for-profit colleges and universities*. Washington, DC: The Education Trust.

Magee, S. (2009). *The open system*. Charleston, SC: BookSurge Publishing.

McKenney, S. E., & Reeves, T. C. (2012). *Conducting educational design research*. New York: Routledge.

McKenney, S. E., & Reeves, T. C. (2014). Educational design research. In Spector, J. M., Merrill, M. D., Elen, J., & Bishop, M. J. (eds) *Handbook of research on educational communications and technology* (4th ed.) (pp. 131–140). New York: Springer.

Meyer, K. A. (2005). Common metaphors and their impact on distance education: What they tell us and what they hide. *Teachers College Record, 107*(8), 1601–1625.

Noble, D. J. (1998). Digital diploma mills: The automation of higher education. *Science as Culture, 7*(3), 355–368.

Norberg, A., Dziuban, C., & Moskal, P. (2011). A time-based blended learning model. *On the Horizon, 19*(3), 207–216.

Pappano, L. (2012, November 2). The year of the MOOC. *The New York Times*. Retrieved from www.nytimes.com/2012/11/04/education/edlife/massive-open-online-courses-are-multiplying-at-a-rapid-pace.html?pagewanted=all&_r=0 [Accessed April 20, 2015].

Picciano, A. (2009). Blending with purpose: The multimodal model. *Journal of the Research Center for Educational Technology, 5*(1), 4–14.

Picciano, A. G., & Seaman, J. (2008). *K–12 online learning: A 2008 follow-up of the survey of U.S. school district administrators*. Needham, MA: The Sloan Consortium.

Picciano, A. G., & Seaman, J. (2010). *Class connections: High school reform and the role of online learning*. Needham, MA: The Babson College Survey Research Group.

Postman, N. (1992). *The end of education: Redefining the value of school*. New York: Random House Digital, Inc.

Powers, W. (2010). *Hamlet's blackberry: Building a good life in the digital age*. New York: HarperCollins Publishers.

Reeves, T., Herrington, J., & Oliver, R. (2005). Design research: A socially responsible approach to instructional technology research in higher education. *Journal of Computing in Higher Education, 16*(2), 97–116.

Roberts, C. (2007). *The unnatural history of the sea*. Washington, DC: Island Press.

Schultz, K. (2011). *Being wrong: Adventures in the margin of error*. New York: HarperCollins Publishers.

Seife, C. (2014). *Virtual unreality*. New York: Penguin Group.

Selingo, J. J. (ed) (2014). The innovative university: What college presidents think about change in American higher education. Washington, DC: *The Chronicle of Higher Education*. Retrieved from http://strategicplanning.fairfield.edu/sites/default/files/innovative_university_140516.pdf [Accessed April 20, 2015].

Setényi, J. (1995, May 12). *Teaching democracy in an unpopular democracy*. Paper presented at "What to Teach About Hungarian Democracy" conference, Kossuth Klub.

Silver, N. (2012). *The signal and the noise: Why so many predictions fail-but some don't*. New York: The Penguin Press.

Straus, D. A. (1988). *Facilitative leadership: Theoretical underpinnings*. Cambridge, MA: Interaction Associates, Inc.

Taleb, N. N. (2007). *The black swan: The impact of the highly improbable fragility*. New York: Random House, Inc.

Vogt, W. P., Vogt, E. R., Gardner, D. C., & Haeffele, L. M. (2014). *Selecting the right analyses for your data: Quantitative, qualitative, and mixed methods*. New York: Guilford Press.

Walster, W., & Cleary, T. A. (1970). Statistical significance as a decision rule. *Sociological Methodology, 2*, 246–254.

Wang, F., & Hannafin, M. J. (2005). Design-based research and technology-enhanced learning environments. *Educational Technology Research and Development, 53*(4), 5–23.

Wang, M. C., Dziuban, C. D., Cook, I. J., & Moskal, P. D. (2009). Dr. Fox rocks: Using data-mining techniques to examine student ratings of instruction. In Shelley, M. C., Yore, L. D., Hand, B. (eds) *Quality research in literacy and science education: International perspectives and gold standards* (pp. 383–398). Dordrecht, NL: Springer.

Watts, D. J. (2011). *Everything is obvious*. New York: Crown Publishing Group, Random House.

Weigert, A. J. (1991). *Mixed emotions: Certain steps toward understanding ambivalence*. Albany, NY: State University of New York Press.

WSU, NLII EDUCAUSE, CNI, & TLT Group (2003). *Assessing transformation*. The Center for Teaching, Learning, Technology. Retrieved from https://net.educause.edu/ir/library/pdf/EDU0251.pdf [Accessed April 20, 2015].

Wurman, R. S. (1989). *Information anxiety*. New York: Doubleday.

Wurman, R. S., Leifer, L., Sume, D., & Whitehouse, K. (2001). *Information anxiety 2* (vol. 6000). Indianapolis, IN: Que.

Index

Figures are indicated by *f*, tables by *t*, and notes by n.